D0425694

A.D. KESSLER

How You Can Get Rich, Stay Rich and Enjoy Being Rich with Creative Real Estate in the '90s

A FORTUNE AT YOUR FEET

REVISED EDITION

IRWIN
Professional Publishing®
Chicago • London • Singapore

This publication is designed to provide accurate and authoritative information in regard to the subject matter covered. It is sold with the understanding that the author and the publisher are not engaged in rendering legal, accounting, or other professional service.

ISBN 1-55738-822-9

Printed in the United States of America

BB

3 4 5 6 7 8 9 0

CB

To those whose love and concern have provided me with the "People Benefits" of health, wealth and happiness; particularly my life partner, Jaclyn.

Table of Contents

List of Illustrations

When . . .

. . . I first heard that A.D. Kessler was writing a book about Creative Real Estate, I said to myself, "It's about time! The world needs to know what A.D. knows!"

I learned much of what I know about Creative Real Estate and building wealth through contact with A.D. and his Professional Educational Foundation. Those of us who know and admire him have been waiting for this book to be written.

Here, for the first time, A.D. Kessler describes his unique, fabulously successful approach to real estate investment. Everything you need to get started is here: the philosophy, the techniques, the formulas—all written in language anyone can understand.

For a generation, A.D. Kessler has been the real estate professional's professional. Through his seminars, his Professional Educational Foundation, his International Exchangors Association, his annual Creative Real Estate Expositions, and his *Creative Real Estate Magazine*, A.D. has helped more people make more money than anyone I know.

Yet for all the complexity and sophistication of the billions of dollars in transactions he's been involved in, he has described the essence of what he does in words the average person can easily read and act on.

Aside from the financial rewards, I have derived a great deal of personal pleasure from working with A.D. Though you may not get the same opportunity to work with him personally, you now have a fantastic alternative: you can learn and use his ideas through this book.

Read it, enjoy it, and put it to work—to create a fortune at your feet!

Robert G. Allen

Author of *Nothing Down*

I Must Say . . .

. . . practically every author, like an Academy Award winner, either expresses gratitude to, or at least mentions, a long list of people whom he either genuinely wishes—or at least thinks it politic—to acknowledge as having been helpful in their endeavours. Truth be known, it's impossible for anyone over the age of two to list all the people who have been influential in their development to the point of an achievement, be it acting, writing or any other publicly recognized accomplishment.

Certainly some of the most painful associations have made lasting impressions on the mental, emotional and spiritual growth of each of us. But nature is kind, and most of us have relegated those experiences to the dark corners of our memories rather than parade them as the grateful growth experiences they probably were.

According to *The Harper's Magazine Index,* the average person has to learn and remember 10,000 faces throughout a lifetime. In my case, I'm sure a significant number of them had some impact on my thinking; and it did take some thinking to complete this book. Can anyone honestly be expected to remember that many names?

That being said, I hope I'm off the hook when it comes to thanking or acknowledging everyone by name who, in one way or another, has been influential in my preparation for writing this book.

When it came down to actually doing the work, my life partner Jaclyn—broker, author, editor and television personality—gave it top priority in our schedule, counseling, consulting, critiquing and helping me automate the writing on a computer system specifically designed and constructed for us for the purpose by my son, Judd, who appeared in my study with the hardware and software one memorable evening. He installed it, tutored us and continues to prompt us computerwise and bookwise. As a lawyer, real estate broker, certified financial planner, software author/publisher and successful businessman, his support and wise counsel are invaluable.

My eldest son, Brian, an attorney and real estate broker with a wealth of contract and litigation experience, both nationally and internationally, and a talent for succinct, cogent expression, provides an ever-ready, resonant sounding board. My sister and brother-in-law, Helen and David Harmelin (another attorney, retired) are ever at the ready for counsel, support, encouragement and reaction.

My editor, Pamela van Giessen, in her refreshingly candid manner, has made me feel comfortable in our relationship, and appreciated.

    My long-time friend and associate Nova Boshear put in round-the-clock hours to provide me with a disk and hard copy of the first edition of this manuscript to ease the ardor of revising and editing. Henry Wakefield graciously translated that disk from MAC to DOS.

    Particularly, I would like to acknowledge my late parents, M.W. and Belle Pastor Kessler, for their wisdom and inspiration. My father showed me at the age of twelve the "people benefits" of real estate. It was my mother who taught me, "Presidents are only people, heroes are only people, and you too, son, are people."

    In so doing, they started me in life with the "can-do attitude," which is probably the single most important ingredient in business and in life.

    In large part, I am what I am and do what I do because of the influence of these people. I am grateful to each and all.

A.D. Kessler

"My God," . . .

. . . said the Queen," I'm pregnant; I wonder who did it?"

No way can I ever forget that phrase, nor the lesson it taught me. Professor McGill, in my freshman journalism class at Rutgers, gave us an assignment. We were to write a succinct piece containing the elements of Diety, Royalty, Nativity and Mystery. He allowed us to toil for just five minutes and then we were each called upon to read our composition. Budding writer after writer read from 100 to 500 words of elaborate text until Mac put us out of our embarrasing misery and shared that never-to-be-forgotten, 12-word phrase with us. He told us that no editor worth his salt would print any of the wordy efforts we had put forth. The lesson was loud and clear. I have since translated it to mean that "less is more," for use in my speeches and writings.

What does all this mean to you? Simply this: the first edition of this book covered the basics of dealing in various types of real estate for profit. Those basics are still valid. I won't embellish them or disguise them in elaborate, new prose. "Some things never change" is a phrase familiar to most of us; however, so is "The only constant is change." Since I give credence to both of those beliefs, in the pages that follow you will find the basics that have prevailed and the changes to their application that adapt their execution to the changes in lifestyle, economy, laws and practices that are most current, and, in some instances, anticipated.

There have been, and are now, many books about real estate available. In this one, you will find one glaring difference. By no stretch of the imagination can you infer that I imply anyone can get rich randomly copying any one of the techniques I describe in successful case histories. Just as for every hand there's a glove, for every practitioner there is a practice that best suits each individual.

You have no doubt heard some of late-night television's so-called gurus of real estate touting their "cookie-cutter" formulas for making millions in real estate. Cookie-cutters are for use with limp dough, not living, vibrant people. Do you believe that you are identically the same as your friend or neighbor? Would you really want to be? Do you have exactly the same needs, wants and desires? Do you want to be an exact carbon copy of anyone else or do exactly what anyone else does? Would you want anyone else to be and respond exactly like you?

So much for the cookie-cutter malarkey. You won't find any in this book. What you will find is a smorgasbord of proven methods that have worked time and again, in good times, bad times and in-between times. You will have the opportunity to pick and choose what you feel and believe will work best for you; what feels good to you, is fun and exciting. That free choice should give you the very best chance to work successfully. If it does, great! And if it doesn't, you'll have many more choices to explore until you hit upon the very one for you.

That's what this book is all about. Choices. And more choices. All of which have worked and do work, but not every one for everyone. I'll give you the ideas—good, solid, tested and proven to be successful. Just one reminder: Ideas don't work unless you do. Henry Ford said it best: "If you think you can, you can."

We've just formed an important partnership, you and I. I will give it all I've got in these pages; you do the same in applying the information from these pages and we'll both succeed magnificently.

I am looking forward to hearing from all of you just as I have from the readers of the first edition: "Your book changed my life"; "I keep your book on my desk for reference"; "Your concepts of people benefits and people being more important than property have helped me put more profitable deals together than I ever thought possible"; "I was broke, used your sweat equity example, and now have five small apartment houses plus my own home"; "With just two ideas from your book I tripled my income and quadrupled my net worth in only 24 months"; "All of our four children have used your ideas to become financially independent"; and many more, for which I am grateful and inspired. Inspired to have this edition mean as much to all of you who are investing your precious time in reading it.

Freud said: "There are no accidents. . . ." "Your destiny is not a matter of chance, it is a matter of choice," according to William Jennings Bryant.

No one can make you feel inferior without your consent. No one can deprive you of your opportunity to become financially independent unless you let them.

More than 50 years ago, the mercantile genius Marshall Field said, " . . . real estate is not only the best way, the quickest way, but the only way to become wealthy." Shortly thereafter, during the worst depression in the history of the United States, President Franklin Delano Roosevelt said, "Real estate cannot be lost or stolen, nor can it be carried away. Managed with reasonable care, it is about the safest investment in the world." More recently an article in *Money* magazine observed, " . . . more and more Americans have come to see real estate as the one investment that offers protection against inflation."

As you read this, all of these statements will still hold true.

No other investment commands the profit potential of real estate. In good or bad times, fortunes can be made almost overnight, using "tax dollars" and borrowed money. Real estate converts taxable income into tax-free income, dramatically reducing or eliminating completely the taxable burden of generating income from other sources—such as wages—and slashes the taxes on profits to an absolute minimum.

Millions and millionaires have always been made in any situation— inflation, recession, depression, bust or boom.

There are only four known ways to acquire a fortune. They are: find it, inherit it, steal it, or earn it.

Of all professions, real estate offers the greatest opportunity to everyone to earn his or her fortune.

Race, religion, color, creed, ethnic background, or sex are no barriers. More women are top money earners in real estate than in any other industry. Profits are made in real estate every day by members of every sect, native and immigrant, living in this country, and by many non-resident foreign investors as well.

There is no better time than right now to become involved in real estate. The cost is low compared to what it will be in 20 years.

No investment enjoys more favorable legislation than real estate. The most important consideration related to profitable real estate investment will continue to be the ability to legally, morally and ethically reduce, defer, or avoid the payment of income taxes. This consideration is a prime advantage of learning and practicing Creative Real Estate. Considering all the layers of taxation, a dollar saved is often the equivalent of two dollars earned!

The successful patterns and practices that have served the Carnegies, Astors, Rockefellers, Gettys, Zeckendorfs, Kennedys, Marriotts, and Hiltons (even Trump—for a reality check) are among those I have researched and studied. With this information I have formulated and structured Creative Real Estate methods and techniques so that you can emulate the proven ways of these fortune-builders to achieve your own financial independence.

Traditional real estate practices may be affected by the economic ups and downs of this decade, but Creative Real Estate will not suffer at all. In fact, Creative Real Estate will prosper because inflation and ever-increasing income taxes will make the need for sheltering income a necessity.

Creative Real Estate provides innovative methods and practical solutions to help you weather the storms of inflation, recession, depression, or any combination of economic disasters that may appear in our rapidly changing times. Above all, Creative Real Estate is a way of life. There is a subtle yet significant difference between traditional real estate, which is practiced as a "numbers game," and Creative Real Estate, which is a "people business."

Those who study only the numbers, computerize the data, and read the computer's answers without cranking in the human equation arrive at incomplete, and as a result inaccurate, decisions. The product of an arithmetical computation is the answer to an equation, not the solution to a problem.

This book provides many formulas for practical and innovative transactions and methods for legally, morally, and ethically keeping your money from the tax collector. All the terms, phrases, and practices you need to know to make your fortune in real estate are here. In this world of constant change, formulas, methods, and practices can come and go. But the basic principles of the people business as applied to sound real estate investment, which are at the core of all the examples in this book, should prove valuable to you for many years. These principles are not theory or guesswork, but practical applications that have been drawn from actual experience.

A number of authors have presented ideas and suggestions for making money in real estate. Many of them often expound ideas originated in Creative Real Estate, and have been active participants in our educational and marketing events, at the annual Creative Real Estate Expositions and in seminar/workshops produced by the Professional Educational Foundation. The best-selling among them have contributed articles regularly to *Creative Real Estate Magazine*. Withal, there are concepts and basic source materials that are being newly published in this book. My purpose is to communicate the complete source materials and the basic principles upon which Creative Real Estate is established.

Whether novice or expert, *A Fortune at Your Feet* will answer your questions and assist you on the road to financial independence. This book has been designed for both the person who has no background in either business or real estate and the seasoned veteran.

For those of you who are already professionals in the field, you have in your hands a working tool that will maximize the development of broker-client relationships. Give a copy of *A Fortune at Your Feet* to all prospective clients and associates. After they have read the book, you can discuss the concepts and techniques of Creative Real Estate with them and rapidly determine the likelihood of establishing a successful and profitable business relationship.

If, after this discussion, the decision is "go," much of the basic client-broker information exchange will already be accomplished. If the decision is "no-go," the book will have saved all parties time and energy while providing a graceful exit from a potentially unfruitful association.

In writing this book it has been my desire to show you how to achieve your own financial independence and enjoy true wealth. In reading it, if you are perceptive, you will be able to create a better quality of life for yourself and those close to you.

The ideas I stand for are not mine.
I borrowed them from Socrates.
I swiped them from Chesterfield.
I stole them from Jesus.
And I put them in a book.
If you don't like their rules,
Whose would you use?"

—Dale Carnegie

PART I

Creative Real Estate: Your Key to Success

> *My interest is in the future because I am going to spend the rest of my life there.*
>
> —Anon.

The Reason . . .

. . . for this book is simple and straightforward: to get your attention. "Expect *anything,* be surprised at *nothing* and you'll be prepared for *EVERYTHING!*" That is **Kessler's Law.** It took me one-third of a lifetime to formulate, another third to write and this third to live by. Applying it, I find that there is a way to get rich, stay rich and enjoy being rich that works for me—and can work for you.

"Many have tried, few have succeeded" has become the sad slogan of a vast legion of unfortunate "wannabees." These are the naive unsuspecting folks who fell for some full-color, wide-screen, after-midnight pitch by a self-proclaimed pundit who promised to impart his secret of success in real estate at a free seminar. Of the thousands who attended, a sizeable number were convinced at that free seminar (where they got what they paid for—nothing) to attend the guru's two-, three-, or five-day event for hundreds, or even thousands, of dollars, and then they would have the real secret of success. (Yeah, right.)

That method of operation became so wide-spread over the last dozen years that virtually everyone who heard of it discredited the possibility of honestly learning how to make good in real estate *except* in the so-called "old-fashioned" way: through hard knocks and experience.

Experience teaches you to recognize a mistake when you make it again; however, the final exam usually comes before the lesson. According to Aldous Huxley: "Experience is not what happens to you, it's what you do with what happens to you." Education is a shortcut to experience. Education will never be as expensive as ignorance. The only book that's too expensive is the one you didn't buy.

Just because one batch of sweet cream turns sour, there is no reason to believe that all sweet cream will sour before you can enjoy it. There is a way to get rich, stay rich and enjoy being rich with Creative Real Estate, the PEOPLEtype, not the stereotype. In those last five words is the key.

With all the real estate books that have been written since the first edition of *A Fortune At Your Feet* in 1981, one or more may have captured your attention. Has any one of them changed your life? Have you attained the promised goals? Through my public appearances in seminars, speeches, radio and television shows, and as Publisher and Editorial Director of *Creative Real Estate Magazine*, I have been in contact with literally thousands of

3

people who are still searching for answers. They want direction in their quest for success in real estate. While many are realistic in their understanding that there are no magic formulas to instant riches—it always takes work, your work, to make it happen—others have just not quite gotten the message.

Scarcely a week goes by that I don't hear from readers that this book made a difference in their lives. When it was first published (1981), many comments were made about the extent of philosophy woven into the case histories. Some appreciated it; others didn't want to be bothered with the ethics, morality and spiritual rewards of Win/Win transactions. All they were interested in was, "How do I make money quickly—walk away with all the chips and let the others fend for themselves?"

Time has proven that practicing a Win/Win philosophy makes it possible to succeed in good times or bad and prevail over the long haul. The quick, hit-and-run artists who grabbed all the chips they could, regardless of the impact on the other players, have all fallen by the way. And the bigger they seemed to be, the harder they fell. The genre of the large public seminar gurus—blanketing metropolitan areas with intensive television and full-page newspaper ads about their "free" seminars—is discredited. The public grew tired of being suckered into free, "teaser" seminars in order to be sold what started out as a $300 and soon evolved into a $15,000 seminar. Too many folks, either out of jobs or living at poverty level, were enticed in their desperation into begging, borrowing, perhaps even stealing, and signing notes for installment payments to pay for those highly-touted seminars. The road is now littered with the broken-spirited disbelievers, who went to the seminars and came out and failed.

Why? Primarily because so many of those super-hyped, high-priced seminars tried to squeeze everybody—smart, dumb, bright, dull, rich, poor, ambitious, lazy and all others—into the same mold. They preached the most spectacular-sounding success stories to illustrate their points and promised everyone if they did the same thing in the same way, they would succeed. If life were that simple, we'd all wear the same size clothing in the same color, eat the same food, listen to the same music, and enjoy the same activities. It would be a world of robots. That ain't the way it is.

We are each and every one of us unique and different, with different needs, wants and desires. As the French say, "Viva la difference!" Because that's what makes life interesting, exciting and beautiful. There is no single answer, reason or rationale for success in anything—least of all in real estate.

That is another reason for this book. To illustrate as many ways as possible, through actual case histories, how success can be attained dealing in real estate. I can state the primary lesson to be learned in one sentence: Real Estate is a People Business. When you learn to practice the Win/Win philosophy, "People are more important than property," lasting success will be yours.

The good news is that the Win/Win philosophy is ingrained in the human spirit and it doesn't take much more than realization of that to let it prevail in your transactions.

This book is dedicated to the good in all of us, recognizing that all we have to do to succeed is formulate good, caring practices and, as Napoleon Hill, Dale Carnegie, Zig Ziglar and many others have been saying for decades, give enough other people what they want and you will get whatever you want out of life.

It doesn't require a one- to five-day seminar costing up to $15,000 to get what you need to succeed. Very often one or two chapters in a book can open up your gateway to success. I hope each of you will find your special chapters in the pages that follow.

"Whatever you can do,
Or dream you can, begin it.
Boldness has genius,
Power and magic in it."

— Goethe

1

Is Creative Real Estate for You?

Know thyself.

—Socrates

ARE YOU READY?

"10 . . . 5, 4, 3, 2, 1." The red light on Camera 1 goes on, then the sound of the director's voice spills from the nearest cameraman's headphones: "Cue talent!"

"Real estate. Is it just something that holds the world together, or does it have another purpose? It can mean the realization of your fondest dreams: success, wealth, comfort, convenience, lifelong security and financial independence—or disaster.

"More fortunes have been made in real estate by more people than by any other means, in good times and bad. As a matter of fact, so-called 'bad times' can prove to be opportunity times.

"There probably isn't a corner in this country where you can hide from the wee-hours infomercials on TV, with self-appointed gurus huckstering their seminars and home-study courses. This is not another teaser about 'getting rich quick' by going to a seminar or buying a home study course. Here you will find documented facts, actual case histories, solid advice, straight answers and functional methods proven over more than four decades of successful work in real estate.

"There are no problem properties, merely problem ownerships. Like Shakespeare said, 'One man's meat is another man's poison'; so if you believe what has been proven since time began—that problems present opportunities—you will learn how to explore each problem situation for the potential benefit to you by knowing what to do with real estate. Should you own, rent, buy, sell, exchange, refinance, option, lease or share?"

That opening monologue from the premiere of "A.D. Kessler's REAL ESTATE ROUNDTABLE," a series of 30-minute feature television shows aired nationwide, prepares you for what this book is all about. Mainly it's about success; your success. And while success itself is good news, the good news about success is that success is beautifully blind. Age blind, gender blind, race blind, religion blind, ethnic blind, physical ability blind and color blind. It is attainable by anyone and goes well with everyone.

Wherever you are at this moment, you are literally standing, sitting, or lying on top of a fortune. No matter where you happen to be right now, under you is a tiny patch of the planet Earth—a bit of land, a piece of real estate—and that piece of real estate is worth a fortune.

Is this an exaggeration? Hardly. If you research the piece of real estate you're occupying, you will find that it's worth many times what it was a century ago and thousands of times what it was a century before that.

As I write this, I'm sitting in my office in Carlsbad, California, a few blocks from the Pacific Ocean. The father of the man who owns the land under this building bought it two generations ago from the heirs of a Spanish conquistador. They'd paid nothing for it and sold it to my landlord's father for $2 an acre, which was a good price at the time. If I offered him $200,000 for one of the same acres today, he'd laugh in my face.

Just before the turn of the century, the original settlers of Bringhurst, Nevada, pulled up stakes and abandoned the town to return to Utah. Shortly afterward, the ghost town they had left behind was "discovered" by the adventurer John C. Fremont. With him came ranchers, a handful of hopeful merchants, saloonkeepers, a sprinkling of the inevitable speculators, and the railroad. The new town, renamed Las Vegas, became a whistle-stop on the railroad's Los Angeles-to-Salt Lake City run. Hailed as a new frontier, this man-made oasis in the valley of the Nevada desert attracted the attention of people taking Horace Greeley's advice, as well as Westerners who didn't want to miss out on what looked like a good opportunity.

On May 15, 1905, the Union Pacific Railroad, a major landholder in the area (because of land originally acquired with their right-of-way), held a land auction in the town square, which today is downtown Las Vegas. In the course of a single afternoon, the auctioneer sold 1,200 individual lots for a total of $265,000. That averages a little more than $200 each. Today, if available, those same parcels are worth as much as $3 million apiece! Think of it. If your grandfather had bought one of those lots and you owned it today, every dollar he paid for it would be worth $15,000 to you today!

In 1803, President Thomas Jefferson sent James Monroe and Robert R. Livingston to Paris to buy the Isle of Orleans (New Orleans) from Napoleon for $2 million. Monroe and Livingston eventually bought the entire Louisiana Territory, 827,192 square miles, for $15 million. Today, not 200 years later, the New Orleans Superdome, which covers less than one-millionth of the area of the Louisiana Purchase, has a value more than ten times Napoleon's selling price.

In 1626, Peter Minuit, first Director General of the Province of New Netherland, bought the island of Manhattan from the Manhattan Indians for the equivalent of $24. The island contains 19,800 acres of land and each acre contains 6,272,640 square inches. In parts of Manhattan today, you couldn't buy *one* of those square inches for $24, and if you could, you would be spending *124 billion times* the price Peter Minuit paid.

Granted, these are not average real estate deals. But even at many times the price paid, the land would have been ridiculously inexpensive compared to its value today. While other forms of wealth have been increasing in value over time, real estate has exploded.

The reason real estate has exploded in value is because it is the basis for all forms of wealth. This is as true today as it was in the past. Because of population growth, technological progress, and new industry, the total wealth of the world is constantly, endlessly expanding. As the wealth of the world increases, so does the value of real estate. This means that there are fortunes to be made with every tick of the clock, in every kind of economic environment, and *you* can make them. You just have to be ready.

To be ready you don't need to have a great deal of money. As a matter of fact, having money *now* actually has little to do with how successful you can be in real estate. Far more important than money are knowledge, the proper temperament, and "wealth consciousness."

Knowledge is a combination of information and practice. This book contains enough information to get you started. As you apply this information to actual situations, you will get practice. By reading and applying what you read, you will have the two ingredients of information and practice that comprise the necessary knowledge for your success in achieving wealth and well-being in real estate.

If you have already made some money in real estate, you may have a head start with the knowledge you have gained. But to keep the money and enjoy it as much as you can and should, you could be lacking knowledge of a different type. This book will provide that type of knowledge for you. The other two aspects of being ready—the proper temperament and wealth-consciousness—do not come from reading one book. You either have them or you don't.

As a beginning, you were curious enough to pick up this book, which demonstrates that you have an inquiring, open mind. In this book you will find details of the concept I call Creative Real Estate. As soon as you are ready for it, this concept will be the golden key to your personal fortune, the fortune you can start to build today. This readiness requires the proper temperament. How well do you handle being in debt? How do you respond to pressure? According to Lee Trevino, "Pressure is when you've got 35 bucks riding on a four-foot putt and you've only got five dollars." Do deadlines spur you into action or scare you into paralysis? Can you deal with being on top of the world one day and deep in debt the next? Are you unable to handle the loss of even small amounts of money? The proper temperament to achieve wealth and well-being through Creative Real Estate is one that can successfully handle uncertainty and debt with resilience enough to bounce back and win. Mark Twain said: "If at first you don't succeed, you're running about average." Success is getting up one more time than you fall down.

Wealth-consciousness is the way you view yourself with regard to money. If you see yourself as someone who will always be poor and struggling, you have low wealth-consciousness. If you see yourself as rich, or at this time potentially rich regardless of your personal net worth, you have high wealth-consciousness.

No one ever became wealthy in actual material possessions until he or she first became wealthy in his or her own mind. The process of thinking wealthy creates a high wealth-consciousness. Do you perceive yourself as wealthy? Can you see yourself as a millionaire? Do you consider yourself deserving of great riches, a life of privilege and luxury? Walt Disney, when asked how he accomplished so much, said: "If you can dream it, you can do it."

It is important to answer these questions right now—before you go any further—to decide if you are ready to pursue the wealth and well-being that is waiting for you, the fortune at your feet.

Creative Real Estate is an exciting adventure, but it is not without some danger. Too many how-to-get-rich books speak only of the dollars and not of the dangers. This is not such a book. If you dislike facing danger, you can keep your money in a bank, where the double-edged sword of inflation and taxation will slowly slice your net worth to net worthless. It's not pretty, but it is predictable. Although that course of action is not immediately dangerous, it is ultimately devastating.

Creative Real Estate can be unpredictable, and recklessly practiced, even dangerous. But at all times it gives you a fighting chance. It allows you to take up your own double-edged broad sword, a sword of creativity and entrepreneurial spirit.

WHAT DOES IT TAKE?

There is no shortage of armchair wisdom about what it takes to make a fortune. One back-porch philosopher will tell you, "It takes money to make money." Another will insist you need a heart of iron and ice-water in your veins. Still others will proclaim that you have to be dishonest or lucky or both.

Forget them all. This is Creative Real Estate. It's a whole new ballgame, and what it takes to make a fortune in this game may surprise you.

YOU DON'T NEED CASH

One thing it does *not* take is a lot of cash. It may not even take a little cash. In fact, there are hundreds of ways to acquire real estate, only one of which requires straight cash.

In the Louisiana Purchase, for example, payment was only partly cash—slightly more than $11 million. For the balance, our government promised to settle almost $4 million in claims by Americans against the French government. The Manhattan transaction involved no cash at all. It was a pure exchange of the island for goods of value. Neither party had any interest in cash.

On March 17, 1775, the Transylvania Land Company exchanged $50,000 worth of goods and trading supplies—no cash—with Cherokee Chiefs Little Carpenter, Dragging Canoe, and Groundhog Sausage for all the wilderness embraced by the Ohio, Kentucky and Cumberland rivers.

History has many such examples. Yet most people think acquiring and transferring ownership of real estate constitutes buying for cash or some simple variation with cash (like a percentage down and the rest in the form of a bank loan). To get anywhere with Creative Real Estate, you must rid yourself of the notion that you need a substantial amount of cash for acquisition of real estate. You don't. What you need far more than cash are: (1) a desire to provide "people benefits," (2) an imagination, (3) willingness to risk, and (4) thought.

A Desire to Provide "People Benefits"

This is a basic key to Creative Real Estate, one that I will mention repeatedly. Providing people benefits is based on the fundamental principle that people are more important than property and that the ultimate test of the soundness of any transaction is the number of people benefits it produces and whether the transaction fulfills a need.

Looking back at the Louisiana Purchase, we see that it was an early example of Creative Real Estate in action. That transaction resulted in more than a change of ownership of property. It solved a problem for people. It provided people benefits to all parties involved.

To analyze the benefits we must understand that Napoleon had just lost the battle of San Domingo and needed cash to pay and rebuild his battered army. He needed that money more than he needed millions of acres of wilderness far across the ocean in America. The sale of Louisiana solved his problem and provided people benefits for his army. The acquisition of Louisiana provided farmland, hunting preserves, and river access to the Americans—the people benefits they needed. That brings to mind another basic fact in the practice of Creative Real Estate. When you provide people benefits by carefully determining and filling the need, you will find that it is virtually impossible to make a bad exchange. It is a fact of life that no one will give up what he has unless he gets something for it that he wants more.

To prosper in Creative Real Estate you must have an unquenchable desire to provide people benefits to everyone you deal with. The three simple rules for doing this are: (1) find a need, (2) determine if you can fill that need, and (3) fill the need. Here's the best part: if you fulfill people's needs and solve people's problems, you have ultimately solved your problem. You will become very rich very quickly. The bigger the problems you solve, the bigger your rewards will be.

Imagination

In real estate as in other life experiences, not all solutions to problems are evident on the surface. Einstein said: "Imagination is more important than knowledge." It may take imagination to provide solutions. For example: a manufacturing company is in serious financial straits. It needs new equipment, raw materials, and cash to pay its employees. The only item of value that it owns is the building it occupies. The company has tried to borrow money by mortgaging the building, but no bank will lend the money because the company's credit is bad. Another manufacturer would like to buy the building, but then the troubled company would have no place in which to operate. Unsolvable problem?

Not to a Creative Real Estate Professional who says, "How about a sale-and-lease-back?" Desperate for a solution, the company takes his advice and sells the building to an investor, then leases it right back again. The company uses the money from the sale to purchase new equipment and raw materials and to pay its employees, stays in business, and becomes productive and profitable once again. The investor gains income-producing property, a tax shelter, a seasoned tenant already in place, and a good measure of security. Everybody is happy, including the Creative Real Estate Professional who earns a substantial commission on the transaction he structured. All it took, in addition to the desire to provide people benefits, was imagination and knowledge.

Willingness to Risk

A capitalistic economy is based on the "entrepreneurial spirit"—the willingness to take a chance. Without this willingness there can be no innovative transactions. "You miss 100% of the shots you never take," Wayne Gretzky reminds us.

Let's take another look at the sale-and-lease-back transaction I just described. Was there an element of risk to the investor? Of course. The management of the company could have taken the purchase money from the investor, shut down the plant, and moved to Argentina. They could have continued to operate unprofitably and failed to make a lease payment. They could have allowed the plant to fall into disrepair. We could list a number of possible situations that might have hurt the investor. Still, he was willing to take the risks in exchange for the possible rewards. The process of evaluating the risk in order to determine his willingness depends on many factors, one of which is . . .

Thought

Don't misinterpret this. You do not have to be a genius to be involved in Creative Real Estate. Not at all. In fact, being a genius might hinder you because geniuses often pay too much attention to unnecessary details.

You should know how to count, to do simple mathematics, to read a contract, and to weigh risks against rewards. If you haven't the particular abilities to do these simple tasks but are smart enough to hire someone who can do these things for you, you will do very well. This concept, which we will explore in depth, is my principle of "leveraging people." Leveraging people was practiced by one of the greatest entrepreneurs of all time, Henry Ford. Though he knew how to do very little in the field of administration and management, he prided himself on the fact that he had a row of buttons on his desk that he could push to summon experts in each field to do whatever he wanted done for him.

Further on in the book we will spend more time on the subject of leveraging people—that is, hiring experts and using OPB (other people's brains), OPE (other people's effort) as well as OPM (other people's money). For now, keep in mind the following advice: know what you are doing or listen to someone who does.

LOOK WHO'S TALKING

If you are going to listen to A.D. Kessler, you would be ignoring my own advice if you didn't find out who I am and why I am qualified to advise you. My credentials are listed in the Publisher's Note in the back of this book. Yet no list of impressive credentials can speak as loudly as accomplishments. The story of my first real estate transaction is a classic example of Creative Real Estate in action. This transaction illuminated the concept of people benefits for me and I would like to share it with you. I turned $100 into a quarter of a million in less than a week. It happened like this.

When World War II ended, I was sent home to New Jersey with $1,200 in separation pay, a chest full of medals, and a temporary disability that kept me in a wheelchair for my first year back in the U.S.A. After buying a specially adapted car, I scouted for work, competing unsuccessfully with thousands of other veterans who were also unemployed. Prior to enlisting in the Army Air Corps for pilot training, I had been touring with a big band and then announcing on network radio. In addition to the post-war demise of big bands and the severe competition for any kind of a job in radio, being in a wheelchair (in that era they were cumbersome, wooden things weighing about 75 pounds) made it impossible for me to gain access to either a bandstand or a radio studio. At the end of a few months, I found myself almost out of money and still out of a job.

In desperation, I petitioned the Real Estate Commissioner to let me take the broker's exam—even though I hadn't put in the necessary time as a salesman—so that I could get started making a living on my own, since I anticipated that no broker would be quick to hire an inexperienced, disabled salesman. Because of my disabled veteran status he let me take it. I passed, and in January 1946, with my license still in its envelope and $100 in cash, I set out to make my mark in real estate.

An item in the newspaper caught my eye. Many of the industries that had done a big business during the war suddenly found themselves with a greatly reduced demand for their goods, yet they were occupying huge, newly built factories. One such company was the Clark Thread Mills, makers of O.N.T. threads, said to have been the brand Betsy Ross used to stitch the first United States flag. Clark was a solid old concern, but without the gigantic government orders for uniforms, it had to close and sell its recently constructed wartime mill in Bloomfield, New Jersey. The mill occupied seven acres and had a total of 600,000 square feet of manufacturing space. It was an albatross around Clark's neck.

The morning after seeing the newspaper article, I put on my uniform, carefully folded my $100 bill in my wallet, and drove to the Clark headquarters at 57th Street and Fifth Avenue in New York. Mustering more courage than I'd ever needed in battle, I wheeled up to the receptionist's desk and asked to see John Clark, the president. The receptionist laughed. No one saw Mr. Clark without an appointment, she explained. I persisted. To get rid of me, she referred me to a clerk, an officious, unpleasant man who probably would have had me thrown out, had it not been for the uniform, medals, and wheelchair. He told me the same story, but I refused to leave, insisting that I had to talk with Mr. Clark about a real estate proposition.

He referred me to a senior clerk, who referred me to a manager, who referred me to a vice-president. When the vice-president finally realized I simply wasn't going to leave without seeing Clark, he arranged a brief meeting.

With my hands shaking, I rolled into John Clark's baronial office and was introduced to him and two of the company's board members, with whom he had been meeting.

"What is it you want?" he asked impatiently.

"I'd like to buy your Bloomfield war plant," I replied.

His eyebrows went up. "Really? That's fine, since we're interested in selling. The price is a million, three-hundred thousand dollars. What are you willing to pay?"

"The full price," I answered, straight-faced.

"Splendid. How much can you put down as earnest money?"

My voice was surprisingly firm. "A hundred dollars," I said.

With that, he and the board members exchanged glances and had a rousing good laugh.

"I'm serious, Mr. Clark," I pleaded. "All I want is a ninety-day contract to sell your property and I'm willing to pay all the money I have in the world—a hundred dollars. If you can sell it to any prospects you may already have, go ahead. But if I can sell it, and I think I can, I'd like the opportunity to profit from it."

"Young man," he said in a fatherly way, "you're either an ambitious entrepreneur or you don't know what you're talking about. In either case, I admire your spunk. And since you're willing to agree to our pursuing our pre-existing sales efforts, we've got nothing to lose by taking your hundred dollars and letting you give it a try."

With that he called in his attorneys, who drew up a contract on the spot. I was on my way.

I left Clark's headquarters and drove over the 59th Street bridge into the old, heavy-industrial section of Queens. The first sign to catch my eye was "Vicks VapoRub." It was perched atop a tottering old building in the most congested, dilapidated part of the neighborhood. Using my special parking privilege, I pulled right up to the plant, went in, and asked to see the president.

Once again I got a laughing receptionist, a string of scornful clerks, and the story about the president seeing no one without an appointment. Once again I persisted and was eventually allowed to see the head man.

It turned out that at that very moment he had been talking with his executive vice-president about relocating. I jumped on this and explained to them that it was a mistake to stay in Queens when they could buy a nearly new plant in New Jersey, where there was room to expand, a good labor force, and many other benefits.

They listened, became interested, and went with me to see the Clark property three days later. It was ideal for them and they loved it. Before the week was out they paid me $250,000 for my contract so that they could buy the property from Clark. Even at the $1,550,000 price ($1,300,000 to Clark and $250,000 to me), it was a great deal for Vicks and they knew it. They were happy, Clark was happy, and needless to say, I was ecstatic.

That was my beginning 48 years ago. I include this story not to boast or bolster my ego or to suggest that you start the same way, but to assure you that when it comes to making money in real estate, I know what I'm talking about.

Lest this story mislead you, I'd like to emphasize that I'm not suggesting that anyone can become a millionaire starting from scratch or overnight. When I wheeled into John Clark's office, I was hardly a beginner. My father had dealt in industrial real estate and I had learned the business at his elbow from the time I was twelve. In fact, I had vowed not to be in the real estate business, but rather in the entertainment business. However, fate deals us the hand we have to play; obviously mine was to be in the real estate business. It became clear to me that I should play it to the best of my ability. I already knew that the dictionary is the only place where success comes before work. Considering all alternatives, or rather the lack of any, my path was clear; I was embarked on a lifelong career in real estate.

If you're just starting out, you can expect that your own fortune will take some time to build. However, you can speed up the process if you learn techniques that work from someone who knows how to use them. With the confidence that comes from more than 48 rewarding years in Creative Real Estate, I can say that I'm that someone.

WHAT THIS BOOK WILL DO FOR YOU

If you do nothing but read this book from cover to cover, you will gain some very real benefits. For one thing, you will be introduced to some great "new" ideas. I put new in quotes because nothing here is really new in the sense that no one's ever seen it before. Every Creative Real Estate technique I describe has been used, tested, and proven for decades—even for centuries. Still, the ideas may be new to you, and that's all that matters.

What these new ideas can do for you is to fire your imagination. They can get you thinking in ways that are different from the ways in which you have been thinking up to now. This book will start you thinking like a Creative Real Estate Practitioner. As I use the term here, a Creative Real Estate Practitioner is someone who uses the principles of Creative Real Estate to invest for his own account and who derives all or part of his income from these investments. A Practitioner is different from a Creative Real Estate Professional, who is someone who makes his living by advising and guiding Practitioners and others in the proper employment of Creative Real Estate techniques. At this writing, there are approximately 40,000 Creative Real Estate Professionals and an untold number of Practitioners.

What these people have in common is a desire to provide people benefits, a unique way of thinking, and a positive, "can-do" approach to real estate that enables them to create profitable transactions from situations that conventional thinkers would view as impossible.

Creative Real Estate, as I describe it for you step by step, will introduce you to that way of thinking. In this book, I will give you the details of proven methods on how to make money in real estate. I will show you how to make money with exchanges, creative financing, "sweat equity," and dozens of other ideas. I will explain more ways to put money into your pockets than you ever dreamed possible. I might even inspire you to create moneymaking ideas of your own. So much the better.

After you've been exposed to Creative Real Estate, you won't ever again have to say, "I never had the opportunity to make big money." Gone forever will be the feeling that only people who have a lot of money to start with can become really wealthy. Success in real estate has been achieved by people who have little or no traditional education, training, or financial backing—and in some cases by people who couldn't even sign their names to the million-dollar contracts they negotiated. You'll be every bit as ready to go out and make your fortune, and enjoy doing it.

... AND WHAT IT WON'T DO

No matter how many good ideas you get from this book, it can't make you act on those ideas. Books do nothing but sit on a shelf. Once you've read them, it takes your own measure of courage and creativity to put the ideas to work. Ideas don't work unless you do.

This book won't give you the determination to stick your neck out and take the risks that are part of any business transaction. You have to provide the judgment and effort to do that.

Even the most ambitious, highly motivated people have a hard time following the advice of the many real estate "experts" who suggest that the way to get started is to buy a small fixer-upper house in a depressed area of your town for little or no money down, rent it, and eventually sell it for a profit.

In my opinion, because of the risks and the work involved, this is not a particularly good way to get started in real estate. Still, it is a way, and with a generation of how-to books advising people to do it, you would think that millions of readers would be out there speculating in fixer-uppers and building real estate empires.

Yet few go out and do it. The reason is simple. It takes work and determination. It takes hours to scan want-ads and drive through depressed areas of town to find a suitable fixer-upper. It may be necessary to go into debt to buy the property. Weekends have to be sacrificed to fix the place up. The new owner has to be able to meet the very real risks that destructive tenants or an economic slump in the market could prevent a profitable re-sale.

No book will search want-ads, scour neighborhoods, or fix faucets. This book is no different. I will be presenting more imaginative ways to build a real estate empire than buying fixer-uppers, but I won't be supplying the work and the determination. That's up to you. You can only benefit from *A Fortune At Your Feet* (or any other self-help book) by helping yourself. Everyone is self-made; only the successful admit it. If you make a commitment to act on the ideas that are presented in this book, I can assure you that you will succeed in good times, bad times or in-between times. Success is 90% getting started and 10% not stopping. Without that commitment, neither this nor any other book in the world can help you.

Finally, a book can't guarantee happiness. I learned long ago that helping people make fortunes in real estate does not always lead to greater happiness for my clients. Of all the people I've helped become very wealthy, many couldn't handle the pressure of wealth. They began to give more importance to money than to people. Their marriages crumbled. Their families were torn apart by jealousy over who got how much of what. Some even lost the good sense that helped them build their fortunes in the first place.

The last part of this book tells you how to keep and enjoy your wealth. Read it carefully. It can't guarantee happiness, but the advice, carefully heeded, puts the odds in your favor.

Any book worth reading is worth reading more than once. To assist you in quickly refreshing your recollection of the key points in each chapter, as you first read them and whenever you later refer back to them, I will provide a list of Kessler's Keys to Success at the end of each chapter. Your knowledge and use of these key points will furnish you with the Keys to Success, to get rich, stay rich and enjoy being rich with Creative Real Estate.

Your first Kessler's Keys to Success are:

- ⚷ Is creative real estate for you?
- ⚷ Are you ready?
- ⚷ What does it take?
- ⚷ You don't need cash
- ⚷ Look who's talking
- ⚷ What this book will do for you
- ⚷ . . . And what it won't do

2

People Benefits:
You Have to Give to Get

He who cannot give anything away cannot receive anything either.

— Nietzsche

TAKE A GOOD LOOK AROUND

If you seek opportunities in real estate, look around. Unless you're in the middle of the ocean, what you see is land. And unless you're in the middle of the desert, you see people as well. To succeed in real estate all you really have to do is understand the relationship between land and people. It seems too simple to be true, but true it is.

The United States Department of Commerce Bureau of the Census typically measures current realities and projects future trends. The Bureau projects that the population will increase from 255 million now to 275 million by the year 2000.

As I write this, a baby is born in the United States every 9 seconds, while someone dies every $16\frac{1}{2}$ seconds. Even though the immigration rate is only slightly greater than the emigration rate in the United States, the country is experiencing a net gain of approximately 2,000 people per day.

Think about it. Every day, 2,000 people "arrive" in the United States. Every day, 2,000 new people need the basic requirements of life: food, water, clothing, and shelter. The basic source for all of these requirements is land. Without exception, each new person requires something to eat, something to drink, something to wear, and a place to stay. Where do they get these things?

All food, not only fruits and vegetables, comes from the land. All water sits or flows on the land or under it. All clothing is made from natural fibers that we draw from the land (or animals nurtured by the land) or from chemicals that we synthesize from the natural products of the Earth. As for shelter, no matter how many stories high you are right now, there's a piece of dirt below you somewhere. Your house or apartment building is made from wood (trees grown on the land) or steel (iron ore taken from the land) or brick (hardened dirt) or stone or cement, all of which come from the land.

With 2,000 additional people each day demanding more food, water, clothing, and shelter from the same supply of land, what do you suppose is going to happen? The answer comes from the most basic law of economics, the law of supply and demand. When demand goes up and supply remains the same, the price rises. This puts anyone who owns real estate in an enviable position.

Yet it leads to a question—perhaps a disturbing one. If real estate is so valuable and increasing in value every day, why would anyone ever want to sell any? Doesn't the fact that there are literally millions of pieces of property for sale right now all over the country cast doubt on the belief that land is rising in value everywhere?

For the following reason, the answer is no.

THERE ARE NO PROBLEM PROPERTIES, ONLY PROBLEM OWNERSHIPS

No matter where it is or what it looks like, real property has no intrinsic worth whatsoever. Whether an acre of land is located in a swamp, in a desert, on a mountain, or in a valley, it is still intrinsically worthless.

Land is only valued in terms of what it is worth to someone. People give land its value by what they believe they can do with it. An acre of sandy soil in the middle of the desert is functionally no different from an acre of sandy soil next to the Pacific Ocean. Neither of them can grow crops, while both of them could potentially house exactly the same number of people. Yet there are people who would not give you a thousand dollars for an acre of desert. Those same people would gladly give you a million dollars for an acre of Pacific beachfront.

Because land of itself has no intrinsic value, its value is relative. This relative value is based entirely on what people think, feel, believe, estimate, calculate, wish, hope, and dream it is worth. The land does nothing to contribute to its own value. It just sits there. People ascribe value to it based on their "circumstances of ownership."

What people do with land—how they use it, how long they keep it, whom they own it with—are the circumstances of ownership. One person buys a piece of property and grows flowers on it, while another builds an office building. One buys an estate to keep in the family for generations, while another needs a condominium only for an eighteen-month assignment in Phoenix. One buys a house in joint ownership with a spouse; another forms a limited partnership with total strangers.

These circumstances of ownership dictate how much a piece of property is worth to any given owner on any given day. If a farmer buys land to grow flowers but the government diverts his water supply, that land is worth relatively less to him because of the circumstances. If an office-building developer can't start construction because his poor credit rating prevents him from buying materials, the land he hoped to build on is worth relatively less to him.

The farmer with no water and the developer with poor credit each have a problem, and their problem involves their ownership of property. In each instance, the problem is not the property itself but the particular circumstances and intentions of the owner. The solution to each problem is determining and providing the benefits each owner needs, wants, and desires from the ownership of that particular property; put another way, it is what each owner wants to *do* with each property.

With this concept of use in mind, we can understand why property is put up for sale. The farmer who has no water knows that his property is rising in value. But in his circumstances, the mere increase in price is not his most important concern. His use of the land is, and he wants land with water flowing to it so that he can grow flowers. To him, land with abundant water is worth relatively more than land without it. So he puts his farmland up for sale. Along comes an auto manufacturer who needs vacant land for a test track. The manufacturer doesn't care that the land won't grow flowers. He wants the open space to use for test-driving cars.

The same concept applies to the office-building developer. Since he can't erect his building and is unwilling to keep paying taxes on the land, he puts it up for sale to someone who has a good enough credit rating to qualify for a loan.

This is where you can enter the scene. If you as an investor or an agent can help someone whose circumstances of ownership present a problem, you will have the opportunity to solve the problem, fill the need, provide people benefits to all involved, and profit from helping or investing in and owning a piece of property. Such opportunities are everywhere—start looking around.

THE ENDLESS LIST OF "PEOPLE BENEFITS"

J. C. Penney, the famous merchant, said, "Give people what they want and they'll make you rich." Without thinking in terms of people benefits you won't get anywhere. Understanding the concept of people benefits is the foundation of your success.

What are people benefits? They are unlimited ways people derive good out of owning—and not owning—property. I include "not owning" because a very real benefit can result from giving up ownership of land, as the examples of the farmer and the developer demonstrated in the preceding section.

In order to show you a point of view you may have never before considered, picture yourself in the role of the professional. In fact, you can be any one of the characters in this scenario. As you begin to creatively deal in real estate, you'll find that sometimes you're the owner of a piece of property and you have a problem with that ownership. Another time you may find you're the holder of cash and that your need is for property that produces a monthly income. Yet again you may find yourself as the middle-man negotiating between two or more parties. So it's good to look at yourself as a potential player of any of the roles I describe in the many examples throughout this book. In any instance, I could be talking about a position you may find yourself in very soon.

Suppose a man in his late sixties walks into your real estate office and says he would like to sell his house, which is free of debt. If you were a traditional real estate broker, you would ask the man how much he expects to sell the house for, get the details on the property, have him sign a listing agreement, and put the house on the market. You would advertise and show the house until it sold for, at, or close to the price the man wanted.

That's the way real estate brokerage is practiced thousands of times every day all across the country. I call that the "numbers game" of real estate. As a Creative Real Estate Professional, you're more interested in the people benefits of ownership and sale than you are in the numbers game of peddling properties for whatever price they will bring. When the elderly gentleman comes into your office and says he wants to sell, you don't ask, "How much?" You ask, "Why?"

The answer might surprise you. It could be that he doesn't really want to sell, but his wife is gravely ill and needs expensive surgery. The man realizes that his house is his only asset, so he decides to sell it to raise the money for the necessary medical care for his wife.

As a professional who deals in people benefits, you immediately see that this is faulty problem solving. The man doesn't need to sell his house, he needs cash. Knowing there are many ways for him to raise cash other than selling, you suggest he place a mortgage on the house. This mortgage could be large enough to cover the cost of surgery, yet carry a monthly payment small enough for the man to meet comfortably.

This gives you an opportunity to provide a benefit to someone else, too. You know people who have large amounts of cash that they regularly keep in low-interest-bearing certificates at the bank, where they are receiving a small but consistent income. Many of these savers would gladly put some of their cash into a higher-yielding mortgage, especially if they would receive a regular monthly payment. And since the mortgage is backed by the value of the house, the lender's investment is secured. Both parties benefit; both parties win. This is the "people business" of real estate.

The key element of people benefits is that everyone involved must win. Everybody must come out ahead as a result of the transaction. This win/win philosophy is not altruistic or idealistic. It is the real world secret to making Creative Real Estate work.

You may be wondering how real estate professionals can make any money turning down brokerage commissions. In the example above, the broker can charge a reasonable fee to both parties in the transaction. True, the fees may not be as much as a commission on the sale of the house, but the broker who acts in this manner has earned the respect and the future business of everyone involved, plus an unknown number of referrals. The word will go out: "This broker really cares about people." Such a reputation and the resulting benefits are worth far more than a single commission.

To further understand the concept of people benefits, you must understand the distinctions among *needs, wants,* and *desires.*

Needs, as I define them, are what a person absolutely must have, such as transportation. This is a need because he must have transportation to get to his job, and his job provides him with the medium of exchange (money) with which he obtains his more basic needs of food, water, clothing, and shelter.

There are many ways for a person to fulfill a need. For transportation, he could walk, hitchhike, roller-skate, take a bus, or drive a car. Any one of these could solve his problem and take care of his need for transportation. He decides that he *wants* a car. The car is not the real need. As we've already reasoned, he could get to work to get his pay and his real necessities without it. Transportation is the real need. Still, he wants a car.

There are any number of makes, models, sizes, shapes, and prices of cars that will fulfill this person's wants. As he shops, he sees something that really catches his eye—a Rolls Royce. Immediately he *desires* that particular automobile (for some reason I just can't say "car" when talking about a Rolls Royce). The person's wants are one requirement; his desires are quite another. And both of them are quite apart from his needs.

To summarize: he needs transportation; he wants a car; he desires a Rolls Royce. Now by filling the need, perhaps with a motorcycle, this person can get to work promptly and regularly, have transportation to take on a second job, and make enough money to buy his want—a car. Then, by using the car, he can broaden his activities, perhaps get promoted, and eventually become successful enough to attain his desire—a Rolls Royce. If he had pursued the desire first (the Rolls Royce), he would probably have gone broke making the payments and would not have been able to take care of his wants or his needs. The person who sold him the Rolls Royce would have to spend time, energy, and money to repossess a used, unpaid-for vehicle.

People benefits are concerned with needs. This does not mean, however, that all you will be doing in real estate is providing people with basic shelter. If that were so, you might well confine your efforts to building huts. There are levels of needs that vary according to the circumstances of different people. A woman who owns a 100-unit apartment building doesn't need all 100 units to live in. But she may need competent management to make her building generate profitable enough income to live on. A man in the highest income tax bracket doesn't need to make huge profits from his holdings, but at his level he needs a tax shelter. And so it goes.

No matter what their income, people will always have wants and desires that are quite apart from the needs their situation demands. Don't concern yourself with wants and desires. To do that would put you in the same category as an unscrupulous car salesman who will sell a luxury car to someone who clearly can't afford it.

Instead, when you begin to deal in real estate, look first for people who have a need. Look for a need you can determine. Look for a need you can fulfill. Those are your only concerns. Stick with them. Satisfy those needs and you will build your fortune.

The list of people benefits that can be provided would be virtually endless. This means that you have unlimited opportunity to succeed, if you do no more than follow the three rules of practice I listed earlier: (1) find a need, (2) determine if you can fill that need, and (3) fill the need. Always remember that any transaction must provide people benefits to all involved parties; it must be a win/win situation. That is to say, *everyone* must come out winning.

Once you have acquired the knowledge that this book provides, your attitude is what makes win/win possible. To illustrate the significance of attitude, think of the two shoe salesmen who were sent to a small underdeveloped country to open new markets. One wired back: "It's hopeless. Nobody here wears shoes." The other wired back: "Opportunity unlimited. Nobody here wears shoes yet."

Being successful depends 10% on what happens to us and 90% on how we react to it.

In the seminar I teach, called "The Key to Creative Real Estate," I distribute a 202-page workbook to the participants. There is enough material in that workbook to discuss for at least six days, eight hours each day. I give this seminar in one eight-hour day. And I begin by asking the participants whether they know the one word that represents the key to success in Creative Real Estate. Invariably, after about fifteen minutes of discussion, someone comes up with that one word. That word is actually the crux of the entire seminar, but it takes some conditioning and explanation (eight hours' worth) to make it acceptable, for it's so simple, so basic. Having read this far in the book, I believe that you are ready to accept and believe the one word that is the key to success in Creative Real Estate: **ATTITUDE.**

THERE ARE HUNDREDS OF WAYS TO BUY REAL ESTATE
AND ONLY ONE REQUIRES ALL CASH

I tell this to people wherever I go, and without fail they have difficulty believing it. Yet it's true.

Here's an example of a way you might actually go about building a real estate empire with no money down. This particular example is based on an actual case history. The dynamics of the situation could work for anyone.

For illustration, assume that you are living in a four-unit apartment building in a respectable but average (not wealthy) neighborhood. You have nothing in the bank, earn $1,500 a month, and pay $500 of that in rent. You want to make a fortune in real estate but don't know how to get started. You look around and discover that your landlady has problems. She's had a succession of part-time managers who have allowed the building to become run-down. If the building continues to deteriorate, your landlady will have to lower the rents or keep from raising them during inflationary times, which is just as undesirable from her point of view. Despite the soundness of the neighborhood and the general climate of increasing property values, your landlady's property is in danger of dropping in value and income.

As a fledgling Creative Real Estate Practitioner, you go to her with an offer. You say, "I've seen a stream of inept managers go in and out of here and do nothing for your building. Repairs, lost rents, and lowered property value are costing you far more than the $500 rent I'm paying. If you give me free rent plus 10% of any rents I collect in excess of what they are today, I'll manage your building."

A reasonable offer? Irresistible. She accepts. Then you add a "sweetener" to the transaction: "An additional benefit for both of us would be for you to share with me 50 percent of the profit in excess of the price you would sell for today when you sell the building in the future. That will be a real incentive for me to improve your building to its utmost." Since this provides her additional benefits that she may not have previously anticipated, your landlady is delighted to "add the sweetener" to your agreement.

With an agreement such as this, you're providing a number of people benefits:

1. You're taking care of your own need for shelter.
2. You're fulfilling your landlady's need for reliable management and increased income.
3. You're fulfilling the other tenants' need for attractive, well-managed shelter.
4. You're creating an opportunity to increase your own wealth by 10 percent of the ensuing rent increases and 50% of the well-managed property's appreciation in value.

What has made you different from the other managers is your understanding of the concept of people benefits. Now you have an interest in the property, a stake in it. You want to see the property improved, the rents raised, and the value increased. You'll take care of the building for your landlady/partner as if it were your own.

If you put down this book right now and get nothing more from it, you will already have the golden key to success in your hands.

That golden key is the realization that people benefits are the first and foremost consideration on the road to success. Determining needs, wants, and desires will permit you to provide solutions and structure people benefit win/win transactions. Your willingness and ability to analyze the needs, wants, and desires of all parties to a transaction and to fit together the proper personalities, situations, and solutions to attain the people benefits objective of win/win are critical to the success of any transaction. All parties, including you, will come out better off than before the transaction.

Let's continue this example. There's another plus in it for you. Now you suddenly have $500 every month that you wouldn't otherwise have had. If you exercise discipline and put that $500 in the bank, at the end of the year you'll have $6,000 to invest in real estate. You can also expect realistically to profit from the sale of the four-unit building and perhaps buy it yourself. But let's say you're impatient. You want something within a year. You decide to use a "piggy-back" strategy. That is to say you hitchhike on the original concept. This process of "hitchhiking" or "piggy-backing" is formally called *idea-tracking* and is a method of using applied creativity, commonly known as "brainstorming." So, let's track the idea further.

LOOK AROUND YOUR NEIGHBORHOOD

Now that you've been managing a fourplex and doing a good job of it, you look for something you can own. Down the block is a ragged old duplex on a large lot with a motor home parked in the backyard. You approach the owner and find out that he's paying someone $100 a month to manage the duplex part-time and that the motor home is vacant and livable (barely).

You make the owner an offer. First, you find out what he feels the duplex is worth today (let's say $50,000). You agree to pay him $60,000 for it in one year on these terms: (1) you will manage his duplex without charge if he will allow you to live in the motor home rent-free, and (2) you will pay him $6,000 down, but not in a lump sum. Instead, you will give him $500 per month for the next year. At the end of the year he will give you a deed to the property, provided you can finance the rest—$54,000.

You might be asking, "How can I do this? Where am I going to get $500 per month and what bank will give me a $54,000 loan with my income?"

By moving into the motor home, you have freed the apartment you've been getting for free in the fourplex (and you are still close enough to continue to provide good management). This enables you to sublet that apartment for $500 per month. Add to that the $500 you're already saving, and you'll have $1,000 per month in extra cash.

By making regular payments of $500 per month to the owner of the duplex, you are building a reputation for reliability; you're building a good credit rating. The payment on a $54,000 loan, with the recently approved longer-term mortgages available at flexible terms, isn't much more than $500 per month. When you show a banker that you've been able to easily make such a payment for a year, and are maintaining a savings account (with the extra $500 a month), you stand an excellent chance of getting your loan, and if not from a banker perhaps from the seller himself.

A year later, you own a duplex, have a 50% portion of the appreciation on a fourplex, and are still piling up more cash. You're well on your way.

LOOK BEYOND YOUR NEIGHBORHOOD

When I advise you to look beyond your neighborhood I mean it in two ways: geographically and generically.

Look Beyond Your Neighborhood Geographically

Many people, particularly in my own state of California, complain that they can't find a decent house to invest in at a reasonable price—that duplexes like the one in the above example simply don't exist at prices under $60,000.

Well, that's not entirely true. They *do* exist. I live in San Diego County, where the price of the average single-family home is more than $100,000. Still, there are parts of this county where prices are much, much lower than that: center-city neighborhoods, older housing tracts, outlying areas, isolated areas in the mountains and the desert, and areas where maintenance has been deferred (real estate jargon for run-down).

It doesn't stop there. Opportunities abound in every part of the country. The specific example above was based on the actual case history of a young client of mine. Here's another one taken directly from real life.

Eric and Jean lived in a $150-per-month apartment in Detroit during the early 1970s. At the time, real estate in that city was in bad shape. As a reaction to the riots of 1967, people were moving out of Detroit at an alarming rate and property values were dropping. Yet Eric and Jean had to live somewhere. They looked in the suburbs, but rents and housing prices both were out of their range. Eric had just returned from Viet Nam and was starting at the bottom of the ladder in the advertising business. He was making $150 a week.

Knowing that if they were going to buy a house anywhere it would have to be right in Detroit, the couple began looking around. They found a house in one of the few desirable neighborhoods Detroit had to offer. It was a small bungalow with a selling price of $17,000, and it had a mortgage at $5\frac{1}{4}\%$ interest with an $11,000 balance owed. The mortgage was assumable, meaning that if Eric and Jean could come up with the $6,000 difference for a down payment in order to consummate the purchase, they could take over that mortgage, with its favorable $5\frac{1}{4}\%$ interest rate and monthly payment of $109.

But they didn't have $6,000. They had no cash at all. Eric went to a relative and convinced her to lend him $5,000 in return for a second mortgage on the house at 6% interest and a monthly payment of $60. That payment, added to the $109 first mortgage payment, totaled $169 per month, just $19 more than they were already paying in rent. By tightening their budget they could make it.

This still left them $1,000 short of the down payment. To raise it they used the $250 refundable security deposit from their apartment and combined it with a $750 loan from a bank. They got the $750 loan by opening a checking account that had an override feature. In those days banks were beginning to stimulate borrowing by means of attaching a line of credit to a regular checking account. Interest rates on such loans were high, but payments were low and could be strung out indefinitely. In addition, Eric knew that if he told his boss he was buying a house (and settling permanently), he could get a small raise.

Even without the raise, buying the house rather than renting gave them other financial breaks. Their property taxes, which were $400 per year, were deductible from their federal income tax, as was the interest they were paying on the three loans. The combined tax savings amounted to almost $250 each year, or approximately $20 per month. Bottom line, it was costing Eric and Jean no more to live in their own house than to live in an apartment.

During the next few years, the couple reduced their various loans to $12,000 and were getting anxious to move. They put the house up for sale and, not unexpectedly, received no offers. But they had a friend who liked the way they had fixed the place up and who was getting married soon. He had no money, but he did qualify for a Veterans Administration loan guarantee with nothing down.

In return for Eric and Jean's willingness to sell the house "VA," which required extra appraisals, paper work and seller's costs, their friend was willing to pay $20,000—$2,000 more than the market price of the house. The sale was made and Eric and Jean paid off the $12,000 in loans and used the $7,500 remainder of the proceeds to buy a half-interest in an eleven unit apartment building elsewhere in Detroit.

For two years the couple managed the building and occupied the manager's apartment rent-free. They banked their rent savings plus their half of the positive cash flow from the building. At the end of the two years they and their partner sold the building for exactly what they had paid (remember, real estate in Detroit was not escalating in value) and they earned back their $7,500. This, combined with the savings of two years of unspent rent plus accumulated cash flow, enabled them to move to Southern California, where they bought a duplex that appreciated at the rate of 20% over the next two years.

While the area of the country in which you live might not hold the right opportunities for you, some other area might abound with them. Right now, in addition to Detroit, cities such as Jacksonville, Cleveland, New Orleans, San Antonio, Kansas City (Missouri), Houston, Biloxi (Mississippi), and Newark (New Jersey) have areas where you can invest advantageously with little or no money down. And you don't necessarily have to live there to do it. Rental homes and small apartment buildings are available in all these places. Most of them generate adequate positive cash flow to pay a resident manager and leave plenty for you, the absentee landlord.

Incidentally, today Eric and Jean are again looking for no money-down investment property back in Detroit, property that one of their relatives who lives there can manage for them. They realize the benefits of not being "area bound" in their asset-building program.

Look Beyond Your Neighborhood Generically

"Generically" refers to the kind of property you invest in. Again, let's say you live in an area where housing prices have made it almost impossible to obtain positive cash flow from residential properties. I suggest you look beyond your neighborhood, that is, look at other kinds of properties in addition to residences.

If you look at the way prices react when an area becomes popular, you'll find that housing always goes up first, followed by food and clothing. Commercial and industrial real estate do not rise as sharply or as quickly as consumer items. So while you're lamenting the state of housing prices, you might be overlooking opportunities in retail stores, warehouses, parking lots, small shopping strips, office buildings, and entertainment centers.

The principles for earning profits from commercial properties are the same as those that apply to residential properties. Find a property with a problem ownership. Define the owner's problem in terms of needs. Determine what those needs are and find ways to fulfill them. Structure a transaction that provides people benefits and you can profit as easily with commercial properties as our friends did in the examples of the fourplex and duplex we explained earlier.

Even in these relatively simple examples, you've been exposed to some fundamental concepts of Creative Real Estate. No situation explained in case histories can be expected to or is intended to precisely fit your current situation, or even one you may find yourself involved with in the future. However, the fundamental principles apply to any situation.

The people in the case histories I tell you about are not super-sophisticated, highly trained investment whizzes; they are the folks who stand next to you in the checkout line at the supermarket.

With practical application of the principles and innovative variations of the techniques and methods described, the practices and solutions can be applied to current opportunities. In the process of applying the principles, you might very well, with only subtle changes, come up with some "new" formulas of your very own.

You're now ready to decide whether building a fortune through Creative Real Estate is right for you.

Here are the new Kessler's Keys to Success to think about:

➤ Take a good look around

➤ There are no problem properties, only problem ownerships

➤ The endless list of "people benefits"

➤ There are hundreds of ways to buy real estate and only one requires all cash

➤ Look around your neighborhood

➤ Look beyond your neighborhood

3

What YOU Have to Do

Nothing happens to you unless you make much of it.

— Plutarch

ARE YOU SURE YOU WANT TO DO THIS?

During my years of teaching seminars to people who want to get started in Creative Real Estate, I've always been fascinated by my students' reactions to two simple questions. First, I ask, "How many of you want to make a fortune in real estate?"

Invariably, everyone in the room thrusts a hand into the air without a moment's hesitation. Then I ask, "How many of you are willing to do whatever—*whatever* it takes to make that fortune?"

The response is significantly different. Only some raise a hand immediately. Most hesitate. Some think for quite a few moments. Some don't raise their hands at all.

It's not hard to figure out why the reactions are so different. The first question promises a reward, the fulfillment of a dream, and a life of wealth and luxury. The second question implies that there might be a sacrifice involved; some risk, some difficulty, some stretching of the self beyond the comfort level. Though nearly everyone claims to *want* a desirable goal, few are willing to make the necessary sacrifices to attain that goal.

Would you like to have a job where you set your own schedule and work as little or as much as you want? Would you like an unlimited income? Would you like to be in a profession that has always been one of the highest-paying in the country? Would you like to work for only 15 or 20 years, then live comfortably on renewal business for the rest of your life?

Did you answer yes to all of these questions? Good. Then you're willing to sell insurance.

With the lure of all those sweet-sounding positives, the insurance industry attracts thousands of new recruits every year. All but a tiny fraction of the recruits leave too soon to experience those positives because they are not willing to do what it takes to get the rewards. Insurance industry statistics reveal that only two out of every five stick it out for a whole year and only one out of every five who remain after the first year lasts as long as three years! They are not willing to work on a commission basis. They are not willing to make unsolicited prospect calls. They are not willing to hear hundreds of people say "no" before one will say "yes." They are not willing to travel across town and spend an evening talking to complete strangers about insurance. They are not willing to learn the thousands of complicated details that a truly professional insurance agent must have on the tip of his or her tongue. They are not willing to do *whatever* it takes to achieve success.

Let's look at the "whatever" you have to be willing to do to make your fortune in Creative Real Estate. *The main thing you have to be willing to do is go into debt.* No big deal? Everybody is in debt, right?

Well, yes—and no. Some people are temperamentally unsuited to being in debt. A few credit card balances, a car loan, even a home mortgage are pretty standard items. With a few exceptions, most of us are quite capable of handling them. But exactly how do you handle them?

Give yourself a quick test. Answer these questions as honestly as you can:

- Do you feel proud and secure when you owe money—lots of money?
- Would you feel proud and secure owing more than a hundred thousand dollars? More than a million?
- Can you readily accept that you are working with someone else's money to build your own fortune?
- When you go into serious debt—that is, when your ability to make the payments is in real question—do you sleep easily the whole night through?
- Are you willing to dip into your savings for a while to make the payments on a loan?

If you answered "no" to any of these questions, you might be temperamentally unsuited to one of the basic requirements of getting rich quickly through real estate investment—the systematic use of large amounts of borrowed money.

There are other potentially uncomfortable aspects to this business that I will touch upon later, but I want to air this one right away because it's so crucial. How you answered those questions will go a long way in determining whether you truly want to get involved in this and how far you're willing to go once you do. A good point to consider is that a diamond was a chunk of coal that made good under pressure.

WHAT DO YOU ENJOY MOST?

It's a fact of life that you do best what you enjoy doing most. People who love to ski spend a lot of time skiing and become magnificent skiers. Crossword puzzle addicts are crossword puzzle wizards. Painting enthusiasts develop into great painters. This principle is equally true in the field of real estate.

- Do you love to speculate, to take big chances with the possibility of reaping big rewards? If so, there's plenty of room in real estate for you to make your fortune.

- Do you enjoy wheeling and dealing? Do you like the challenge of making complicated exchanges with numerous negotiations and ramifications? There's room for you, too.

- Are you a handyman or handywoman? Do you love to paint and fix and tidy up? Or does the mere sight of a paint brush turn your blood to turpentine? Either way, you can find a piece of real estate to fit your favorite way of getting things done.

No matter what you enjoy, you can use it to your advantage in Creative Real Estate. What is important is that you decide in advance exactly what it is you like to do—and then do it.

Suppose you have no particular ability or desire to be a fixer-upper. Yet, according to the "experts," there is money to be made in real estate on fixer-uppers, depressed properties that with paint and putty and clever management can be turned over for handsome profits. If you have no stomach for paint or putty, you are better off not investing in fixer-uppers, because you probably won't do a decent job of fixing them up. You'll hate the repairs while you are making them and hate yourself after the fixing is completed. That doesn't make you less of a person. It just means that you're being true to your nature. So just be true to yourself and do something else. Success comes in cans, failure in can'ts.

Just a word of caution to those who contemplate hiring someone to do the fixing-up and anticipate making a profit. Be certain to get precise contracts for the repairs from a licensed, bonded contractor. Include a penalty clause to reimburse you for delays and a guarantee of a fixed price, not subject to any extras or overcharges. Without these assurances in writing, you may find that the actual fixer makes all the anticipated profit, leaving you with only the property and a lot less in your bank account than you had before you started.

On the other hand, though you might hate fixing things, you might love dealing with people. You might have a knack for helping them out, mediating disputes, and calming folks in times of stress. If so, you might be perfect for real estate situations calling for property management. There are limit-less opportunities for you to make fortunes with those talents.

Whatever talents you have are inherently no better and no worse than anybody else's. They are just different. What counts is that you use them and use them in ways you enjoy. Use them and you will succeed. Enjoy yourself and you will succeed. Have an absolute ball at it and you will succeed magnificently.

Take a few moments to write down the activities you most enjoy. Make a few notes in the margin of this page, or on a separate sheet of paper. If your favorite activity is lying in the sun getting a tan, write it down. It doesn't matter if you can't see any connection right now between what you enjoy doing and real estate. For the moment, just get a clear idea of what you like. Save your list because you'll want to refer to it later when we get into the nuts and bolts of how Creative Real Estate is practiced and how you can participate.

As you glance over your list, you will find at least one or two items that you would classify as work. These form the basis for the productive part of your activity. These are the activities you will use to start building your real estate empire.

In getting started, there is another major consideration for you to con-template:

DO YOU WANT TO PRACTICE CREATIVE REAL ESTATE FOR A LIVING?

Although I am personally fascinated by the real estate field and choose to spend a good deal of my life involved with it, I don't expect everyone to feel the same. Obviously, many people prefer to spend their lives acting or servicing motorcycles or teaching school. If that or anything else you choose to do is what you enjoy, that's what you should do. It would be a mistake for you to immerse yourself totally in real estate solely because there's money to be made in it. Choose a job you love and you'll never have to work a day in your life.

Fortunately, you don't have to give up your chosen occupation to benefit from Creative Real Estate. You will be pleased to know that it's not necessary to work at real estate full-time to be successful. In fact, most people who practice Creative Real Estate are *not* professionals as I define that term. They are plumbers and secretaries and engineers and teachers and others employed in many other types of work. They make their living doing what they enjoy and were trained to do and make a handsome extra income from their real estate investments on the side.

Consider my friend Kathy. Kathy sells magazine advertising for a liv-ing and is good at her work. The nature of her work is such that Kathy spends much of her time driving around the city, calling on clients and

soliciting advertisements for her magazine. Her hours are her own to schedule most effectively and her gasoline is paid for by her employer. This puts
Kathy in a marvelous position to practice Creative Real Estate. In her travels
about town she sees properties with "For Sale" signs on them. Rather than
blithely driving by as other advertising salespeople probably would, Kathy
does one of two things. If she has time, she stops and inquires about properties that look interesting. If she's in a hurry, she slows down long enough to
note the agent's name and phone number. She then calls and inquires later.

In doing this, Kathy has found some tremendous buys. Often, she will
notice a "For Sale" sign the first day it goes up. Sometimes she'll learn that
the seller, in seeking a quick sale, is asking a price lower than the market
price. Other times, she finds an owner who is so delighted to get an interested prospect on the first day that he will agree to very advantageous terms
or to a no-cash-down transaction or a tax-free exchange.

Kathy makes a good living selling advertising. But in the past few
years her profits from Creative Real Estate have far exceeded her sales
commissions. Despite her substantial real estate income, you couldn't con-
vince Kathy to give up her advertising job. She enjoys it too much. Besides,
she feels that if she devoted all her efforts to real estate, it would become too
much like work and all the fun would go out of it. She'll be a strictly
part-time Creative Real Estater forever.

Above all, and this is the important point, my friend Kathy is having a
great time. She's selling her ads, dealing in real estate, and enjoying the best
of both worlds. She's doing what she enjoys doing in her chosen worlds of
advertising and real estate.

Many people I know are just the opposite. After discovering, learning
about, and becoming involved in Creative Real Estate, they quit their regular
work and become either full-time investors for their own accounts—Creative Real Estate Practitioners—or Creative Real Estate Professionals, counseling others. Whether you will want to become a full-time Creative Real
Estate Practitioner or Professional is a decision you will have to make based
on how much the material in this book appeals to you and on your own
experience with Creative Real Estate once you get started.

DO FOR YOURSELF WHAT YOU DO BEST

Let's face it, as human beings we all have limits. No matter how smart a
person is, no matter how multi-talented, well-read, or well-informed, one
can't do everything. This is not a negative aspect of humanness to be lamented or avoided; it is a plain fact of life that you can use to your advantage.

In real estate there is always much going on and there are too many
aspects to the profession for one person to be familiar with them all. A

partial list of specialties within real estate includes: buying, selling, exchanging, financing, appraising, building, escrow, mortgaging, law, accounting, tax shelters, government regulations, maintenance, property management, rehabilitation, and refinancing. These barely scratch the surface.

You could spend a lifetime becoming an expert on improving desert lands through irrigation. Another lifetime could be spent structuring time-share arrangements for vacation condominiums and another setting up limited partnerships to invest in government-subsidized apartment projects. And it could take three more lifetimes to learn the ins and outs of holding property in foreign lands.

Any specialty you choose will require some learning time, and then some time to practice toward success. If, however, after a fair trial time you find that what you've chosen does not meet your expectations and happiness quotient, don't be afraid to admit you were wrong. It's like realizing you're wiser today than you were yesterday. The thing to try when all else fails is: again.

When I was a college student, one of my part-time jobs to finance the tuition was assistant to the owner of a paper box factory. One day he directed me to call the National Biscuit Company (NABISCO), one of the factory's regular customers, and ask the vice-president for Fig Newtons a question about a delivery we were to make. I thought my boss was pulling my leg about the "vice-president for Fig Newtons," but I followed the instructions to the letter and asked the National Biscuit telephone operator for the vice-president for Fig Newtons. Without hesitation she asked me whether I wanted to speak to the vice-president in charge of baking Fig Newtons, the vice-president in charge of packaging Fig Newtons, or the vice-president in charge of selling Fig Newtons! Now that's specialization. You know the old saying: "One doesn't quarrel with success!"

No matter what aspect of real estate you decide to get into, you cannot possibly know all there is to know about it yourself. You can't possibly do all there is to be done yourself. You *must* rely upon others for advice, counsel, and assistance.

LEVERAGE PEOPLE

The key to success in specialization is: Find out what you do best and do that—*only* that—yourself. Then, be like a postage stamp; stick to one thing until you get there. Get others to help you with all other aspects of your real estate transactions. Pay them or give them a percentage of the profits, but always use others whom you have carefully selected for their expertise, to guarantee that you and they will only be doing what you enjoy and do best and most efficiently. This is effectively using OPB—other people's brains, OPE—other people's effort, and OPM—other people's money.

This idea is part of a larger concept that I call my two-word course in economics. The two words are *leverage people*. This concept employs the theory of leverage, that is, using a small amount of one force or resource to control a much larger force or resource. When you leverage money, you may control a large apartment building by placing a small down payment on it. When you leverage people, you find specialists to do whatever they do best for you, and thus your single force controls a much larger force working toward the same goal.

To illustrate I'll go back to my friend Kathy. Finding bargains and negotiating great terms are her unique talents. Does she go out and try to find financing? No. Does she research the tax ramifications of her transactions? No. Does she scurry around hunting for tenants for her rentals? No. She could do these things, but why should she bother? For one thing, she's too busy selling advertising. For another, there are many experts who can do these aspects of her real estate transactions better and faster than she can.

These experts are well worth the fees they charge her. Kathy is simply leveraging people. If she didn't, she'd spend the bulk of her time botching up the things she doesn't do well and ignoring what she does beautifully.

A lighthearted example that illustrates this truth of leveraging people is a legend about a famous physicist. The great physicist was asked to go on a university lecture tour across the country, telling graduate students about his latest theories. He accepted and was given a car and chauffeur to take him on the trip. In each place they stopped, the chauffeur sat at the back of the lecture hall and listened while the professor explained his complicated theories to the scientists in his audiences.

One day near the end of the tour, the aging genius was so tired he was barely able to stand up anymore, let alone lecture. He instructed his chauffeur to call and cancel the next engagement. The chauffeur said, "Professor, we've come all this way and these people want to hear you so badly, we can't disappoint them now. I've got an idea. They don't know what you look like and I've heard your lecture so many times I could give it from memory. Why not let me lecture while you sit in the back and watch?"

The professor was reluctant, but there was no better alternative and he agreed. As a lecturer the chauffeur was brilliant. He had memorized the theories, formulas, and explanations perfectly. When he finished, the audience applauded as the amazed physicist sat at the back.

Flushed with success, the chauffeur took a dangerous step. When the applause died down, he asked, "Any questions?" The professor was thunderstruck. Memorizing a lecture was one thing. Fielding random questions was quite another. If the chauffeur couldn't answer something, the professor would look like a fool, for he was supposed to be the man at the lectern.

A local physicist stood up and asked the chauffeur a complicated scientific question based on one of the points in the lecture. The chauffeur was momentarily stunned but, amazingly, didn't show it. With a touch of bra-vado in his voice he chided the questioner, saying, "Sir, I certainly expected more from this august gathering than such a patently simple question. In fact, it's so elementary I'm going to let my chauffeur, who is sitting at the back of this hall, answer it for me." A perfect example of using OPB—other people's brains (the professor's) and OPE—other people's effort (the chauf-feur's).

Right from the start you can and should make use of your ability to leverage people in Creative Real Estate. While you're looking for the right properties, look for the right people as well. Find people with whom you like to work and who know what they're doing. Surround yourself with these people. Keep in touch with them. Use them. Take good care of them because as time goes by they will inevitably take good care of you.

Think of the college student who desperately wired home: "Am with-out friends or funds." The prompt return telegram from the student's parents advised: "Make friends."

Above all, as you progress keep your own focus on what you do best. When you see what it is that you do very, very well, key in on it. No matter how small an aspect of the business it is, stick with it. Learn it better. Become the foremost expert at it. And keep doing it again and again so that you continually get better at it. Only some of us learn by other people's mistakes; the rest of us have to be the other people.

A familiar adage is "Practice makes perfect." Just because that's an old saying doesn't mean it's true. It's not. What *is* true is this: Practice makes permanent. If you're doing something wrong, you'll continue to do it wrong no matter how many times you repeat it. Continued practice will only make your error permanent.

In a television interview the late Vince Lombardi, legendary coach of the Green Bay Packers, said it right: *"Perfect* practice makes perfect." In other words, perfect what you do right and continually repeat doing it right. During Lombardi's tenure at Green Bay, his team had a play that they executed particularly well, the "Packer power sweep." They practiced it perfectly and when they took it into a game it was an invincible tool. They ran the play successfully even when their opponents knew it was coming. They did for themselves what they did best, and the Packers were one of the most successful football teams in history.

You can be just as successful. Simply remember to do for yourself what you do best. Leave to others the task of doing for you what they do best. If you put this advice to work in your life, you cannot fail in real estate or anything else.

There's one more concept to discuss at this time. It is an integral part of the recipe for success and is best expressed in three words . . .

DON'T LOOK BACK

This attitude is a particularly good one for the Creative Real Estate Practitioner to adopt. When you're involved in a transaction, you make your decision based on the information available to you at the time, on the market conditions surrounding it, and on the advice of the people you hire to assist you. After you make that measured decision, go with it. Don't look back. Once a transaction is complete, there's no past potential, only a future. Look ahead and do your best to make it work.

If you constantly look over your shoulder, hindsighting a better interest rate or more favorable terms or a lower price, you're wasting energy and time that you should be directing toward scouting and planning for your next real estate transaction.

I call this negative expenditure of energy and time "down time," like a computer that is "down" and not functioning. Why waste all that time and energy on something dead, past, and down when you could be creatively forging ahead with a plan for the next successful venture? Whenever you find yourself slipping into reflections of remorse, ask yourself whether or not you want to pay the price for that down time. The price is the expenditure of irretrievable time—time that could and should be used positively rather than in negative reflections of remorse.

To do something over, the actual cost in opportunity time is three times what it costs to go on and do something new and positive. The original effort was a waste; the second try puts you back to ground zero opportunity-time-wise (if you get it right the second time), and then you have to use a third opportunity time to get ahead the one positive step where you wanted to be in the first place. Three moves. Whereas you could put the mistake behind you and make one fresh, new positive move and be in the same place. Which makes more sense to you? And that's not even considering the emotional distress of revisiting a disaster!

In any transaction there are many variables. Not all of them will necessarily work out to your satisfaction, but you can't look back. If you do, you'll drive yourself crazy and sabotage your future success at the same time. Don't carry old baggage any longer than you have to.

One of my employees has a grandfather who sold a tract of land with a stand of trees many years ago for $500 because he had to pay some doctor bills. Shortly thereafter the land he sold became more valuable and the person he sold it to made $12,000 profit on it. Years later, the grandfather is still berating himself for having sold too soon. The sad part of the story is that (1) if the circumstances ever came up again, he would probably do exactly the same thing; (2) all his hindsight isn't changing for a second the fact that the transaction is done with; and (3) the down time he expends being negative about the irrevocable past prevents him from doing some-thing positive in the present.

I'm not saying you can't learn from the past. There is a saying: "Those who ignore history are doomed to repeat it." It's valuable to review a pre-vious transaction analytically and unemotionally to discover how you might do better in similar circumstances in the future. The grandfather should now realize he could have sold the stand of trees and kept the land. (In a later chapter you'll find one of my favorite formulas to accomplish this: "Yank the Land.") Analyzing the past is one thing. Second-guessing yourself and persecuting yourself for it are entirely different.

The same holds true for your good decisions. If you overindulge in the luxury of congratulating yourself for a well-made decision in the past, you can easily fail to notice problems arising before you in the future.

Again, this doesn't mean you shouldn't look back to see what you did right so that you can repeat it in a future transaction. This is the heart of the "perfect practice" concept we looked at a moment ago. But egotistical back-patting is as worthless as masochistic self-deprecating when a transaction is already part of history.

Now, as you plan for the future, you can choose from a variety of specific, beneficial routes to success described in *A Fortune at Your Feet*. In Part Two you will have the opportunity to chart your way to success with perfect practice as you select what works best for you.

And now, these Kessler's Keys to Success:

🔑 Are you sure you want to do this?

🔑 What do you enjoy most?

🔑 Do you want to practice creative real estate for a living?

🔑 Do for yourself what you do best

🔑 Leverage people

🔑 Don't look back

PART II

How to Make It Work for You

It is not enough to be busy—the question is what are we busy about?

— H.D. Thoreau

4

The Language of Creative Real Estate

In good speaking, should not the mind of the speaker know the truth of the matter about which he is to speak?

— Plato

Every form of organized human activity has its own language—special words and phrases that have precise meanings for the people who carry out that activity. A strike means one thing to a labor union leader, something else to a gold miner, and something entirely different to a baseball player.

Real estate, of course, has such a language—a jargon that is at once intriguing and confusing. A term that represents a certain concept to a real estate agent in Florida may evoke a completely different image to an agent in Arizona, and a word used by the same people in the same place may change its meaning over a period of years.

To eliminate confusion, most books on real estate have a glossary printed at the back, dictionary style, with academic definitions spelled out. I suspect many readers ignore such glossaries. I know that I prefer more lively reading myself.

It is essential that we understand each other. At this point I've included the real estate terms used in this book in narrative style rather than dictionary style, so you can find it more interesting to read and understand my usage of the words. You should at least scan this chapter with an eye toward clarifying terms that are new to you. Even if you are familiar with real estate terminology, you might be surprised to learn that a definition has changed or that I use a term in a special sense you hadn't anticipated. If you're a beginner, learning the language is a necessity and you should read this glossary straight through. Whether you are looking, buying, operating, selling, or exchanging, these are words you need to know in the world of Creative Real Estate. If you need to recheck a word later, for quick reference you will find it listed alphabetically in the index which will refer you to the page number (in bold face) for the definition in this chapter.

PEOPLE IN REAL ESTATE

Someone who organizes, manages, and assumes the risks of a business or venture is called an *entrepreneur.* Someone who only puts money into that business or venture is called an *investor.* The investor who puts up his money hoping to profit from a quick rise in the market price of the investment is a *speculator.*

The real estate profession is directed by *brokers,* people who represent buyers and sellers in real estate transactions. For the most part, brokers are independent business people, and all are licensed by the state in which they operate. *Realtors®* are brokers who belong to a local real estate board that is associated with the National Association of Realtors® (NAR). A *licensed salesperson* who works for a broker is commonly known as a real estate salesperson or *agent,* with the broker being responsible for the agent's actions.

When a property owner wants to sell, he signs a contract with a broker, giving that broker the right to sell that property for a certain length of time. The contract is called a *listing agreement* or an *employment agreement* and is one of the tools used by brokers to make money.

When a broker sells a property for an owner, he is paid a *commission,* usually a percentage of the sales price. The broker who represents the buyer may also receive a commission and is called a *buyer's broker.*

Real estate consultants are people who, because of their knowledge of the field, advise others on the desirability of entering into real estate ventures, though they may not be licensed as brokers. They are usually paid *fees* rather than commissions.

The special part of the profession that I discuss in this book and one that almost defies brief definition is *Creative Real Estate.* Essentially, it focuses on benefiting people in every aspect of real estate, in the belief that all things are possible to people who want them badly enough and who are willing to think in new and different ways in order to get what they want. Believing that *people are more important than property* and that *there are no problem properties, merely problem ownerships,* those who practice Creative Real Estate know that real estate is simply a vehicle to be used to fulfill needs by applying practical solutions in innovative ways to achieve goals and objectives. Hence the slogan, *Creative Real Estate is the PEOPLEtype, not the stereotype.*

A *Creative Real Estate Professional* is one who is licensed as a broker or salesperson, who has taken specialized educational courses in Creative Real Estate, and who practices the principles of Creative Real Estate for hire.

A *Creative Real Estate Practitioner* is someone who uses the principles of Creative Real Estate to invest for his or her own account. When you finish this book, you will be equipped with the information and knowledge to become a Creative Real Estate Practitioner.

A *Creative Real Estater* is the all-encompassing term for one who, licensed or not, operates in Creative Real Estate primarily for his or her own account as a full-time *or* part-time professional or amateur.

A *licensed exchangor* is a licensed real estate professional broker or salesperson who belongs to one of the organized Creative Real Estate *exchange groups* or associations that regularly meet throughout the country to further increase their specialized education in exchanging and to market properties for clients through exchanging. An increasing number of Creative Real Estate Practitioners who are not licensed as brokers or salespersons are studying and becoming exchangors for their own accounts.

An *exchange counselor* is a Creative Real Estate Professional who is qualified through specialized education to perform the functions of a counselor and to determine the objectives of the clients in the interest of exchanging properties for clients and fulfilling their needs.

A *moderator* is an experienced exchangor who guides the presentations and conducts the problem-solving sessions at exchange marketing meetings.

IRS is the acronym for *Internal Revenue Service*, the branch of the U.S. government responsible for collecting income taxes and regulating and enforcing the *Code* applying to income taxes.

A *client* is someone who employs a Creative Real Estate Professional to assist in accomplishing the necessary steps involved in real estate acquisition or disposition in order to achieve his or her objectives.

A *don't-wanter* is someone who doesn't want to retain ownership of the property he has and is highly motivated to dispose of it for virtually any reasonable price or exchange.

A *taker*, the opposite of a don't-wanter, is someone who will take ownership of a property or properties each with its own specific set of existing circumstances.

Area-bound is the term applied in exchanging to the individual who does not want to acquire property in any area other than a specific one, generally close to home.

NEGOTIATION

Your first venture into Creative Real Estate will probably involve the creative purchase or acquisition of a piece of property. You will need to determine the *market price*, the price one actually would pay for a property. This is not to be confused with the *appraised value*, which is a professional estimate or opinion as to value as of a specific date. The appraised value is, however, one of the factors that should be considered in arriving at the market price. Another of the factors to consider while looking for property is *directional growth*, the geographic trend of developing and building in a growing urban area. It's one of the factors used in evaluating location.

If you've heard of real estate, you have probably heard of the importance of *location*. It has been said that the three most important factors to consider in respect to real estate are location, location, and location. What this really means is that you should pay strict attention to directional growth so as not to find yourself the once-proud owner of a luxurious one-family residence now in the middle of a neighborhood of heavy industrial manufacturing and chemical plants.

Another item of major importance to you as a buyer is *terms*. Simply stated, terms are the specific conditions and details of the transaction. They can materially affect whether the transaction is a good one or not. You will find as you progress in the practice of Creative Real Estate that you can pay almost any price justifiable by future rising values, providing you can structure advantageous terms that you can easily comply with now.

When you find a property you like, you'll make an *offer*, which is a written statement of the price and terms you're willing to agree upon. This offer is usually accompanied by *earnest money*, a small amount that shows the seller you're serious about the transaction. If your price and terms are not objectionable, the seller will sign an *acceptance*, binding both of you to the price and terms in the offer as written. If your price or terms are not acceptable, the seller will either reject the offer or sign a *counter-offer*, setting out a different price, different terms, or both.

When you get back a rejection or a counter-offer, the *negotiation* usually begins, a process of discussion in which people try to settle their differences about the details of a transaction in order to reach a mutually acceptable compromise.

A *can-add* is something that can be "thrown in" in addition to the prime properties in the transaction to balance equities or generally to provide a *sweetener* to the transaction. The sweetener can also be terms and conditions that are particularly favorable to the other party, enhancing their desire to accept the proposed transaction.

Some, though certainly not all, of the topics you may discuss in your negotiations are *contingencies,* those clauses added to an offer or counter-offer that would give the one making the offer a chance to back out if the contingencies are not met. You might, for example, make your offer in writing, contingent upon passage of a *house termite inspection.* If your offer is accepted and it turns out that there are no termites, your offer would then *"ripen"* into a *contract.* If there are termites in the house, you're not bound to buy it, even if the seller has accepted your price and all your terms, because that specific contingency has not been met.

In negotiation, one can use a *front porch,* a clause added to an offer just for the purpose of bargaining. It is a non-essential condition of an initial agreement and can be waived by either party without adversely affecting the transaction as you would eventually like to see it take place. An example would be: " . . . providing the seller repaints the basement and the attic." The repainting really does't matter significantly to the buyer, who will "reluctantly" give it up, as a compromise, if the price and all of the other terms are acceptable to the seller.

One of the most important terms in an offer is the *down payment,* which is the amount of money the buyer must give the seller in order to get possession (and usually the title). The down payment is always less than the purchase price and can be as little as zero unless the purchase is made entirely for cash.

If the item you're buying is not the property itself but a piece of paper showing an interest in property, you might buy it at a *discount,* which is something less than its *face value.* A piece of paper that says that it is worth $20,000, would be bought for $2,000 less than the face value, or $18,000, if discounted 10%.

A *weasel clause,* or as I prefer to call it, a *whistle clause,* is a general contingency clause in an offer permitting the offeror to renege. A typical example is, "Subject to inspection and approval by the buyer."

An item that might enter into the negotiations is your *credit rating,* a score you receive indicating how much risk you are to someone who is selling you something for less than all cash. If you pay all your bills on time, have extra money in the bank, and have never defaulted on a debt in the past, you'll get a good credit rating. This will increase your chances of borrowing money.

When your negotiations are complete, you'll set a date for *closing,* the day on which the transaction formally takes place. On that date, *deeds* are signed (or delivered), money changes hands, and legal possession of the property is transferred.

In negotiating, the primary concept to keep in mind is *people benefits.* As I use the term, people benefits means all the ways people can derive good out of owning (and not owning) property. As people benefits are increased, the quality of the transaction increases for everyone. A companion concept is *problem solving.* It involves solving whatever problems people have as a result of owning or not owning property. The more problems a transaction solves, the better that transaction will be in providing people benefits for all involved parties.

Inherent in a successful negotiation is the *win/win* situation, a transaction in which everyone involved comes out better off than he would have if he hadn't been involved. A basic principle of Creative Real Estate is that the best way for me to win will be for you to win too, even though you might be on the "other side" of the transaction. When there are more than two people involved, all must win to provide a win/win situation. "You give enough other people what they want and you'll get whatever you want in life." Remember?

TYPES OF TRANSACTIONS

Most transactions involve change of ownership of the property involved. To the buyer, that type of transaction is a *purchase,* to the seller it's a *sale.* There are many kinds of purchases and sales discussed throughout this book.

A kind of transaction that results in change of ownership but is not a sale is an *exchange.* An exchange has many forms and ramifications but basically involves passing title of property for property rather than for money.

When the right to possession or use of property but not ownership is passed in writing, it's usually a *lease.* Under a lease, one party gives written permission to another party to use and occupy property for a specific time and at a specific price.

Fee simple refers to the ownership of the land and the entire bundle of rights that go with it, whereas a *leasehold* is merely the right to use the property owned by someone else. *Leased land* refers to the land that is held in a leasehold.

An *option* is the right to acquire title at a fixed price, on fixed terms, for a fixed amount of time.

MECHANICS OF TRANSACTIONS

A *deed* is a written document that says that one person is transferring ownership of his property to someone else. In the days before deeds were written, the act of changing ownership was an actual deed—that is, the property owner in the presence of witnesses would reach down, grab a handful of dirt from the subject property, and hand it to the buyer, while declaring that "with this deed" he was passing ownership to that person.

In those days, the deed was effective when it was done. Today, it's effective between the parties when the document is signed and delivered. If the buyer wants the deed to be effective as far as the rest of the world is concerned, he must *record* it, that is, have it copied into the public records of the community in which the property is located.

If a deed is signed but for some reason the signer doesn't want it delivered right away, he can deliver it into an *escrow,* a neutral third party who holds it until instructed to do otherwise. In addition to deeds, money, notes, and other documents can be held in escrow. In some states escrow is used to complete all transactions. Instead of the buyer and seller getting together, each deposits the necessary money and documents into an escrow.

On the closing date the escrow company completes the transaction by delivering the deed to the buyer and the *proceeds* or net cash or other consideration to the seller.

A *preliminary title report* is a written summary of the status of a particular property delivered by a *title insurance company* upon request and prior to closing. This report shows in whose name title is held, easements, restrictions, conditions, and matters of record as of a specific date. The cost of the preliminary title report is generally credited against the cost of the *title insurance policy* when issued.

Title insurance is insurance against loss or damage resulting from defects in or failure to receive perfect title to a particular parcel of property.

TYPES OF PROPERTY

For ease of discussion I'm going to divide real property into two types: *residential* (the kind you live in) and *investment* (the kind you buy to make money on).

Presuming no one buys property for the purpose of losing money, investment real estate can be further classified into two kinds: *income-producing,* in which the land itself or the improvements on it bring in a flow of money at more or less regular intervals, and *vacant (raw) land.* While vacant land may produce income, as occurs when a farmer rents it for cultivation, I use the term differently here.

Before vacant land is built on, or developed, it is subdivided. *Subdivision* is the process of breaking large tracts of land into smaller ones by drawing lines on a map and filing that map to be recorded in the public record. Once the map is approved, the *subdivider* can sell the smaller parcels to separate individual buyers. Thus, vacant (raw) land is transformed into income-producing land.

You can construct buildings for *commercial* use by businesses, for *industrial* use as factories, or for *residential* use for people to live in. Most single-family houses are used as personal residences, though they can be bought as investments and rented out. A house consisting of two separate living units is called a *duplex* and one with four units is called a *fourplex.* Generally, a building with more than four units that people live in and rent is called an *apartment building.*

A *condominium* can be an apartment in a high-rise building, one dwelling unit of a multi-dwelling building of any size or shape, or a single-family, detached dwelling in a cluster or complex. It is a unique type of ownership. People who buy condominiums buy the apartment within the walls in which they live and an undivided part interest (in ownership with all of the other individual condominium owners) in the rest of the condominium complex, including land, stairways, outside walls, swimming pools, clubhouse, and so forth. Though you can buy a condominium to use as a residence, you can sometimes use it as an investment, too. Another kind of residential ownership of apartments is called a *cooperative* (or just *co-op*). That type of ownership is not discussed in this book.

FINANCING

The term *financing* is an all-encompassing catchword for the limitless ways you can put together the money for a purchase. When most people use the term, however, they are referring to the ways you can borrow part or all of the purchase price. Thus, buying with *nothing down* is often called *100% financing.*

There are hundreds of definitions of the word *capital.* As I use it in this book, it means the money that a buyer has in his possession or control to use for the purchase of real estate. If you had, for instance, $5,000 in capital that you used to buy a house, some of it would go to cover the expense of the purchase and the rest would actually go to pay for all or part of the house. The amount of your capital that goes into the property is called *equity.* If the house were bought for $45,000 and $4,500 of your $5,000 went into it as a down payment, that $4,500 is your equity.

Your equity can be raised or lowered in a number of ways. For example, if the market price of your property rises, the amount of that rise is an increase in your equity. If the market price falls in those same circumstances, your equity will decrease. As you make payments against an *amortizing* mortgage loan, part of the payment is for interest, and part repays the principal amount of the loan, increasing your equity.

The technique of controlling a large amount of property with a small amount of capital is called *leverage.* If by means of a lever you could move a 100-pound rock with only 10 pounds of force, the 90 pounds you didn't have to exert is your leverage. Similarly, to buy a $100,000 building with $10,000 down is to use 90% leverage.

Generally, when you use leverage to buy property, you put a small percentage down and borrow the rest. Most often you will borrow from an *institutional lender* such as a bank, a savings and loan company, an insurance company, a finance company, or a credit union. Other times an individual will provide the loan, which is *private financing.* When the lender is an individual, he or she most commonly is the seller of the property.

The language of lending is a fascinating study in itself. For our purposes we will divide loans into two general types: *personal loans,* obligations that you take on as an individual, guarantee with and promise to pay out of your personal (not real estate) assets; and *real property loans,* which you borrow against the value of your real estate assets.

It's safe to say that lenders always require some *security,* that is, something of value that is pledged to assure repayment of the debt. The security can be an oral promise, a written promise, or a promise plus the pledge of some tangible property. When you make a personal loan, you'll usually be asked to put up some *collateral* as security. Collateral can be a personal asset (stock, bonds, an automobile, or jewelry), the control of which you relinquish to the lender to cover all or part of the loan balance if you don't pay it. *Substitution of collateral* may be agreed upon between the parties and should be in writing. It permits the borrower to substitute another asset (personal or real, as agreed upon) in place of the one originally pledged. This can be a very valuable condition to have in a loan document for both lender and borrower.

In real estate loans the security—and the collateral—is almost always the property that you're borrowing money to acquire. Because land cannot be moved and the lender can't physically control it, the security for the debt is evidenced by a number of different kinds of paper.

Paper is a general term that encompasses many kinds of documents that in turn stand for various types of agreements and promises. The chief distinction with regard to paper is between *notes* and *mortgages.* A *note* is a signed document in which a borrower acknowledges a debt and promises to pay it according to terms spelled out on its face. A note does not give anyone any interest in property. A mortgage, however, does. And in real estate loans the note is in most instances secured by a mortgage. In a *mortgage* a specific property is designated as security for a debt and gives the lender the right to take the property if the debt isn't paid.

Soft paper is the term applied to notes with an easy or very flexible repayment schedule, often secured by items or property of questionable value.

To *hypothecate* is to borrow against and pledge something of value as security for the repayment.

To *subordinate* is to permit your position in line for repayment to become next or lower in priority to repayment and recovery of a new debt.

When you as a borrower sign a mortgage and pledge your property as security, you are the *mortgagor.* The lender is the *mortgagee.* Sometimes the mortgagee will agree to *substitution* of mortgagor, allowing another person to step into your place but leaving the rest of the mortgage terms as written.

There are many different kinds of notes and mortgages. With notes we will limit ourselves to *straight notes,* in which the amount owing (the principal) is paid in one lump sum, and *installment notes,* which provide for payment of the principal in two or more amounts at different times. Installment payments are usually equal in size and due at regular intervals.

In addition to the principal, you as a borrower will be expected to pay *interest,* a charge made for the loan of the money. Interest is usually expressed as a percentage of the principal. When you borrow $1,000 at 12% interest, it means that each year you must pay 12% of $1,000 (or $120) for your use of the money.

Points are the lump sum amount payable up front, calculated as a percentage of the loan—one point equalling 1%—charged by the lender for making the loan.

With mortgages we will limit ourselves to:

- *First mortgage,* one that gives the mortgagee the right to take back the property before any other secured party.

- *Second mortgage,* one that gives the mortgagee the right to whatever is left after the first mortgagee has obtained satisfaction for the debt. If a first mortgagee foreclosed or took back a piece of property to satisfy a $50,000 debt and sold the property for $70,000, there would be $20,000 left for the second mortgagee. That's all the second mortgagee could get, even if the second mortgage had more than $20,000 owing on it.

- *Purchase money mortgage,* a private arrangement in which a buyer who is unwilling to pay for the property entirely with cash gives the seller the right to take back the property if it's not paid for according to the agreed-upon terms. By law in some states a purchase money mortgage is first in line even when there's a first mortgage ahead of it.

- *Blanket mortgage,* a mortgage that pledges more than one piece of property to secure one debt.

- *Wrap-around mortgage,* one that secures a new debt that is larger than all the combined debts of the mortgages already on a property and includes those debts within it.

- In some states *trust deeds* (or deeds of trust) are used instead of mortgages. Although there are subtle legal differences between mortgages and trust deeds, we will consider them synonymous for our purposes. In trust deed states, a wrap-around mortgage is called an *all-inclusive deed of trust (AITD).*

There are many uses for mortgages in addition to signing a new one to secure a debt. You can *assume* a mortgage, that is, take over primary liability for the debt. This makes the original mortgagor liable only if you don't make the payments (unless they secured a release from the lender when you assumed).

You can buy property *subject to* a mortgage, where you just take over the payments on the loan, not the primary responsibility for it, leaving the original borrower liable for the payments if you default.

As a seller you can *carry back* a mortgage, that is, accept a mortgage instead of money for part of the sales price. A mortgage carried back in that way would be in line behind the previously existing mortgages in case the buyer didn't make the payments.

When you borrow under an *installment contract,* you promise to pay a specific schedule of payments over an extended period of time. Your payments are usually set up so that part of the money is applied to pay back the principal. The process of paying off the principal bit by bit is called *amortization.* It's a word that comes from the Latin word for death. As you amortize a loan, you are killing the principal (which is the amount you originally borrowed) a little at a time, until at the end of the payment term, it is dead. In real estate transactions the amount of money that goes for principal and interest is called *debt service.*

When a property has an old mortgage on it and for one reason or another the owner wants to get more money or consolidate a number of loans, he may *refinance* it. All that means is that he's getting a new mortgage with different terms and is (usually) paying off whatever mortgages are already on the property.

In borrowing money, you might face a *tight money market,* the term used to describe a shortage of cash available for lending among the institutions. In a tight money market it's harder to qualify for a loan. If you can get a loan at all, you will have to pay a much higher interest rate. People generally should refrain from refinancing at times when money is tight.

REO is the acronym applied to the category on financial statements of lending institutions for *real estate owned.* This is the title under which the lending institutions must report the value of all real estate owned to the regulatory agencies. Generally, lending institutions are not permitted to own more than the property that houses their business. If the REO item discloses additional holdings, it is usually a result of bad loans and resultant foreclosures. This excess property must be divested and favorable creative transactions with the institutions can be structured involving such property.

OPM refers to the use of *other people's money,* and is a major concept in leveraging. Using OPM permits maximum leverage, and often allows purchases with nothing down. In my concept of "leveraging people," I also use the acronyms *OPE* for *other people's effort,* and *OPB* for *other people's brains.*

EXCHANGING

In addition to buying and selling property, you can *exchange* it. Take careful note that in an exchange, no one is either buyer or seller. The parties to an exchange are identified according to their properties, which are usually designated A, B, C, etc., or Number 1, Number 2, Number 3, etc. The properties would be referred to as *"the A leg,"* *"the B leg,"* or *"the C leg,"* or *"the Number 1 leg,"* *"the Number 2 leg,"* or *"the Number 3 leg."* An exchange involving more than two properties is called a multi-legged exchange. In another reference, an exchange of four properties would be said to have four legs and be a *four-legged exchange.*

As you will see, some exchanges unavoidably involve some cash as well as real estate. This is not prohibited, but if one party to an exchange gets cash or something else of value in addition to real estate of like kind, or something of determinable value in excess of the equal value of the properties being exchanged, that something is called *boot* and is taxable.

The provision of the Internal Revenue Code that covers exchanging is Section 1031. Thus, an exchange made in compliance with that section for tax purposes is called a *Section 1031 exchange.*

The term *country store* refers to the display of written descriptions and photographs of all types of property, both real and personal that is pinned, tacked, or taped on the walls or bulletin boards in or adjoining an exchange marketing room.

Idea-tracking, also known as *piggy-backing* or *hitchhiking,* is the process of building on one possible solution to examine the resulting alternative solutions. It is a focused form of brainstorming.

A *package* contains information about the client, the property, and the situation offered in the exchange marketplace in concise, written form. This is the document that is circulated as an offering and from which the exchange counselor makes a presentation to the assembled group at a marketing meeting.

A *back-up package* or *property brief* is the file of documented details pertaining to the package. It provides all available information relating to the property and the situation.

Broker-owned is the term applied to property owned by the licensed exchangor who is presenting it for sale or exchange.

Accommodator or *facilitator* is the *qualified intermediary* who holds the funds in trust and conducts the legally prescribed steps of a *delayed exchange* (also called a *Starker* exchange after the litigant who prevailed in a classic case).

EXPO is the brief term of reference for the Annual Creative Real Estate Exposition. It is the largest educational and marketing event in the world at which the innovations, changes, and improvements in the exchange marketing process are tried, proven, and disseminated throughout the world. It is the place to get started for anyone interested in Creative Real Estate and exchanging. It is also the most active and productive national market for the seasoned veteran.

OWNING AND OPERATING REAL ESTATE

Most likely, once you've bought and financed your property, you will want to get some income from it. *Income* is a recurring benefit, usually measured in money, that is derived from the investment of capital or labor. With some properties, particularly vacant land that is leased for cultivation, you can get income simply by owning the land and doing nothing else. Sometimes, if you own land that has buildings on it that are owned by someone else, you can collect *ground rent,* a regular sum paid to an owner for letting someone else use it.

In most cases, however, you will own both the land and the buildings on it and will be responsible for the *property management.* This activity includes renting the buildings, maintaining them, keeping up the grounds, and keeping track of the money taken in and spent.

Tenants are people who have no ownership rights in real estate that they occupy and use. They usually pay *rent* in the form of regular cash payments to the owner or owner's representative.

As property is managed, rent is collected and expenses are paid out. That in-and-out activity is called *cash flow.* When more money is taken in than is paid out, it's called *positive cash flow.* When more is paid out than is taken in, it's *negative cash flow.*

When repair of property has been put off for some reason, some *deferred maintenance* may be required. This is usually major repair work like new roofs, furnaces, sidewalks, and so on. If the property has been so neglected as to be almost unlivable, it may require rehabilitation. *Rehabilitation* is nearly complete restoration, without changing building plans, style, or structure.

A popular term among investors referring to properties that need repair is *sweat equity,* which describes the increase in a property's value that results when the owner paints, cleans, and fixes it. In a real sense, the owner's "sweat," more than any other investment, such as capital, increases the value—and the owner's equity.

REAL ESTATE LAW

Real estate is land and everything permanently attached to it. Is a building real estate? Yes. Is wall-to-wall carpeting real estate? Maybe. Curtains are not real estate, although permanent curtain rods probably are. Lawyers in different jurisdictions and cases argue endlessly about these details.

It's not necessary for you as a practitioner to define terms as precisely as lawyers do. All you need is a basic idea of the meaning of common legal terms. Leverage people by employing the services of a lawyer who specializes in that type of law when you become involved in legal contracts.

In real estate, there's much talk about title. *Title,* an elusive concept, is evidence of a person's right, or the extent of his interest, in property. Most of the time when people say title they mean ownership or ownership rights.

Title can be either *free and clear* or *encumbered.* When it's free and clear, the property is free of mortgages, liens, and the like. "Clear" indicates that there are no so-called clouds on the title. *Clouds* are lawsuits pending against the property and unresolved questions as to whether someone other than the owner of record has an interest in it.

Encumbered property is said to be burdened with an encumbrance, which is anything that limits free and clear title. *Liens, easements,* and *restrictions* are examples of encumbrances.

If you or anyone with whom you deal does not meet the terms of a loan agreement, you will become familiar with a legal process called *foreclosure.* In foreclosure proceedings the secured party (such as a mortgagee) uses the power of the courts and the sheriff to help him regain possession of the property and sell it to pay the debt.

If the foreclosure price is not enough to cover the debt, the borrower may have to pay a *deficiency judgment.* This is a chilling term to careless speculators because it is a court order requiring the borrower to pay the balance of the loan when the proceeds from the sale of the property aren't sufficient to cover it. The deficiency must be paid using the borrower's other assets.

Foreclosure may be avoided by issuing a *deed-in-lieu* of foreclosure, also known as a *deedback,* giving the property back to the mortgagee in full settlement.

There are ways investors can limit their liability, not only from deficiency judgments, but also from other kinds of lawsuits. A common method of so doing is the *limited partnership.* This is a legal arrangement written and filed on public record showing that some of the partners (called *general partners*) have unlimited liability and the rest (called *limited partners*) are liable only to the extent of their investment.

If each of ten limited partners in a simple limited partnership invested $10,000 in an apartment building operated by the general partner, and because of the general partner's negligence someone was hurt and sued the partnership for a million dollars, the most the limited partners could lose would be their original investment. The general partner would be liable for the rest.

A method of holding property that has become widely popular in recent years is called *time-sharing.* Time-sharing is usually practiced with expensive properties in highly desirable locations, such as resorts. In a time-sharing arrangement, you buy much the same rights as you would if you bought a condominium, but instead of having the right to occupy the property all the time, you only have the right to occupy it for a designated period each year.

If a condominium apartment in Vail, Colorado (the ski area) were priced at $520,000, only the rich would be able to afford it. If no rich people were buying, the condominium owner theoretically could sell 52 shares in the unit at $10,000 each. (In fact, state laws limit the amount of weeks sold to provide for at least one week for repair and maintenance, and have stringent consumer-protective regulations for time-share operators.) Each share would buy the use of the condominium for one week per year for as long as agreed, or in perpetuity. Another term for time-sharing is *interval ownership.*

An added benefit in the ownership of most time-shares sold today is the right to *exchange the use of your time-share ownership* for the use of another time-share ownership in some other part of the world. This is accomplished through membership in a central time-share exchange-facilitating organization, of which there are several in operation world-wide. They currently report a successfully completed exchange of facilities for approximately 80% of the requests made.

TAXATION

Please be advised that taxation is a tricky business. Tax laws and interpretations change continually. This book is not intended to be technically precise in defining or advising on tax matters; for that you should consult accountants and attorneys who specialize in tax matters. Leverage people, remember? I am simply hoping to explain some general concepts.

As a *taxpayer,* your income is divided into two general types: *ordinary income* and *capital gains.* Types of ordinary income are wages, rents, royalties, and bank interest. Depending on the amount of that income, you can be taxed on a variable percent of it. This means as much as 50 cents (or more) of every dollar in ordinary income can be taken by the government for taxes. A person who is paying this lofty rate is said to be in the *high tax bracket.*

Capital gains is income generated when you sell material possessions for a profit. If you buy a vacant lot for $10,000 and sell it for $20,000, you must pay tax on the capital gain of $10,000. How much tax? Generally, if you have held the property for one year or more, the capital gains tax is less than the amount would be for your ordinary income tax bracket. This lesser figure is called the *long-term capital gains rate.* Thus, if you were in the high income tax bracket, you would have to pay less tax on the gain of $10,000. If you had sold the land for the same profit in less than a year, you would have to pay tax at the *short-term capital gains rate,* which is essentially the same as the ordinary income rate.

Since the percentage of tax increases as income increases, everyone tries to show the government how little income they have at tax time. There are a number of ways to reduce your reportable income for tax purposes. *Deductions* are subtractions you can make to reduce your income in this way. For example, the cost of operating an income-producing building is deductible. If you collect $2,000 in rents and pay $1,500 in expenses during the year, you could deduct the $1,500 and only pay tax on $500. If you had paid out $2,500 in expenses, your loss of $500 could be deducted to offset tax due on your other income from other real estate.

Losing money on the operation of a building will reduce your taxes, but it certainly won't help you build your wealth. There are devices to show losses (for tax purposes) and still build your wealth at the same time. These devices are called *tax shelters.*

In real estate, the principal way of sheltering income from taxes is through *depreciation.* Defined as a loss in value of real property brought about by age, deterioration, or *economic obsolescence,* depreciation is based on the theory that virtually all improvements upon the land will be worth nothing some day. By estimating when that day will be, you can progressively lower the stated value of the property over the elapsed time. For an example of the arithmetic only (not tax law), a $100,000 building that you estimate will be worth nothing in ten years is theoretically depreciating at the rate of $10,000 per year. In making out your income tax return for the year, you could subtract $10,000 from the net income on the building. The loss of value is theoretical (depreciation), while the deduction you make is unquestionably real; therefore, you pay no tax on money that you did not actually lose. You can also subtract that "loss" from money you actually made, so that the tax on the money you made will be less. It is really a legal way of having your cake while eating it. This is the tax shelter aspect of depreciation.

Taking $10,000 per year for ten years is an example of *straight line depreciation.* Methods in which you take a larger percentage of depreciation in the first few years and smaller percentages in later years is called *accelerated depreciation.* People who planned to hold properties for just a few years often preferred the accelerated method in order to take advantage of larger deductions as soon as possible. However, recent tax law revisions do not permit accelerated depreciation. It is an investment advantage that is continually sought and prayed for. Perhaps Congress will reinstate it in the future.

When you plan to sell a building, you must calculate the profit you made on it because the government will want to collect tax on capital gains, if any, and you will want to take a deduction on capital losses, if any. Calculating profit would be a simple matter of subtracting your cost from your sale price, but the real question is, "What is *cost?*" For tax purposes, it's the *adjusted tax basis,* that is, the original price plus capital (permanent) improvements minus allowable depreciation. It is also known as *book value* and *cost basis.*

Suppose you find someone willing to buy your building at a huge profit. You might want to make an installment sale rather than to sell it outright. An *installmemt sale* is a sale in which, for income tax purposes, the seller does not receive full payment of the sale price in the first year, thus minimizing and spreading the tax liability over a number of years under a special set of installment sales provisions in the Internal Revenue Code.

The term *tax-free* technically refers to a transaction that is free of any tax liability. However, the term is freely used in exchanging, along with the term *nontaxable,* to refer to the *tax deferred* status accorded qualifying exchanges under Section 1031 of the Internal Revenue Code.

Now that you have read the language of Creative Real Estate, we should be on the same wave-length. When I explain in various ways how to acquire real estate with little or no cash, I will be able to make a number of points more easily and quickly as a result of your understanding of my specific use of technical language. You will be able to start making Creative Real Estate work for you at once.

You now know about Kessler's Keys to Success for:

⊶ People in real estate

⊶ Negotiation

⊶ Types of transactions

⊶ Types of property

⊶ Financing

⊶ Exchanging

⊶ Owning and operating real estate

⊶ Real estate law

⊶ Taxation

5

Time and Money

Dost thou love life, then do not squander time, for that's the stuff life is made of.

— Benjamin Franklin

One of the most elusive concepts in the field of economics is that of value. Philosophers and economists endlessly discuss the meaning of value, what things have value, how to calculate value, and whether value is absolute or relative. No wonder it's been said that if all the economists in the world were placed end to end, they still wouldn't reach a conclusion.

But this is a book about real estate rather than economics or philosophy, so I'll ignore the debates and get down to the practical aspects of what you need to know about value in order to make money.

In Part One we saw that real estate has no *intrinsic* value, meaning it's not worth anything by itself. It only has value in relation to what it's worth to someone. I mentioned that there are people who would gladly pay a million dollars for an acre of beachfront property. Let's say you owned such an acre, an undisputed million-dollar value, and were willing to sell it. You advertise it and soon the investors come running with million-dollar checks in hand. One of them accepts your price, and as he hands you his check, you say, "There's a catch. You can only have this property for one minute."

What do you suppose that investor would do with his million dollars? He would make it disappear so fast, you'd think he was a magician. Why? Because that million-dollar piece of property is no good to him for only one minute. It's no good to him without sufficient time to do something with it, such as build on it, subdivide it, sell it, will it, or even keep it for appreciation. Real estate only has value when linked to possession of the property by specific individuals or groups. Possession only has meaning when linked to the concept of *time*.

Suppose someone offered to give you a million dollars, tax-free, as a gift. Great! But if you could keep the million for only one minute, would you want it? No, not without the time you would need to spend it, invest it, or do whatever you chose with it.

The essential ingredient in both of these examples is time. The concept of value has meaning only when it's linked to the concept of time. If you were to ask an aging, sickly billionaire what his most valuable possession is, he would most likely answer, "The time I have left." In the face of limited time, no amount of money, no possessions have any significant value, if indeed they have any value at all. In 1813, John Randolph said: "Time is at once the most valuable and the most perishable of all our possessions."

Time—dear, sweet, precious time—is the only resource of any intrinsic value at all.

This book would be of no value to you without the time it takes to read it. The information in it would be of no value to you without the time you need to put it to work. Nothing has any value without time.

If you want to learn how to build wealth, you have to learn how to increase and concentrate value. The critical aspect of doing that is knowing the use and value of time. And, in particular, you must be responsible for effective use of *your* time.

YOUR TIME IS VALUABLE

One of the most often used but incorrect statements is "time is money." Time costs money. Time is worth money. But time is not at all like money. You can't earn it, save it, or earn interest on it. You can't store it to use for a rainy day, lend it, or borrow it. You can't multiply it, invest it in order to make a profit, leverage it, or manipulate it.

No matter how rich or industrious you are, no matter how poor and lazy, you only have 60 seconds to a minute, 60 minutes to an hour, and 24 hours to a day. I don't care how hard you work, you'll never get more than that. Money can be increased, time can't.

If you have a few dollars you don't need right now, you can save them and use them another day. Not so with time. If you have a few extra hours, you must spend them when you have them.

There are ways to multiply, leverage and manage your money to accumulate more than the next person. But no amount of manipulation will get you more seconds in this minute than anyone else has.

There is always talk, especially among busy people, of "time management." Time management refers to the practice of keeping track of your time and scheduling your day to get more accomplished. Taken literally, the term is meaningless, because you cannot really manage time. You can only manage yourself and what you do with the time that's available to all of us equally. Nevertheless, for ease of communication, I'll use the term and share with you my *10 Rules of Effective Time Management.* I would like to have you think of them as 10 ways for more effective management of yourself, bearing in mind that time is nature's way of preventing everything from happening at once.

Recognize and act on the knowledge that:

1. The root cause of poor use of your time is poor time habits.
2. You must control your time or others will control it for you.
3. You can only spend time, you can't save it.
4. You must learn to say "no."
5. If you don't take time to plan, you cannot work efficiently.
6. You must organize your time or lose it.
7. Your time has a precious, determinable dollar value.
8. Your greatest asset in life, in achieving your goals, is time.
9. You must continuously strive to defeat the time wasters.
10. The key to successful time management is to build good time management systems and then act within them.

A time management system is an organized way of doing things. You give a higher priority (and you allot more time) to important tasks, and a lower priority (thus allotting less time) to unimportant tasks. A number of books have been written on the subject. Two that I recommend are *How to Get Control of Your Time and Your Life* by Alan Lakein and *The Time Trap* by R. Alec Mackenzie. It doesn't matter whether you use one of these systems or one that you develop yourself. What does matter is that you *use* a time system. This is especially critical in your dealings in Creative Real Estate. If you are going to practice Creative Real Estate full-time or part-time, the way you budget your time will strongly determine whether or not you succeed.

Most time management systems are based on a combination of organizing or listing what you have to do and determining priorities for effective action. Let's say you wake up on Monday morning with the vague notion that you have a busy day ahead, a day that promises too few usable hours for all the tasks you hope to accomplish. Before attacking those tasks in a helter-skelter way, sit down and list them, as they occur to you. For example:

To Do Today

- Renew driver's license.
- Record deed to newly purchased property.
- Check on zoning change for planned addition to duplex.
- Clean out and reorganize desk.

- Sign and deliver acceptance of offer on property for sale.
- Go to bank to cover check overdraft.

As you look over your list, first decide which items absolutely *must* be done today. Renewing one's driver's license is unquestionably important, but unless today is the day it expires the task does not absolutely have to be done now. On the other hand, if you don't cover the overdraft on a check that will be presented to your bank for payment today, the check will bounce and cause you embarrassment, expense, and wasted time. Thus, the trip to the bank has a higher priority today than the trip to the driver's license bureau. After you list your priorities, the list might look like this:

Priority	To Do Today
1	Go to bank and cover overdraft.
2	Sign and deliver acceptance of offer.
3	Record deed.
4	Check on zoning change.
5	Renew driver's license.
6	Clean out and reorganize desk.

Now that you have a complete list of priorities, do the tasks on the list *in their order of importance.* If you don't get them all done, that's all right. You can transfer the incompleted tasks to the next day's list. Theoretically, the incompleted tasks will rise on the priority list as time goes by. If a task remains a low priority, it probably isn't worth doing and you might eventually leave it off your "To Do Today" lists. (It could help you to know that the only person whose work was all done by Friday was Robinson Crusoe.)

Whichever system you use, make effective use of your time by doing only those activities that are the most productive for you. Spend your time doing what you do most efficiently. Realize the value of the concept of leveraging people and use it for your benefit.

However you choose to use your time, the essential element is that you keep track of it. Get a notebook, a diary, or a calendar book and jot down the time you spend on your real estate activities. A simple annotation about what you did and how long it took will be a valuable tool later, when you sit down to figure out how you're doing. If you don't keep track of your time, you'll be amazed at how much of it you waste. If you do keep track of it, you'll also be amazed at how much time it takes to accomplish certain tasks. It's not unusual, for example, to spend an hour looking through want-ads without finding a single interesting piece of property. As you keep track of your time, you may find that you just spent twenty-five minutes on the phone with your real estate broker talking about something you could have handled in five.

All this time is "wasted" in the sense that it's nonproductive and must be counted when you sit down and figure out what you ultimately "paid" for a piece of property. Remember, the time you invest is often more valuable than the money you put into a real estate transaction. When you figure the cost of a real estate transaction, calculate your time at a certain number of dollars per hour and add the amount to the cost. You must do that, because if your time is indeed worth a certain number of dollars per hour, it stands to reason that if you hadn't spent the time working on your real estate transaction you could have been paid for doing something else.

For people who have never been in business for themselves or who have never been required to account for their time on the job, time accounting is at first a difficult practice to learn. So you might have some trouble with it initially. But I urge you to stick with it. If you don't, the wasted time will prevent you from being as effective as you could have been had you counted and properly evaluated your precious time. Once you learn the value of time, you'll learn something directly related to it. . . .

YOUR SERVICES ARE VALUABLE

This information is part of my seminar for Creative Real Estate Professionals. Regardless of how you make your living, it's valuable to know these principles.

Know your own worth. Many people say, "I'd like to make $50,000 a year." How many of them actually sit down and figure out what that means? If you work 40 hours a week, 50 weeks a year, you'll put in 2,000 hours. In order to make $50,000 a year, you have to be paid $25 for every one of those hours. That may sound like a little or a lot to you, but either way, the figure itself realistically has no significance. It's almost impossible to charge for every hour of a 40-hour week. Who are you going to charge for the extra half-hour you spent in a traffic jam on the way to an appointment? Who are you going to charge for the twenty minutes you waste looking for a lost file folder, the hour you work on your books, or the five minutes you spend on the telephone on "hold"?

If you keep track of the productive time you spend each day, you're doing very well if you can total four hours out of eight that are income-producing. In fact, the national average of income-producing time is less than four hours per day. For the sake of simplicity, let's say you do put in four hours of productive time. To make $50,000 a year you have to be paid $50 for each hour you work. And that means every minute of your precious time is worth 83 cents. Consider this fact for an 83-cent minute.

All a professional has to sell is time and experience. In the words of Abraham Lincoln, "A lawyer's time is his stock in trade." What Lincoln was saying is that the time, including the experience that enriches it, is all the lawyer, or any professional who provides advice, really has to sell. The same wisdom applies to anyone who wants to make the most effective use of time to achieve a goal. It then follows that before you do anything, you must ask yourself, "Is this time being used or wasted; is it being paid for or given away for free?"

The classic example of being paid for time plus experience is that of the old plumber who was called in by the building manager because the ancient heating pipes in the town hall meeting room made such a noise during town meetings that it was difficult to hear the speakers. When the old plumber, suffering from arthritis, hobbled in, the building manager had some doubts about his ability to handle the job. With no hesitation, the veteran plumber painfully eased his way toward a joint in the pipes on the wall, took a ball-peen hammer from the hanging loop on his overalls, and sharply hit the pipe at the joint. Instantly, the clanging and knocking noises in the old pipes ceased. When the plumber submitted his bill for $200, the building manager exclaimed: "But you just hit the pipe with a hammer and only spent 5 minutes on the job!" The wise old plumber replied: "Yes, and my $200 bill consists of $5 for the 5 minutes when I hit the pipe with my hammer and $195 for the 25 years of learning when and where to hit the pipe."

If you allow your time (or the experience that is part of it) to be wasted, you'll never make money. Anyone who takes your time or your advice without paying is a thief—as much a thief as a shoplifter, a burglar, or a pickpocket. There are a number of ways to guard against time wastage and to protect yourself from time thieves.

If you work as a consultant for a fee, decide what your time is worth based on what you want to earn and the number of productive (paid) hours in your week. When someone asks for your advice, don't be afraid to say from the start what that advice is going to cost. You might be uncomfortable about this at first, but it's better to get the matter of price taken care of *before* you give advice than it is to explain afterward that you expect to get paid for what you already did.

When someone wants your advice, even if it's at a party or a ballgame, ask warm, friendly questions to show that you care about him or her as a person. For example, "Are you seriously or casually interested in real estate?" You can then politely say, "I know you realize that what you're asking me for is professional advice. I'm very interested in discussing it with you; would you please call my secretary (or me at my office) so we can set aside some private time to give it full attention?"

You'll get one of two reactions to this. A person might say, "I was just making conversation," meaning "No, I won't pay for your advice." If so, that's fine. You both have politely established your positions and can enjoy the event you're attending. If you don't lay the terms out that way, that person could milk you for all the free advice he could get, whether or not he could use it. And he probably would not value your advice enough to use it. The old adage explains it best: "What we get for nothing is usually worth only that to us."

Another reaction might be, "Oh, I'm sorry. I didn't realize you're a professional. I really do want the advice and would be happy to pay you for it." Hang on to such a person. He'll make a great client.

If you are an investor, you might suggest at this point that you don't take fees for your advice, but do provide it to your investment partners and associates. This could be a great way to find co-investors.

If you work on a commission basis, you have to be just as careful about your time and your advice, if not more so. Before you talk to someone in your professional capacity, make sure he is a *bona fide* prospect, not just a "suspect"—that is, make sure he is a serious investor or a committed buyer or seller. After a while, you'll be able to tell the difference between prospects and suspects. Here are some clues:

1. How specific are they about what they want to do?
2. Can the situation they're talking about be handled in a reasonable time?
3. How realistic are the terms they're discussing?
4. Are they talking as if they already have the means to transact the business, or do they say, "Gee, if only we had the money" or, "If we did own some property . . ."

Cultivate prospects and avoid suspects

If you're going to be a professional, act like one. Be prepared, be organized and do your homework, and you won't be charging people for wasted time. When you're acting in a professional capacity, be businesslike and efficient and deliver what you're selling. People will recognize that you value their time as much as you do your own and that the services you're giving them have value. They'll be willing to pay any reasonable sum for your services. This also pertains to valuing your sweat equity in investments.

Being a professional has two basic requirements: (1) perform a service that others can't or won't do for themselves, and (2) get paid. Whether you are a professional or an amateur, the most important point to remember when dealing with others is to give and expect consideration.

THE TIME AND SERVICES OF OTHERS ARE VALUABLE

Earlier I mentioned my two-word course in economics: leverage people. The concept is directly related to the subject of time and money and is based on this simple formula:

$$V + Q + S = \$$$

Here's what it means: **V**alue plus **Q**uantity plus **S**peed equals **W**ealth. Anything of value that you would like to have performed (**V**), plus the quantity (**Q**), plus the speed or velocity at which it gets done (**S**), provides wealth (**$**). **V**alue refers to how well a particular job is done; **Q**uantity to how much is done; and **S**peed to how fast it gets done. Together they produce **W**ealth.

For example, let's say your kitchen sink is stopped up and you want it cleared. You decide to fix it yourself rather than pay a plumber. First you scrounge around your closets until you find a plunger. You apply the plunger to the drain and start working it up and down. In so doing, you splash greasy water over the counter, the floor, and your new suit. But eventually the water goes down and the job is done—until your next meal, when some artichoke leaves slip down the drain and the sink gets stopped up again. So much for the quality of your work. You did a poor job because the drain really needed to be cleaned out all the way down.

Next, you locate a do-it-yourself tool rental service and rent a mechanical snake. You return home, spend half an hour trying to figure out how it works, another half-hour running it down the drain, and yet another half-hour cleaning up the mess you made. After that, you return the snake to the rental store and the job is done to your satisfaction. You're proud of yourself.

Now let's figure out what it really cost you to do that job. There's the time it took for the plunger operation and the cost of cleaning your suit. There's the time it took you to change clothes, look through a directory to find a store that rents snakes, go to that store, get a snake, and bring it home. Then there's the rental charge and the hour and a half you spent doing the job, plus the time it took to return the snake and get back home again. Add it up. What did that job *really* cost? Multiply your time by your hourly rate and add the out-of-pocket expense of the cleaners, the rental, and the gas it took to drive to the store and back. Don't be surprised if your total comes to hundreds of dollars. Now check what it would have cost to call a plumber and have it done professionally. It's probably less than $60. You have decreased your own wealth by hundreds of dollars in an effort to save money. And, worst of all, if you didn't do the job properly, you might have to call a plumber after all. And, the new suit might be permanently stained.

If you had called a plumber, you would have been leveraging people. You would have been using his time and his experience to get something done properly and quickly. While he was working, you could have used your time to do what you do properly and quickly, thus creating wealth for yourself rather than decreasing what you have.

I have mentioned before this vital principle of Creative Real Estate and I will again, to remind you to form the habit of leveraging people. Use your time for what you do well and use others for everything else. Let's examine how this works in an extreme example.

Suppose you are a successful young engineer, earning $55,000 a year, and you don't know the first thing about real estate. What's more, you don't care to learn the most basic principles of real estate. All you want to do is to augment your income from the profits of real estate investment. You just want to invest and forget about it. Can you do it? Of course. Just leverage people.

First, find yourself a Creative Real Estate Professional* to discuss your goals, your financial situation, your ability to incur debt, and the measure of risk you can handle. Next, find someone who is good at locating the kinds of properties that fit your particular profile. Find a lawyer to handle the legal aspects and an accountant to figure the tax requirements. Seek out a handyman who can do the necessary work on your property and a manager to take care of the day-to-day operations. Ultimately, you'll want a good salesman who can sell the property for you at a handsome profit. Now, all of these people are going to cost you money, and you have to estimate these costs in your real estate ventures, but that's OK.

There are enough profitable situations that would allow for all of those services and still leave a healthy chunk for you. When you really get going in real estate, you'll have teams of such support people working for you in a number of locations.

The most rewarding aspect of this arrangement is that while all these people are working for you, you're merrily toiling away at your engineering and getting better at it, so you'll soon be making more than $55,000 a year.

On the other hand, if you can do one or more of the tasks involved in a real estate transaction and do them properly and quickly, then by all means do them. In that way you'll save whatever it costs for the services of someone else. But do so only if it won't take away from the time you could spend more profitably and productively at your own work. I can't stress this enough.

If you get a kick out of scouring want-ads for good properties and would waste 45 minutes of your lunch hour doing crossword puzzles anyway, go ahead and scour those want-ads at lunch time. But if you usually spend 45 minutes at lunch boning up on new developments in your profession, don't divert yourself from that activity unless in those 45 minutes you

---

* See Chapter 16 for information on finding a Creative Real Estate Professional in your area.

can find better properties than someone else could—properties that pay off more handsomely than the 45 minutes of professional reading would.

Understanding the concept of leveraging people is not the same as practicing the principle. When you have learned to actually leverage people at all times, you will be a master of economics and will be using a tool that has been used effectively by everyone who has ever become wealthy.

The final aspect of leveraging people that you need to practice is to learn to follow the advice you pay for. I know you might think this goes without saying, but it must be stressed.

The biggest mistake people make in dealing with professionals is failing to take the advice they're paying for. Ask any doctor or lawyer what his biggest frustration is, and he or she will probably reply that it is patients and clients who don't take his or her advice. A doctor says, "Stay off your feet and don't eat junk food." The patient nods gravely, pays the doctor's fee, then goes to an amusement park and eats cotton candy and popcorn. He spends the next few days in bed wondering why the doctor didn't help him. A lawyer says, "Don't sign anything unless I see it first." The client nods affirmatively, pays the lawyer's fee, and three weeks later comes back begging the lawyer to help him get out of an unfavorable contract.

As a real estate consultant, I have seen this happen hundreds of times and to this day I can't figure out why. Maybe people decide they know more than the professional. My advice is, if you do, fine. Use your own judgment. But if your judgment is so good, why pay someone else for his? Advice not taken is a waste. It's a waste of time, a waste of money, a waste of effort. You'll never get rich wasting those valuable commodities.

You will, however, get rich if you read—and heed—the advice in the next chapter.

Remember these Kessler's Keys to Success:

☛ Your time is valuable

☛ Your services are valuable

☛ The time and services of others are valuable

6

Finding the Right Property

Understanding human needs is half the job of meeting them.

—Adlai Stevenson

The ability to identify a property that will increase in value more quickly than others is not a trait we are born with. I find this fact refreshing and encouraging because it means that any of us can learn this important skill. It is a skill because it requires specific information and perfect practice to achieve.

In the pages that follow I will supply the information. You will have to add the practice—perfect practice—that will, together with the information I supply, form your knowledge of the skill.

Whenever you become impatient practicing, think of the young visitor to New York City who stopped a kindly looking gentleman carrying a violin case and asked: "Can you tell me how to get to Carnegie Hall?" The kind gentlemen leaned over and whispered in the young visitor's ear: "Practice, practice!"

FILLING THE NEED

First, it is essential that you know what needs, wants, and desires the "right" property will fulfill. Obviously, these needs, wants, and desires have to be the requirements of someone. That someone is an investor. For it's the investor who actually establishes the value of any piece of property in the marketplace by his requirements (needs, wants, and desires).

Now that we know the who and why of it, let's talk about the what.

A real estate investor desires only two basic considerations. Those two things also represent the investor's wants and needs, as you will clearly see. The two considerations are: (1) a return (profit) on investment, and (2) a return (security) of investment.

Always remember that irrespective of the circumstances surrounding the investment, the two basic considerations of any real estate investment are always the same: *profit* (in some form, such as dollar returns, exchange for other property, other goods and services, tax-savings, or personal use) and

71

security (a reasonable assurance that the original investment will at least remain intact and be recoverable). When an investment fulfills these two basic considerations, it is a perfect example of a case of needs, wants, and desires that can all be filled at once, using identical considerations.

P.S. As a memory jogger, whenever you consider an investment, if you haven't initially examined it in light of these two basic considerations, remember this *P.S.* and continue your examination to ascertain if this investment provides:

P for profit (return on investment), and

S for security (return of investment).

WHY REAL ESTATE?

By now I hope you've noticed that we are not just talking about real estate but about *a way of life*. People benefits and the fulfilling of needs, wants, and desires applies to *everything* we do in life, not just real estate. I maintain that the proper "life attitude" will provide the basis for a proper "business attitude" in real estate or any other endeavor, and will result in success and fulfillment. However, since this book is particularly about my expertise in Creative Real Estate, let me explain four specific benefits of real estate investment as compared with any other type of investment:

1. Cash flow (also called spendable).
2. Equity build-up.
3. Depreciation.
4. Appreciation.

Each of these benefits is a unique characteristic of real estate investments.

Cash flow, or spendable income, is the money that is available for personal discretionary use after all the operating expenses (including real property taxes) and debt service (payments on loans against the property) are paid, but before the payment of income taxes.

Equity build-up is the increase of your own share (your capital investment, or the amount of money that is yours over and above the total loan debts against the property) of the value of the property. This increase occurs automatically when you make payments that include principal and interest against the mortgage. The portion of each payment that is applied toward the principal or repayment of the original amount of the loan increases your equity build-up.

Depreciation is that deduction that you take "on paper" to offset your income from that piece of real estate. If the depreciation is more than the income from the subject property, the excess may be used to offset income taxes on your income from real estate sources other than the subject property. This benefit, depreciation, is a major source of *tax shelter* or *tax umbrella*. The concept permits you to deduct the prescribed amount that represents the supposed decrease in value of the improvements (buildings) due to aging each year. In fact the property may be increasing in value, but you can derive the tax benefits on the amount of the scheduled depreciation.

Appreciation is the increase in fair market value of the property created by demand, enhanced desirability, inflation, or anything else that causes the price to escalate. The amount of appreciation also increases your equity build-up.

Keeping in mind the two basic considerations for a real estate investment, **PS** (profit, security), and the four unique benefits of a real estate investment, **CEDA.** (cash flow, equity build-up, depreciation, appreciation), you are ready to . . .

FIND PROPERTY THAT IS INCREASING IN VALUE

Rather than rely on the projections of economists, who have unabashedly predicted 23 of the last 17 recessions, we can always expect and plan for the next recovery, which inevitably succeeds the next downturn.

Long-term statistics reveal that the *total* value of all property in the country is increasing every day. That's nice to know but, of itself, doesn't help you much. The reason it doesn't help is that not all properties are increasing at the same rate, and more importantly, some properties are actually decreasing in value while others are increasing astronomically. So the trick is to be able to look at properties and decide which are increasing, which are decreasing, and which, if any, are staying the same.

Obviously, the best property to buy is property that is appreciating in value faster than the average. It is possible to make money on property that is increasing slowly or staying the same, but initially it's more difficult and requires extensive knowledge of complicated principles that may not be the most effective use of your time. For now, let's concentrate on building wealth quickly. That means learning how to recognize property whose value is likely to increase rapidly.

MY PROFIT FORMULA

Learning to recognize property whose value is rapidly increasing is a matter of understanding my "**PROFIT** formula." Do this and you'll be on your way. The word PROFIT is an acronym for **P**rofitable **R**ealty **O**wnership **F**or **I**nvestment **T**actics. This formula has four simple points, and if you follow them when acquiring property, the odds for acquiring a good property will be weighted heavily in your favor. In fact, it has been a rare occurrence that anyone who followed these points acquired a piece of real estate that didn't appreciate in value quickly.

While writing this book, I had a most enjoyable visit with my editor of the first edition, Bill Gladstone, now a nationally prominent literary agent at Waterside Productions, Inc. It was particularly gratifying to learn that while he owned no real estate at the time the first edition was published, he told me he has since benefitted from applying my PROFIT formula. He now owns his office building, which sits on a hill overlooking the Pacific Ocean in a seaside town that has been included in a megalopolis, as well as a number of other properties in various locations, which met the test of the PROFIT formula. Although still a young man, Bill's major concern is now perfecting his estate so that his children may benefit from his wise real estate investments.

1. Buy in the Path of Progress

As populations grow, they generally move outward from a city core or area of concentration. It's easy to see where these areas are. Look around your own city. If there's a reservoir to the south, a mountain range to the east, and government park land to the north, growth has to take place to the west. So, "Go west, young person." Go out there and look around. What do you see? Land being cleared for subdivisions? Shopping centers going up? Roads being widened? Bright new office buildings gleaming in the sun? That's progress. Land in those areas, and immediately beyond them, is in the path of progress and is multiplying in value faster than land in other areas. Right there in the path of progress is where you want to be.

A prime example of this phenomenon exists in my own county, San Diego. The city of San Diego is in the extreme southwest corner of the United States with Mexico to the south and the Pacific Ocean to the west. There's no land available in either of those directions. That leaves north and east. Vacant land lies east of San Diego and progress is slowly inching its way in that direction. The trouble is, most of the land to the east is desert, and finding sufficient water is a continuing problem. If you go out there, you'll see some progress, but not much. That leaves the north. As you drive into north San Diego County, you find temperate weather, an adequate water supply, and a booming real estate business. Land values, you can rightly conclude, have escalated much faster than in the deserts to the east.

There are ways other than physically going to an area to look for the path of progress. Check the newspapers. When builders develop a subdivision, they place big, splashy ads enticing people to come out and buy. Locate these subdivisions on a map. They will undoubtedly be in the path of progress.

Notice where companies are building factories. Often a new factory seems to be in the middle of nowhere, surrounded by "worthless" land.

Companies building factories are as interested in bargains as anyone else, so they buy and build where land is inexpensive. But the land around those new factories does not remain "worthless." Factory workers will need places to eat, to relax after work, and to shop on the way to or from their jobs. Soon that worthless land around the factory will be sprouting restaurants, cocktail lounges, and shops of all kinds.

I don't mean to suggest by these examples that you have to look for vacant land. Not at all. Houses, apartments, and commercial buildings in partially developed areas in the path of progress also quickly rise in value. You can find many kinds of property in the path of progress. The kind you buy depends more on what your investment objectives are than on the area. So get out there and start looking.

2. Buy on the Water Side

In real estate, there's something magical about water. People love to be near it. They love to swim in it, boat on it, fish in it, play in it, even just look at it. And they'll pay dearly for these privileges. Take advantage of man's natural affinity for water. If the area you're looking at has water anywhere near it, buy as close to the water as you can. You'll be well rewarded for your judgment.

About a hundred years ago, a number of fast-buck artists were traveling about the country selling "waterfront" lots in Miami Beach. The "pigeons" who bought these lots, sight unseen, found out later that the property was actually *under*water swampland and not on the waterfront.

Nevertheless, in the early 1900s a man named Flagler dredged and filled huge tracts of this land, creating what is now the Golden Strand. The people who kept their underwater lots found themselves with property worth $1,000 per front foot! More than 100 times what they had paid for it!

Today, water is more valuable than ever, and with projects to clean up rivers, deepen lakes, restore and preserve coastlines and build canals, the opportunities to buy property near newly developed, usable bodies of water are increasing. Get close to that water and you'll get rich. To avoid the risk suffered by the flood victims in the early part of this decade, make certain your waterfront property has sufficient elevation to survive a 500-year flood. The county and state planning departments usually have records and projections to determine 100- and 500-year flood levels, check them before you buy.

3. Buy on the Hill Side

People love to live on hills. Maybe it's because they like to look at a nice view, or maybe they enjoy being "king of the hill." Whatever the reason, they are willing to pay more for hillside property than flatland or bottom land. And they'll pay astronomically for hilltops! In all my years of development marketing, the price of hillside and hilltop lots has averaged over 50% more than the rest of the lots in the development.

4. If You Have the Choice, Combine as Many of the Three as Possible

If you can find property in the path of progress that is near the water, buy it. If it's in the path of progress and on a hill overlooking the water—BUY IT! In fact, you can make a specialty of dealing in properties that have all three of these qualities. If you do, your net worth will start to multiply faster than you can figure it.

THE IDEAL INVESTMENT

An old maxim in the real estate business is that the three most important things are location, location, and location. That's true, but it's not the whole story, especially when it comes to the investment aspect of real estate.

If you buy with location as your only consideration, you are thinking of only one of five factors that make for the ideal investment. You are anticipating appreciation. It's a good point by itself, but to do extraordinarily well you need to learn how to acquire property having all five factors working for its profitability. Together, these five factors make up what I call the **IDEAL** theory of investment. They are:

- Income
- Depreciation
- Equity build-up
- Appreciation
- Leverage

Income is a flow of revenues that exceeds the costs of holding and managing a property. In areas where property prices are extremely high, as in Southern California, positive income from property investment may be hard to come by. It's difficult to have income from an investment in vacant land. Yet income is desirable, for obvious reasons, and you should strive for income-producing property whenever possible.

Depreciation can be used to some extent on any property that has improvements on it. Improvements are usually buildings, although the term can include blacktop paving, fences, indoor/outdoor carpeting, decorative walls and canopies, as well as other things permanently fastened to the property. Depreciation is a tax-saving device that works like this: if you buy a $100,000 piece of property consisting of land and a four-unit apartment building, you must first figure what the land is worth in order to figure the depreciation. Since the land will presumably always be there, by definition it cannot depreciate. You must exclude it from your calculations. Let's say the land under your building is worth $20,000. That means the building is worth $80,000. The next step is to try to estimate when that building will be worth nothing at all. Customarily (in the past, before the Tax Reform Act of 1986 prescribed fixed cost recovery periods) this estimate was based on the actual expected life of the building. For now, it's a fixed figure arrived at using guidelines acceptable to the Internal Revenue Service.

Presume that the life expectancy of your building is 27.5 years, as permitted under the Tax Reform Act of 1986. Then your $80,000 building will be worth nothing in 27.5 years and is depreciating, or going down in value, at the rate of $2,909 every year. If you use the prescribed "straight line" method of depreciation, you can deduct $2,909 each year from the income on your building when you're paying income taxes. You can take this deduction even if the income from the building was less than $2,909. If that happens, you have what investors lovingly call a tax loss, or a reduction from your taxable income whether or not you might have had a positive cash flow, of up to $2,909. This is why investors love depreciable, income-producing real estate.

Like most good deals, though, it does have a catch. When you sell the property, you have to use the depreciated value as your cost basis for the purpose of figuring capital gains taxes. Thus, if you sold in five years after depreciating this building a total of $14,545 and received $120,000 for your building and land, you're actually selling $20,000 worth of undepreciated land and a building that only cost you $65,455 ($80,000 less $14,545 depreciation) for tax purposes. Since $100,000 ($120,000 less $20,000 for the land) of your sales price is attributed to the building, you have to pay capital gains tax on $34,545, not the $20,000 that was your actual profit (calculated on your purchase price).

Having to pay tax on the extra (that was depreciated) is not that bad, because long-term capital gains, which this profit is, are taxed at a lower rate than ordinary income. So, for five years you haven't paid ordinary income tax on $2,909 a year and at the time of sale you're only paying the lower rate of capital gains tax on that money. It's much better to pay tax on long-term capital gains than on ordinary income or short-term capital gains. I've really oversimplified this matter and there are many other considerations that you should discuss with a good tax accountant (again, leveraging people), I'll even show you how to defer paying the capital gains tax later in Chapter 14. But now you at least have an idea of what depreciation is and how to use it to make money.

Equity build-up is, in part, the amount of money you pay on the principal part of the loan on the property as you amortize (repay) your loan. Suppose you bought your $100,000 apartment building with $20,000 down and took a bank loan of $80,000, with payments of $800 per month, principal and interest, for 30 years. Fully amortizing bank loans are structured so that you pay the lion's share of the interest in the early years, with the part of the payment that goes to the principal starting small and gradually increasing, while the interest part of the payment becomes less as the loan matures. The payment amount remains constant.

For simplicity's sake, suppose the first payment you make is $780 worth of interest and only $20 worth of principal. This means that $780 goes to the bank for the use of their money. You'll never see it again. The remaining $20, however, goes to pay the principal; that is, it actually goes to pay back the original amount of the loan on the building. After the payment, the principal balance on your loan is $79,980. The other $20,020 of your $100,000 property is your equity—the amount you own, not owe. By making this payment, you will have built up your equity by $20.

Another source of equity build-up is the increasing value of the property. The amount that the property increases in market value over your purchase price, as long as the loan isn't increased, is also equity build-up, as is an increase due to inflation. Equity build-up is available in every real estate situation except those in which the property is decreasing in value faster than your ability to pay off the loan. Stay away from those kinds of ownerships.

Appreciation is the amount property is rising in value because of desirability, improvement, inflation, market conditions or any or all of the above. If your $100,000 building is slightly run down, you can increase its value by fixing and painting it. If you put $2,000 worth of repairs into it, making it worth $5,000 more on the market, you have appreciation tied directly to desirability. When you actually do the work yourself, this is referred to as "sweat equity." If you do nothing to the building but it goes up because the price of everything (including cars, corn, and Chivas Regal) is going up, you have appreciation because of inflation. If you do nothing to the building and it goes up because of a shortage of apartments in your town, you have appreciation because of conditions in the apartment market. Because there are so many ways for values to increase, appreciation is one of the chief reasons people buy real estate.

Leverage is the ability to control a large asset with a small amount of input. Just as a lever enables you to move a big rock with little effort, the combination of good credit, income, and a property's increasing market value enables you to buy a big piece of property with a relatively small amount of money down. In the case of your $100,000 apartment building, if you paid cash, you would have zero leverage. If you bought with only $1,000 down, you would have 99% leverage. The lever is a powerful tool, as powerful in real estate as it is in rock-moving. It is a key ingredient for making Creative Real Estate work. Use leverage properly and wisely, and you will prosper.

Every one of the elements I have just discussed is desirable to have in a real estate transaction. In order to have a good transaction, they are essential. If you are clever and fortunate enough to include all five, you have, indeed, the IDEAL investment. Even though it may be impossible to get all five every time, I urge you always to try for as many as possible. Because of the vast amount of real estate available for investment and because of the thousands of opportunities that present themselves constantly, I personally pass up situations that don't offer all five elements. Why settle for less than the IDEAL?

Your Kessler's Keys to Success now include:

🗝 Filling the need

🗝 PS

🗝 Why real estate?

🗝 CEDA

🗝 Find property that is increasing in value

🗝 My PROFIT Formula

🗝 The IDEAL investment

7

How to Get Rich—Quickly!

Believe in yourself.

— Norman Vincent Peale

Actually, this whole book is about how to get rich. This chapter will reinforce the general ideas we've already looked at and will give you some additional, specific techniques that will help you get rich more quickly. Just simple little truths and ideas, about which Henry Ford said: "Paying attention to simple little things that most people neglect makes a few rich."

The key word is quickly, because what's important is not only how much money you make but how fast you make it. If you make $25,000 a year for forty years, you will have made a million dollars. If you saved half of that income, you would still have $500,000—and that's "rich" by most people's definition. Still, for most of those forty years you would not be rich; you'd be living moderately, like everyone else on your block.

The people who most enjoy their wealth are those who accelerate their incomes so that they accumulate money while they still have time to retire early and enjoy their wealth. In purchasing this book, you have demonstrated your interest in making money. My purpose is to show you how to make it quickly—more quickly than inflation, more quickly than your ability to spend it, and more quickly than Uncle Sam's ability to tax it away. According to Abe Lincoln, "Things may come to those who wait, but only the things left by those who hustle." In other words, get rich quickly, because getting rich slowly is hardly better than staying poor.

A WORD ON PYRAMIDING

Don't.

The best definition of a pyramid that I've heard is: "A pyramid is constructed by carefully laying the blocks of the foundation on a wide area and working hard tapering it up to the top where it will narrow off to nothing."

Real estate speculators may tell you they have pyramided their way to a fortune and that pyramiding is the only way to multiply your wealth. There may be an isolated story of success among speculators, but pyramiding is bound to fail in the long run.

A typical real estate pyramid could start with a rental house bought for $50,000, with $10,000 down. If you fix the place up, increase the rent, and are in an escalating real estate market, you may see the value of the house rise to $55,000 in a year.

Next, you spot a four-unit building selling for $120,000. You borrow $15,000 from a private lender on the equity in your house, put the $15,000 down on the building and finance the $105,000 balance. Your pyramid has begun. You "own" $175,000 worth of property, but your total investment of capital is only $10,000. The other $165,000 is a combination of appreciation and loans.

A few years later your four-unit building rises in value to $140,000. You find a ten-unit building selling for $250,000, so you borrow $35,000 from a private lender against your fourplex to use as a down payment on the larger place. Your pyramid now consists of your $55,000 house, a $140,000 four-unit building, and the new $250,000 ten-unit building—for a total value of $445,000. And still you've only invested $10,000. Seems to be great, but let's take an analytical look at your position.

There's one obvious problem. While you're pyramiding your equity and your properties, another pyramid is growing, a pyramid of debt. You now owe $55,000 on the house, $140,000 on the four units, and $215,000 on the ten units. The trouble with this debt pyramid is that it's upside down— narrow at the bottom and huge at the top. The slightest wind can blow over pyramids built in this fashion.

If you owe $410,000 (the total cost of the properties) on properties worth $445,000, you are leveraged at over 92% with no cash reserve on hand. A fire in one of the units, a few slow-paying tenants, a change in the neighborhood, or a normally insignificant event that only slightly affects your ability to promptly meet the payments on all this debt could place you in serious financial difficulty. A mere drop of 8% in market values (a common occurrence in recessionary times) would leave you owing more than the properties are worth.

If you find yourself in cash-flow trouble and the lenders foreclose, they'll first look to the equity in the buildings to repay the debts. If that equity isn't sufficient, and sales commissions and costs could eat up such a slim margin, they could hold you personally responsible to make up the difference out of your other assets. The school of hard knocks is an accelerated curriculum.

When I said earlier that you have to be willing to take risks to make money, I was not referring to taking too great a risk to be able to maintain reasonable control of a situation. Jumping out of an airplane with a parachute is risky. Jumping out of an airplane without a parachute is just plain crazy. The kind of risk you take in pyramiding is of the no-parachute variety. It's just too great a risk to justify whatever potential reward you might anticipate.

So if you're thinking of pyramiding, remember this one word of advice from A. D. Kessler: *Don't.* Mark Twain reminds us: "It is easier to stay out than get out."

NEGOTIATING SO THAT EVERYONE WINS

With proper negotiating, you can turn a marginally good transaction into a great one and a barely profitable venture into a substantially profitable one. Sometimes more money can be made in the negotiation than at any other point in the actual transaction.

The essential point to remember in negotiating is to think win/win. Everyone involved in the transaction must come out better off than before the negotiation started. Remember the main theme of Creative Real Estate: people benefits.

Although the crass version, "He who has the gold, rules," is in wide practice, living by the Golden Rule, "Do unto others as you would have them do unto you," has been effective for many centuries. Idea-tracking on that great concept, I offer a piggy-back concept for Creative Real Estaters, the Platinum Rule: "Do unto others as *they would have you do unto them.*" Simply explained, the Platinum Rule suggests that you should provide the benefits for others that *they* need, want, and desire. Let's say that I happen to like to own apartment buildings and welcome the opportunity to acquire apartment buildings, and you like to own vacant land and would like to dispose of your apartment building. What possibility is there of your accepting an offer to exchange one of my apartment buildings for yours? On the other hand, if I offered you some vacant land for your apartment building, you would probably be very interested in consummating that transaction, wouldn't you?

In win/win negotiating, it is important to offer what someone else wants, so that he also can win when you win. Always bear in mind the concept I expressed earlier in this book: No one will give up what he has unless he gets something he wants more.

Do your homework. Determine the needs, wants, and desires of the "other side," and make your best effort to fulfill them. In that way you will seldom miss an opportunity for all parties to benefit from win/win negotiation.

BACK TO THE BASICS

In addition to the Platinum Rule, there are three basic keys that are vital to include in your practice of win/win negotiating. These three keys, each preceded by "always," are:

1. *Leave something for the other fellow.*
2. *Make full disclosure.*
3. *Let there be no surprises.*

Always leave something for the other fellow to benefit from as much as you do. Don't try to squeeze the last dollar of value out of the situation before you dispose of it. By leaving some visible benefits, you will have a salable package that will be much more attractive to a greater number of people than if you take all the benefits for yourself and try to dispose of the stripped "carcass."

Always make full disclosure of all the facts and details of which you are aware. The only thing you should have up your sleeve is your funnybone. It is also good practice to update your knowledge before you enter negotiations so that you can honestly and sincerely represent all of the aspects of the situation. This will result in building credibility and confidence early in the negotiations and make it easy for everyone to save time and energy by being able to make decisions based on solid facts. As John Burroughs put it: "To treat your facts with imagination is one thing, to imagine your facts is another."

Always let there be no surprises, so that once you start negotiations you can be reasonably certain they can continue to a fruitful conclusion. Nothing should be left to chance, to upset the boat in midstream. This would only cause a distressing and useless waste of everyone's time, energies, and good faith and would be counter-productive to success.

I suggest that you memorize these three basic keys and include them in every negotiation. By using them, you will soon find that more, if not all, of your transactions are falling into place more easily and profitably.

MAKING TRANSACTIONS WORK

Francis Bacon wrote: "A wise man makes more opportunities than he finds." An elderly gentleman, represented by an elderly traditional broker, wanted to sell his $250,000 apartment building because he was tired of managing it. He owed $100,000 on the building and was willing to let a buyer assume that mortgage. But he insisted on the rest—$150,000—in cash as a down payment. His plan to put the $150,000 in bank certificates that would yield him $1,000 per month in income was disclosed only after I got permission from his broker to ask some discreet counseling questions. The real solution to a problem is found with a properly stated question.

Our prospective buyer didn't have that much cash. Even if he did, $150,000 is 60% down, meaning the leverage would only be 40%—ridiculously poor terms for this buyer. Rather than have the buyer walk away, we constructed a creative offer. We offered the seller $50,000 down (20%). The buyer would assume the $100,000 debt and would sign a note in favor of the seller, secured by a mortgage on the property, for the other $100,000, payable at $750 per month. And, finally, the 'sweetener': we offered to give the seller an apartment, rent-free, for as long as the note is in force.

Superficially, the seller would appear to be accepting less than he originally asked, but in terms of people benefits, he is not. Presuming that the apartment would rent for $250 per month, the free rent plus the $750 monthly payment on the note equaled the $1,000 he would earn from the bank certificates. The gentleman would have to pay rent somewhere if he sold his building on normal terms. Since he has to live somewhere and moving would be a distasteful and costly chore, the sweetener was a real inducement to accept the offer.

Even more important to the man as a retired person was the fact that the rent-free apartment protected him from inflation. People who exist on fixed incomes live in constant fear of the next rent increase. With this offer, the retired seller would never have that worry.

The benefit to the buyer in the arrangement is that he could take over the building with a down payment only one-third the size of what was asked. Thus, every percent of appreciation on the building was worth three times as much to him. By skillful negotiating, we tripled the buyer's potential return without changing the price a penny, while giving the seller even more people benefits than he had asked for!

There was a bonus benefit that you might have already noticed. The elderly seller-turned-tenant still had a $100,000 interest in the building. He wanted to make sure the building kept its value and he wanted to make sure the buyer was able to continue paying him his $750 per month. So he kept a close watch on things, advised the buyer when something was broken, even did a little gratuitous puttering around the place. In effect, the buyer had an unpaid resident caretaker at no extra cost, and the seller continued to feel important, protecting his proprietary interest.

There's something vitally important for us to notice in the above example. The way I, as a negotiator, made this deal work was by increasing the people benefits to both parties involved. People benefits is the key to proper negotiating. It is even more important than money.

To repeat a most significant point, a good negotiator finds out what everybody needs, wants, and desires, then proposes a transaction that will fill as many of those needs, wants, and desires as possible. This is the essence of the win/win situation. Another point to realize is the necessity to educate other parties; in this case, the broker, in order to counsel his seller.

And that is one more significant reason for this book: to expand the community of brokers and investors knowledgeable about Creative Real Estate. In that way, many more win/win transactions will be embraced and completed.

Many amateur negotiators believe that good negotiating means coming out a winner while making the other fellow a loser. That's the exact opposite of the truth. Making the other fellow a loser usually leads to hard feelings, often to lawsuits, and too often to transactions that fall apart at the last minute.

TWO BASIC NEGOTIATING TECHNIQUES

Only practice can teach you to be a master negotiator. To start you in the right direction, I will give you proven tools that will immediately increase your effectiveness. They are (1) the *Suppose . . .* technique and (2) the *Front Porch* ploy.

Suppose . . .

As a practical matter, it's best not to start with a direct offer. A direct offer may intimidate people and make them nervous and defensive. But when you begin your proposition with "Suppose . . . " you're making it hypothetical, non-threatening, and noncommittal. The other person is more relaxed, more receptive, less on guard.

In the previous example of the elderly apartment owner, if you were the negotiator you would say, "Suppose I could show you a way to earn as much income from this sale as you were counting on, plus a free apartment for the rest of your life. Is there any reason why you wouldn't want to listen to what I have to say?"

The answer is obviously "No!" (while the head nods "Yes"), meaning: There is no reason I wouldn't want to listen.

Now, why did I phrase the question to prompt a "no" answer? Because in our culture we have become conditioned to saying "no." It is a virtually automatic, protective reflex. We say "no" to the hundreds of advertisements bombarding us every day. We say "no" to spending on luxuries because we have been taught to save. We say "no" to salesmen, to our children, to everyone. "No" is an easy, comfortable and safe answer to give, even if it means "yes!"

In this example, the "no" that means "yes" opens the door to your purely hypothetical offer and has you a long, long way down the road to getting it accepted. The buyer benefits as well from this negotiating technique because he will have an easier time accepting an innovative concept that actually brings him more benefits than his original idea, as in our case history.

In his first book, *Winning Through Intimidation,* Robert Ringer convinced many people that they could bully and bluff their way to success. I wasn't one of those he convinced. I call my technique "winning without intimidation," and it is not only a more consistently effective technique but also one that will help you sleep better at night when the negotiation is completed.

An important ingredient in this technique is the phrase, "Is there any reason why you wouldn't . . . ?" This phrase is part of an old device that's been used by good salesmen for generations. After the salesman has made his presentation, he comes to the "close." He says, "Now, Mr. Prospect, if this product does all that I've shown you, is there any reason why you wouldn't buy it today?" What the salesman is doing is boiling down all the possible objections into one. He's giving the prospect a way out that takes into consideration all our protective negative conditioning. If the prospect says "No," (there is no reason why he wouldn't . . .) he will buy, and willingly.

Look at the proposal in the apartment transaction again: "Suppose I could show you a way to earn as much income from this sale as you were counting on, plus a free apartment for the rest of your life. Is there any reason why you wouldn't want to listen to what I have to say?" Unless there is some unknown element, such as the seller having bought a house, the only possible answer to that question is "No." As we've seen, this "no" answer implies that he *would* agree to it. If the seller gives you any other answer, he's implying that you're not, in fact, going to show him what you've just said. If you do, he would be foolish not to take it. The only way out for him is to call you a liar, which is something he is not likely to do, especially since he has not even heard the offer yet.

So when you say, "Is there any reason why you wouldn't . . . ?" you're getting a preliminary commitment from the seller to accept your offer. All you have to do to merit that acceptance is to spell out the terms of a transaction that delivers exactly what you just said you were going to deliver. When you do that, everybody wins!

In the event the seller doesn't agree to the terms, you could always say, "Well, it was just supposing," and the door remains open for further negotiation.

The Front Porch

Just as your hypothetical question gives all an opportunity to "win" in negotiating, it is essential to give the other party a chance to see that he can win early in the discussion. So that's exactly what you do, and very early in the negotiations. In offering to buy the elderly gentleman's building, you make your terms realistic and reasonable except for one condition. You say, "I'm not satisfied with the front porch. As a condition of my purchase, I want you to tear down the old porch and build a new one of brick, across the entire front of the building, with a shingled roof over it and new shrubbery all around."

When the seller hits the ceiling over your outrageous demand, you spend time explaining how important it is to you, until you let him win, whereupon you reluctantly agree to go ahead with the other terms of the transaction, giving up your "important" front porch.

This way the seller wins early in the game and in his elation over winning he realizes you will be reasonable and has no resistance to the rest of the terms of your original offer.

Naturally, it's not necessary that the negotiation literally involve a front porch. Your front porch can be anything that would legitimately make the transaction more attractive to you: new landscaping, elaborate repairs, custom painting—whatever you can think of. Exactly what you propose isn't that important, as long as it's something—not really outrageous—you would truly benefit by having yet can easily do without when the seller rejects it, if he rejects it. If he accepts your front porch, so much the better.

That's it for techniques. Bear in mind as you start negotiating that the purpose is not to win "battles" at someone else's expense. The purpose is to make a transaction work. And the only way it can work is if it works for everyone. When everyone sees the possibility of getting what he or she wants, there are no unworkable situations; everyone will bend over backward to make it happen. When someone feels he's getting the short end of the stick, he'll start looking for ways to sabotage the transaction. "Nine-tenths of the serious controversies which arise in life result from one person not knowing the facts which to the other person seem important . . . or otherwise failing to appreciate the other's point of view."—Supreme Court Justice Louis Brandeis. Think win/win and you'll be a master negotiator—a rich master negotiator.

PERSUASIVE PRESENTATION

Research data reveals that person to person—one on one—is the most effective means of communication.

Meaning is conveyed:

- 10% by words
- 40% by tone of voice
- 50% by body language

How you say something, accompanied by your gestures and facial expression, constitute 90% of the meaning of your message.

Based on these facts, a letter can only convey 10% of the full meaning of your message, telephoning only 50%. Only face to face can you transmit the full impact of your ideas.

The art of simple, direct communication is immeasurably helpful in negotiating. It is not difficult to master when you know how to organize and deliver your presentation. Heed the dictum, "Put brain in gear before starting mouth." Do your homework and you will greatly enhance the possibility of success in any presentation.

My suggestions for effectiveness are:

1. Evaluate how much your listeners already know about the subject. This will prevent you from talking down to them or over their heads.

2. Start by clearly stating what you intend to prove.

3. Use only relevant facts. Many people overload their presentations with too much information. Talk is cheap because supply exceeds demand.

4. Use simple words. Many speakers use long, confusing words and phrases that they think sound important. One of the world's outstanding speakers, Winston Churchill, appealed to the United States at the beginning of World War II for war matériel. He didn't use pompous words. He said, "Give us the tools, and we will finish the job."

5. Don't take the attention of your listeners for granted. Sometimes speakers don't appreciate all the distractions going on in their listeners' minds. Ad lib and get the listeners to participate.

6. Talk with the listeners, not at them.

7. Finish with a bang. Always sum up, repeating your basic points. The end of your presentation often is remembered longer than the beginning.

8. When you are finished, remain silent. Silence at the right time is just as effective as saying the right thing at the right time.

9. Be as succinct as possible. According to Mark Twain, "Few sinners are saved after the first 20 minutes of a sermon."

CLOSING TIPS

Unclutter the Contract

Often, at the conclusion of negotiations, while the major points are resolved, some minor details remain to be satisfied. These are known as contingencies. Many real estate professionals, in writing purchase offers, include a number of these contingencies. For example, "subject to a satisfactory termite inspection," "subject to a satisfactory septic tank inspection," "contingent upon buyer qualifying for a mortgage," and innumerable others. These many contingencies can dishearten a seller and perhaps cause him or her to reject an offer.

The same purpose can be accomplished by including only one catch-all contingency such as, "subject to buyer's consultant's approval." After all, the reason any contingency is included is to make certain the transaction will close in a manner satisfactory to the buyer. All the details can be attended to regardless of how many contingencies are actually written in the contract. Once the contract is signed, everyone is in the same boat, working to close the transaction.

The necessary contingencies should be listed on a separate piece of paper, and a clear understanding of whose responsibility each is should be determined, but don't clutter the contract with them. Your transactions will proceed to closing more smoothly and you will be covered by the single contingency in the contract. Should you choose to waive any or all of them, it can easily be done with a brief, separate letter of agreement, without disturbing the contract.

I don't personally like the term, but the single, catch-all contingency is often called the "weasel clause." The reason is obvious. It provides a chance to "weasel" out of the deal.

Perhaps you'll join with me in getting people to call it the "whistle" clause. If things aren't right, it provides an opportunity to "blow the whistle" (and end the play).

Above all, keep the paperwork as short and to the point as possible. Only a lawyer can get away with writing a document containing 5,000 words and calling it a brief.

Decisions

We've seen that sound transactions are based on the circumstances of ownership, not merely the circumstances of the property. Always remember: *there are no problem properties, only problem ownerships.*

Regardless of the depth and quality of the analysis of the economic and tax consequences of a real estate proposition, most real estate decisions are based as much on the emotions of the parties as on hardheaded analysis. Hugh Downs says: "A happy person is not a person in a certain set of circumstances, but rather a person with a certain set of attitudes."

It is important to remember that the transfer of real estate depends not so much on the amount of the down payment but on solutions to make people comfortable. Provide the needed people benefits and you will have little difficulty using very little cash.

CREATION OF WEALTH

Wealth doesn't come from nothing. Somebody has to create it. Farmers create wealth by turning seeds into food. Manufacturers create wealth by turning raw materials into marketable products. And Creative Real Estate Practitioners create wealth by turning accumulated equity into purchasing power. Here's how:

Suppose I own a house worth $50,000 that has a first mortgage of $30,000 on it. My equity is $20,000. You own a duplex that you would like to sell for $80,000 with $20,000 down. Now I'd like to buy your duplex, but I don't want to sell my house. What can I do?

Well, I could go out and borrow on my equity, but that would put me in a highly leveraged position and it would in effect be pyramiding.

An alternative would be for me to create (write) a note for $20,000 and give it to you directly as a down payment on your duplex. This might bother you for two reasons: (1) you're not receiving any cash, and (2) you're unsure of my ability to pay this note in addition to meeting payments on the $60,000 loan on the duplex.

First, with regard to the cash, my cashless down payment might not bother you as much if cash were hard to come by at the time and if there were no cash buyers around who were willing to pay your price. Rather than drop your price to $76,000 to lure someone with a cash down payment, you would do better to accept my $20,000 note, then sell it at a 10% (or $2,000) discount of face value. Or, you could just accept the note and let me pay it off with interest.

I could wipe out your insecure feelings about my ability to pay by giving you a "created" note secured by a "blanket" mortgage including my house (with its entire value of $50,000) in addition to the mortgage on the duplex. This blanket mortgage protects you in case of default. With a blanket mortgage, if I default, not only can you get your duplex back through foreclosure but when you foreclose on the blanket you get my house as well. It's double security for the $20,000 note.

I'm not likely to default on the $20,000 note because in so doing I'd lose the roof over my head in addition to the duplex.

So there you have it. In creating and signing the note, I have created usable wealth from accumulated equity. I have increased my real estate holdings and have at the same time taken your unwanted property off your hands in a way that makes you feel secure about getting paid for it.

This is a simplified explanation of the "creation of wealth" formula. There are dozens of ramifications to it, especially in the area of exchanging. No matter what form your real estate dealings take, you can use "creation of wealth." It is a principle you can use for the rest of your life; a principle that will instantly create wealth for you.

SUBSTITUTION OF COLLATERAL

Now that we have completed the previous transaction, let's say I decide to sell my house and am still unwilling to give you the cash. I can substitute other collateral (another house, stocks, or other items of value acceptable to you) as security for the note, and deliver my house to the new buyer free of the encumbrance of the blanket mortgage. This allows me to use the proceeds of my equity to buy another piece of real estate. You will see this technique fully described later as "walking the mortgage." With walking the mortgage, you substitute another piece of real estate as collateral for a mortgage that already exists. The technique of substituting other kinds of property besides real estate (such as stocks, automobiles, and other personal assets) is a variation of the walking the mortgage technique. The process is called "substitution of collateral" and it can be written into any real estate transaction you make. In fact, I recommend that you make it a practice to write a substitution of collateral clause into every promissory note you sign. The specific clause to be used varies with the area in which you operate. It is essential that you seek the advice of a local attorney who specializes in real estate. When you tell him that you want to include a substitution of collateral clause in the document you have brought to him for examination, he will be able to add the precise wording for your area of the country.

The clause is practically a magical device. It gives you a degree of flexibility you may never have thought possible and permits you to continue to use the previously borrowed money for subsequent acquisitions without incurring new loan origination fees or costs and without having to submit a new application to qualify.

IT'S ONLY MONEY—WHO NEEDS IT?

One of the most difficult concepts to explain to people is that they don't need money to get rich. "It takes money to make money," they say. That's an exaggeration and an excuse for lack of knowledge and for not trying. What it really does take to get rich, as I explained in Chapter 1, is:

1. A desire to provide people benefits.
2. An imagination.
3. A willingness to risk.
4. Thought.

When you want to buy property, don't be scared off by a seller's demands for a cash down payment. There are many quick, cashless ways to fund down payments. All of them are based on the principle of offering something of value other than your cash as a down payment. "Nothing down" doesn't mean that no cash is used, it means that none of *your* cash is used.

A partial list of the ways to fund down payments includes:

1. Creation of wealth.
2. Wrap-around mortgage.
3. Purchase-money note.
4. Blanket mortgage over more than one property.
5. Your vacant lot as a down payment in exchange for seller's equity.
6. Your car, boat, trailer, or other personal property as a down payment.
7. Instead of giving up the use of your possessions, give the seller a chattel (or personal property) mortgage on them, while you keep possession and use.
8. Buy two properties from the seller. Refinance one and use the resulting cash as a down payment on the other.
9. Use a bank's money. Buy the seller's house, get a "consumer's equity" loan on it, and use the loan as a down payment. If you have a line of credit at a bank, pledge that as security for down payment. Poor credit? Have the seller co-sign your note to get cash, then give him a wrap-around mortgage to secure repayment of the note.
10. Use credit cards. Some allow you to borrow as much as $5,000 or more in cash which you can use for a down payment. All carry easy terms for installment repayment over an extended period of time.
11. Use sweat equity. You put in the effort to fix-up and find a partner to put up the funds.

In my seminar and home-study course, I explain more than 169 ways to buy property without using any of your own cash. The variations are virtually limitless. When you are involved in Creative Real Estate you continue to find new formulas.

NO-CASH OPTIONS

Without cash you can also buy options. An option is a contractual right to buy property at an agreed upon price within a specified period of time. Usually, you pay for this right in cash. But if you don't have cash, you can offer other goods or services.

You already saw the "sweat equity" option at work in Chapter 6 and the "effort equity" option is described in Chapter 12. Here's another one. You find a farm that you'd like to own, but your cash supply is low. You figure it will be at least five years before you can come up with the money for the down payment. The farmer who owns the land isn't eager to sell right now anyway, but he says that in five years he will be. How do you get a "lock" on the property?

In doing your homework and counseling with the farmer, you discover he is using a 20-year-old tractor that is not as efficient as he would like it to be. You get an idea. But ideas don't work unless you do, remember?

So, you hustle down to the local John Deere dealer and have him deliver a new tractor with an air-conditioned cab and a stereo tape/CD player to the farmer for a demonstration run. After the farmer has had a chance to fall in love with the machine, tell him he can have it to use with no cost to him for five years if he lets you buy the farm at the end of that time for a stipulated price.

Results:

1. You get the option.
2. Because you lease-purchase the tractor, you haven't tied up much cash. (Lease contracts require very little cash down.)
3. You take depreciation on the tractor, so you benefit as far as taxes are concerned.
4. At the end of the lease, you get the tractor back, and if history is any indicator, the tractor will be worth close to what you paid for it, or more!
5. The farmer gets the use of the tractor, but since it's not his, he doesn't have to pay income taxes on it as he would if he had taken either cash or title to the tractor.

Again, the principle is simple. Anything of value can be used to obtain an option, as long as the parties agree on it.

Don't consider these your only no-cash options. Use your imagination to create others. The potential list is endless.

THINK BIG

At the beginning of this chapter, I mentioned that the importance of getting rich is really a matter of getting rich quickly. To do that, you're going to have to start thinking *big* quickly. You won't make millions unless and until you start thinking in millions. And the sooner you start thinking in millions, the sooner you'll see them rolling in.

If you want to be a millionaire ten years from now, it won't do you any good to start thinking, ten years from now, about making millions. You have to start thinking and doodling in seven figures *today*.

This may seem implausible, especially if the most expensive item you've bought to date is a used $5,000 car with $500 down and three years to pay. But I can ease your doubts and fears by pointing out some comfortable aspects of thinking big.

My earlier examples of $100,000 properties apply just as readily to $10 million properties. The principles are the same. The mechanics of the transactions are the same. Everything you learn practicing Creative Real Estate, even as a sweat equity beginner, works the same for you as it does for a multimillion-dollar wheeler-dealer. So relax. Remember, if you're doing what you've already learned how to do successfully, you're on familiar ground. Only the numbers are different. A few more zeroes. So what? A great oak is just a little acorn that held its ground.

Actually, it's easier to deal in large numbers than in small ones. When you're dealing in large numbers, people treat you better and show you more respect.

If you visit a bank meekly asking to borrow a thousand dollars, you probably won't be given first-class service. When you stride in confidently asking to borrow a million dollars, a vice-president ushers you into his paneled office and sends someone to get coffee while you discuss your requirements.

Big transactions tend to be better transactions. A $10 million apartment building is prime property. A $10,000 apartment building is generally in poor condition. Big buildings have larger cash flow, appreciation, depreciation, tax benefits, and more substantial tenants. They hold their value longer. In a big transaction, while the total dollars involved are greater, the actual risks are fewer than in a smaller transaction. So, for the reasons listed above, don't let the numbers scare you. Think big. After all, it's only money.

MAKE YOUR CHOICE

Some people are born wealthy, but no one is born knowing how to get wealthy. Many of those who are born rich become poor and many who are born poor become rich. The difference between them is not how much money they had at birth; the difference is what they learned about making and keeping money during their lifetimes. Ayn Rand told us: "Wealth is a product of man's capacity to think."

Getting rich is a learned skill. Genetics and talent play small roles, if any. Money helps but is by no means the sole, essential ingredient. How many stories have we heard about people who lost everything in the Great Depression, dug themselves out of deep debt, and went on to become millionaires all over again? How many people came to this country as penniless, illiterate immigrants, unskilled and unable to speak the language? Yet how many of those rose to positions of great wealth and power?

In the great democracy of nature, everyone at birth has an equal opportunity to learn how to get rich. We are not all born with the same color skin or with rich parents or influential friends, but race, color, creed, education, and social position are not the controlling ingredients of a person's success. The controlling ingredients are precisely the ones I've listed earlier: a desire to provide people benefits, an imagination, a willingness to risk, and thought. Applying those four ingredients and nothing more, you can become as wealthy as you choose.

If you choose to use what *you already know* about Creative Real Estate from reading this book, the whole world will open up with opportunities for you.

WHEN A HOUSE IS NOT A HOME

Ophelia was Jack Benny's "little old lady from Pasadena" personified. Petite, with pure white, neatly coiffed hair, pink cheeks, sparkling blue eyes behind wire-rimmed, round spectacles, and Chiclet-like dentures.

Widowed early, she continued her late husband's residential sales brokerage, putting her only daughter through college and law school. Doing her mother proud, daughter Jenny graduated with honors and went to work as an assistant district attorney in an infamous Nevada county. One of her assignments was to make certain that prostitution was practiced in compliance with the law permitting it in that county. As Jenny eagerly shared her day-to-day work experiences with her mother, it wasn't long before Mother Ophelia sensed opportunity.

While a number of "big-name" brothels had made the headlines, many more were operating with a lower profile. Nonetheless, the business was highly profitable for all. Proprietors and investors—who ranged from farmers to doctors, lawyers, bankers, schoolteachers, entertainers, and others—made a lot of money quickly. It was the kind of business people got in and out of frequently.

Since Jenny's job was to keep tabs on those operators, she was surprised at how often one or more of those establishments changed hands, so to speak, and remarked at that fact to her mother.

The opportunity Ophelia saw was to be a broker specializing in those properties. They were each not only real estate, either for sale or lease, but a going business opportunity with a large cash income. Such properties were high-priced, and brokerage commissions would be substantial.

Ophelia lost no time in soliciting listings from just about all of the legally operating brothels. Before long, she was successful in signing an exclusive (very) listing agreement with one. Now she had to sell it. Realizing that she had already taken a creative step, she decided to learn more about Creative Real Estate, which she had heard about during her years in the brokerage business. She took a number of seminars on creative financing, counseling, and exchanging.

She then became acquainted with the exchange marketplace and joined a local Exchange Group. There she found out that the most active marketplace for any property was at our annual Creative Real Estate EXPO. She registered to attend the very next one, and sent in her brothel listing package to be exposed (pardon the expression) to the exchangors who came from all over the country seeking opportune transactions. When her turn came to personally present the merits of her listing package to the assembled professionals at the marketing session, she surprised them. No; rather, she shocked them. Picture this innocent-looking, "little old lady" on the podium pitching a brothel, with color slides to boot! She not only aroused them, she received a dozen good offers (for the property) as soon as she left the podium. Before the session was over two days later, she had a signed offer and acceptance! Her commission was over $200,000 when it closed thirty days later.

Needless to say, she liked that—so much so, that she made that kind of property her specialty. And every year, for the next decade, everyone at EXPO would look for Ophelia, the little old lady from Pasadena, with another House of Pleasure to market.

Ophelia finally retired after 10 years. Each and every year she had successfully marketed her special kind of property and pocketed a six-figure commission at least as large as her first.

She saw opportunity, seized it, applied Creative Real Estate, filled needs, wants, and desires, stayed with it, provided plenty of people benefits, had fun doing it and became wealthy. Isn't that a rousing story?

TAKE ONE FORMULA AND STICK TO IT

Exactly how you go about getting rich is up to you. I've already suggested many formulas in this book. Which formula you eventually decide to use is not important. What is important is that you learn one formula very, very well and keep using it.

"Do what you do best." Find one formula that you understand, are comfortable with, and like to work with. Try it. Try it again. Get good at it. Get better. "Perfect practice makes perfect," remember? When you have a success, reinforce it with another. When you miss, analyze and correct your mistake and do better the next time. Keep refining your pet formula until no one else can implement it as well as you do. Success is no accident; it takes commitment. A young lady rushed up to Jasha Heifetz at the end of a brilliant performance saying: "Oh, Mr. Heifetz, I'd give my life to play like you do." The maestro quietly replied, "I did."

The best example of commitment I can give you involves my eldest son, Brian. Now a full Colonel in the United States Air Force, he graduated from the U.S. Air Force Academy in 1970 with a Bachelor of Science degree in Economics and Engineering Management, continued his education at University of California at Los Angeles while assigned to duty at the Los Angeles Air Force Station, graduating in 1973 with a Master of Science degree in Management and Juris Doctorate. He then took the California Bar examination and passed on his first try.

Throughout his Air Force career in various assignments, he has been the recipient of professional awards such as: Outstanding Young Judge Advocate of the Year in Air Force Logistics Command, Outstanding Young Judge Advocate of the Year in Air Force Systems Command, and Outstanding Senior Attorney of the Year in Strategic Air Command.

In Brussels, he served as general counsel to the European management office at NATO for the $1.6 billion F-16 aircraft coproduction program involving the United States and four other NATO countries. At the same time, he was legal advisor for the United States Delegation to the 13-Nation NATO program to procure and operate a fleet of E-3A aircraft comprising the NATO Airborne Warning and Control System. He has had major responsibilities during his entire career which he has fulfilled with commendable efficiency and honor, earning—among other military decorations—the Meritorious Service Medal with four oak leaf clusters and the Air Force Commendation medal with one oak leaf cluster.

If all this, which touches on only a fraction of his illustrious career, sounds like the claims of a proud father, it is! However, the point of this story is the commitment Brian has displayed.

He is a gifted artist and musician whose talents were visible at age three, when he started drawing outstanding pencil sketches, and at five when he picked out melodies on the piano. Subsequently, he learned all that several piano teachers were able to offer by the time he was twelve. As a teenager, he led a bohemian life style. A licensed ham radio operator, he would play chess at all hours of the night over short wave radio with people all over the world. He would draw, paint and play piano whenever the mood dictated.

With all of this going on, he maintained a sufficiently high scholastic average to be one of the less than three dozen who were admitted to the prestigious Cornell University School of Architecture. He has a distinct style and flair for design which was impressive for his years.

When our congressman announced the qualifying examination for the Air Force Academy, Brian decided to take it. With my background in aviation, I had continued to fly and all of the boys participated. Brian was a licensed pilot when he was sixteen.

When the results were in, Congressman Minish told us that he wanted to appoint Brian as his candidate for the Air Force Academy. We were honored, pleased, and wondrous. Brian had secured a coveted post at Cornell and was really well-suited to a career in architectural design. It was as much of an artistic, free-form laissez-faire type of life as someone with Brian's bent might choose.

He asked my advice. The best I could offer him was to be true to himself and make his own decision.

The next morning, making a rare appearance at early breakfast, Brian announced that he had made his decision. "I've decided to accept the appointment to the Air Force Academy and notify Cornell that I will not be attending," he told us.

When I recovered from the surprise, I asked, "Why?" He promptly replied: "Because I need the discipline."

At that tender age of 18, Brian made the commitment to pursue a career in the Air Force. His first year at the Academy was a difficult one. The discipline was rigid, a complete reversal of his prior life style. He rose gallantly to the challenge and committed to press on and complete the four-year course. During his four years there, a significant number of his former classmates resigned or were obliged to leave the school. Of his entering class of 1035, only 735 graduated.

At each phase of his career, Brian demonstrated his commitment. Despite his difficult first year, he committed to complete his education at the Air Force Academy. He persisted in his studies until he graduated from the Academy. He committed to graduate schooling with the diligence required to pass the challenging California Bar examination on his first try. Upon entering active duty, after completing his graduate education, his commitment to excellence in each assignment earned commendations, promotions, and career advancement. He has deported himself as an officer and a gentleman of whom his country, commanders, colleagues, friends, family and father are justifiably proud.

When you commit to learn, practice, and perfect one formula, not only will you make a considerable amount of money with that formula on your own, but you'll find people coming to you for advice. They'll pay you consulting fees. They'll share brokerage commissions. They'll make you a partner in joint ventures. They'll lavishly reward you in ways you don't expect. All because you're the expert, the best, the top banana in your area of expertise. "That's the time to remember not to confuse fame with success. Madonna is one; Helen Keller was the other," Erma Bomberg reminds us. Keep a level head and you'll continue to prosper.

Once you perfect your formula, you'll find money coming in from many directions, and very quickly. The more people you help and the more ways you help them, the more sources of income you'll have and the quicker you'll get rich.

To enjoy *maximum* benefits from your wealth, use your knowledge to get rich quickly.

Your knowledge has expanded to include these Kessler's Keys to Success:

☞ A word on pyramiding

☞ Negotiating so that everyone wins

☞ Back to the basics

☞ Making transactions work

☞ Two basic negotiating techniques

☞ Persuasive presentation

☞ Closing tips

☞ Creation of wealth

☞ Substitution of collateral

☞ It's only money—who needs it?

☞ No-cash options

☞ Think big

☞ Make your choice

☞ When a house is not a home

☞ Take one formula and stick to it

PART III

Acquiring Property with Little or No Cash

Do what you can with what you have, where you are.

—Theodore Roosevelt

Yes, You Can!

If you think you can win, you can win.

—William Hazlitt

There are countless ways to buy real estate with little or no cash. In the following chapters I explain techniques I personally have used or advised clients to use. I have divided the methods into six basic categories, with a representative case history and explanation of each. More methods are listed for those situations available to the average buyer than for those requiring special circumstances. Not all techniques may apply to your particular situation, but all are worth reading for the insights they contain about transactions you can create yourself, even beyond the techniques mentioned here. For consistency and ease of understanding, I have used rounded numbers in the neighborhood of $100,000. Actually, the numbers are irrelevant. Every example will work just as well with a $10,000 property as it will with a $10 million property. The principles and techniques are the same.

The essential points to remember are the basics we have been mentioning throughout this book. In order to structure win/win transactions, you must always provide people benefits. Remember that people are more important than property and there are no problem properties, only problem ownerships; transactions have to be structured by finding a need, determining the need, and fulfilling that need.

It is important to discover the intentions of the parties and to analyze their objectives. Once this is done, you will be able to fit the personalities of the people to the situations most compatible with their needs, wants, and desires. Matching the objectives of the various parties to a transaction is critical to the success of the transaction. That specific step, matching, is the single most important element in creating a win/win situation. There are times you will require expert advice and counsel. At those times, leverage people by employing the services of the most capable specialists available.

By the time you are in a position to structure creative transactions, you should also have established rapport with experts in the fields in which you are not particularly skilled. Legal aspects, tax consequences, "paper," and finance are only some of the areas that may require consultants when you are structuring involved transactions.

Don't get fancy and "create" yourself right out of business. Keep your feet planted firmly on the ground and always examine each step of every transaction for practicality, feasibility, and *necessity*. In my years in this business, I have seen many creative-minded people carried away with their ability to structure innovative transactions. They have so much fun doing it that they completely ignore the simple solutions to fill the needs because the fancy ones feel so good.

For many years I made it a practice to visit a marketing session, somewhere in the country, at least once a week. It was always refreshing to witness the interchange of ideas, suggested solutions and brainstorming that followed a listing package presentation by one of the members to the group. Oftentimes the creativity flowed for many times the amount of time it took to make the original presentation. Formula upon formula, new combinations of formulas, and sometimes outrageous ideas came forth. At one very active session in the sunny South, the presentor had just introduced a splendid, downtown ante-bellum home, and the charm of it stimulated a particularly exuberant flow of suggested creative formulas to dispose of the property in the most advantageous way. After 15 minutes of this enthralling display of creative minds churning and spewing forth, my turn to contribute came— even though I was a visitor I was graciously afforded the opportunity to speak—and I offered the most logical solution I could think of: "Why not just put a 'For Sale' sign on the front lawn?" After an instantly chilling group silence, several started to chuckle, and before long we all had a rousing good laugh together.

I told them how impressed I was with their creativity and willingness to share, but why overlook the obvious?

The sign went up that afternoon; there were three inquiries before dark and one became the proud, new owner of that beautiful, ante-bellum mansion.

The moral of the story is, don't take an axe to the fly on the baby's nose.

Your purpose in structuring creative solutions is to provide better, trouble-free solutions. Litigation is a luxury. Avoid any situations, either existing or created, that involve lawsuits There is no better example of a no-win situation than litigation. "The wisdom of life is in the elimination of non-essentials."—Lin Yutang.

Be aware, also, that many of the techniques that worked well in the past are either overworked or no longer workable. The old "buy low, sell high" platitude sounds good, but how often can you do it in today's sophisticated world? The very success of the formulas you are about to study is the fact that most of the world has become so much more sophisticated in the last decade that it more readily understands and accepts innovative ideas.

Acquiring run-down, multiple dwellings and applying magnums of sweat equity doesn't accomplish much anymore, except in rare, isolated instances.

Whichever formulas, techniques, or strategies you decide to use, make certain that you are able to maintain full control. By control, I do not mean manipulation and force. I mean the type of control that a helmsman maintains over the rudder in order to competently fulfill his responsibility of steering that ship to its destination.

Remember, if you want real wealth you can't overlook the unlimited potential of real estate, particularly if you can handle the tax aspects by deferring or avoiding that erosion of your profits. No matter how little cash you have available, through the use of Creative Real Estate strategies, techniques, and formulas, your opportunities to make huge profits on tiny investments are limitless.

Use the examples of techniques that follow as a continuing reference source. Vary them; combine them; customize them as you see fit and necessary. Use the techniques illustrated here as starting points for new transactions in which you begin to acquire real estate, Creatively.

Bernice Fitz-Gibbons said: "Creativity often consists of merely tuning up what is already there."

CREATIVE VISUALIZATION

To exercise your creativity, here is an opportunity to practice creative visualization (looking for potential). Looking at the illustration below, with one continuous stroke of your pencil, make that a six.

I X

You'll find the correct answer in Chapter 8.

8

Person to Person

More money has been made in real estate than in all industrial investments combined.

—Andrew Carnegie

Every transaction is a person-to-person transaction. Even if it is between a large institution like an insurance company dealing with another large corporation like a national bank, the transaction ultimately involves one person negotiating with another. However, in this section, for simplicity I will explain only those transactions that involve an individual dealing with another individual, both sides dealing in their own personal accounts. While the motivations may differ, a large organization's transactions would be conducted by individuals representing them in similar fashion to these one-on-one examples.

WATERWAY FOR WATERHOLE

A friend of mine, Ace, had been living on a houseboat that was the only personal asset he had retained after a difficult marital dissolution. After two years of this lifestyle, he met and fell in love with a woman who preferred living in a country club community rather than on a waterway.

A few weeks before Ace discussed his situation with me, a contractor had stopped in my office to tell me that he had recently been paid for a job with two mortgaged condominiums on the seventh fairway of a nationally famous golf course. After counseling with him, it was apparent that he neither wanted to live in golf-course condominiums nor undertake the responsibility of renting them. At that time, we were in the throes of the infamous, unpredicted 1973–74 real estate recession.

The country club development had an oversupply of condominiums, and they were not selling. While the contractor was not hurting for money, he did not relish the idea of making the monthly mortgage payments, and there were a number of properties he would rather own than condominiums. He executed a listing agreement with me and departed for a long-planned, two-week vacation with his family to go fishing on the river.

When Ace discussed his problem with me, I asked him to bring his future bride to look at the builder's fairway condominiums. I asked her how she felt about being a landlady, and she was delighted at the prospect.

When the contractor returned from his fishing trip, I had lunch with him and couldn't get a word in edgewise. He told me about the beautiful trip he and his family had on a rented houseboat and how much he would enjoy being able to do that again, as often as every month. At the end of his hour-long tale of "paradise found," I dropped the first shoe. "How would you like to own a houseboat in exchange for those two golf-course condominiums?" I asked him. His expression indicated that it was too good to be true, while he said: "I might consider it, but who would want to trade if he owns a houseboat?"

I told him that the possibility existed and that the chances of structuring the transaction looked promising. With that, he authorized me to negotiate and complete the exchange as soon as possible.

The details went together smoothly. Ace and his bride were delighted to assume the two $45,000 mortgages on the condominiums and exchange the $21,000 houseboat for the builder's $18,000 equity in the two condominiums. The builder was equally happy to make the exchange, giving $3,000 cash, which Ace used to furnish the condo he and his new bride moved into. She convinced a friend to rent the other condo, and a month later the three couples went on a fishing trip together in the contractor's "new" houseboat.

The builder gladly paid his share of my fee in cash and Ace gave me a note for his share, secured by a second mortgage on the condominium that he moved into.

ASSUME THE MORTGAGE, SELLER YANKS THE LAND

Burt and Terry wanted to buy an apartment building with no money down. They had looked for months, and when they came to me, I found them a $100,000 building owned by an agreeable man who was nearing retirement. The building had an $80,000 mortgage on it. The seller planned to sell the building for a cash payment above the amount of the loan and move to Florida, using the income from banking the $20,000 cash he received for his equity in the building to supplement his Social Security check. He wanted no part of managing the building or worrying about it from a distance.

I suggested that Burt and Terry offer him this alternative: they would assume his $80,000 mortgage and let him keep the land under the building as a $20,000 down payment. They would lease the land from him, structuring the lease payments to exactly equal the amount of income he would earn from depositing $20,000 in a bank CD to draw interest. The land lease was written to be exactly as long as the mortgage, with an option to buy the land on the date of expiration at a negotiated price.

The benefits to all the parties were enormous. The seller was able to move to Florida with no worries about the building. He earned as much income as he would have by selling the land, but with two additional benefits: (1) during the term of the lease, the land was appreciating in value, whereas money in the bank would not, and (2) with the $20,000 tied up in the land, he would never be tempted to draw out and spend what was in essence a pension fund.

Burt and Terry took possession of a beautiful building for no cash and for almost as much net income as they would have if they'd bought the land, too. A positive aspect of the arrangement was that Burt and Terry couldn't depreciate the land anyway, so it wouldn't have done them much good in terms of tax benefits to buy the land.

People benefits made this transaction work. Everyone involved came out a winner, with all their basic problems solved. My fee was paid by assignment of the rent from three apartments for a year. As you've already learned, people benefits are the key to Creative Real Estate success, and these examples demonstate people benefits in action.

EFFORT EQUITY

This technique is especially good if you're long on ability and short on cash. It differs from sweat equity, the fixing-up you would personally do to improve a property's value. *Effort equity* is more sophisticated, but you don't have to be a genius or even a lawyer to do it. (Lest I unnecessarily offend any of my good readers, please consider this remark an inside joke: two of my sons are lawyers—and probably geniuses too, although we've never admitted it.)

Glenda had recently left her job as an escrow officer at a large real estate firm in California. Escrow officers prepare the paperwork for transactions in every kind of California real estate transaction, so Glenda knew more about real estate documents than the average person. Out of work, and not anxious to take another nine-to-five job, Glenda was looking for ways to use her know-how to make money and consulted with me. She found a natural solution in effort equity.

In talking to her former boss, a real estate broker, she learned that he had a listing on a $500,000 building that wasn't selling. The owner wanted no less than $100,000 down and had rejected every offer that didn't include that much cash.

Now if the broker could sell the building, he would earn a commission of 6%, or $30,000. The situation was critical because the listing was about to expire and the broker was distressed to lose the opportunity to earn a $30,000 commission.

At Glenda's suggestion, the broker discussed the problem with me and agreed to share his commission if I could assist with a solution. I counseled with him and Glenda separately; after both had agreed in principle to my suggested solution, I counseled them together.

Here is how it went. Glenda went to work to implement my solution for everyone's ultimate benefit. In her escrow dealings she had come to know the names of real estate investors who loved to buy property but who couldn't possibly come up with $100,000 in cash on their own. She called each investor and asked him if he would be interested in a cooperative investment requiring $20,000 each. After making only seven calls, she had five commitments.

The offer was simple: for $20,000, each of the 5 investors would receive a 19% interest in the property. Five times 19% is 95%. The other 5% would go to Glenda for putting together the transaction. Each investor considered the arrangement fair, especially since he didn't have to do anything.

We drew up an offer to purchase. Glenda went to each investor for his signature, added her own signature, and presented the offer. The owner, delighted to at last be paid his $100,000 in cash, accepted immediately. The broker, $15,000 richer (the other $15,000 of the $30,000 commission was mine), was understandably pleased.

Glenda's work was far from over. She had to hire a lawyer to show her how to draw up a limited partnership agreement. She had to arrange the financing because the old loan could not be assumed and she had to write up all the closing papers.

When the transaction was consummated, Glenda had a 5% interest in a $500,000 property, a part-time job managing the building, and enough experience to launch her on a new career. Since then, she has used her abilities to put together far more complicated deals and has built up her effort equities and her cash positions considerably. She learned her lesson well, is sticking to what she knows best, and providing people benefits with win/win solutions.

CREATE PAPER

Take another example. Howard was in a slightly better position than Burt and Terry, who assumed the mortgage while the seller "yanked the land." Howard had no cash either, but he did own a house with $20,000 equity. He noticed, when the Multiple Listing Directory came out each week, that the real estate market was going soft and that the number of unsold properties was mounting. Howard decided it was a good time to buy. But buy with what?

Looking through the Multiple Listing Directory in my office, he recognized a property that had been on the market for months. The seller, a recently married woman named Mrs. McGuire, wanted to move out of her five-unit apartment building and move in with her new husband, who was living alone (and somewhat impatiently) in his own house. Yet she steadfastly refused to take less than $85,000 with 15% down. Her original asking price had been higher, but she decided to lower it because of the inactive market.

I advised Howard to make an offer that Mrs. McGuire both loved and hated. What she loved was his price: $100,000, more than 17% above the listed amount. What she hated was his down payment: $10,000 in the form of a second mortgage on Howard's house. I coached Howard, and he had to do some straight talking. I then arranged a meeting between Howard and Mrs. McGuire.

"Mrs. McGuire," he began reasonably, "you want to sell this building, don't you?"

"Of course," she replied.

"Well, I'm willing to buy it at a price that's more than fair. In return for that price, I'm asking you to make a few, equally fair concessions—a 10% down payment and a mortgage instead of cash."

"But I'll be giving up my building and not getting any money out of it," she replied.

"Do you need cash to buy another house?"

"No, I'll be moving into my new husband's house."

"So cash isn't really the problem, is it, Mrs. McGuire?"

"I guess not," she admitted.

"Then what's *really* bothering you?" he asked.

"I'm afraid you won't pay me the $10,000."

With confidence mounting, Howard continued, "But Mrs. McGuire, I live in the house that I'm mortgaging to you for security. I have equity in it. If I don't make regular payments on that second mortgage to you, then you can foreclose and I would lose it. Do you think that I would let that happen to my home and be left with no place to live?"

"I suppose not," she replied, weakening.

"Besides, look at my background," Howard added, "I've lived in this house for five years. I've worked steadily at General Motors for twelve years and every other thing I own is fully paid for. You may check my credit and my employment, just like a bank would."

She finally agreed. Howard purchased the building on his terms and the McGuires were able to live together in Mr. McGuire's house with a dependable income from the paper Howard had created (the $10,000 note secured by a second mortgage on his home.)

Though Howard didn't use any money to make this acquisition, he did use a number of other valuable assets that millions of people possess: his built-up equity, his reputation, his employment record, his credit, and his powers of persuasion. He leveraged people (including me). I agreed, along with Mrs. McGuire, to take a portion of the payments Howard would make over the next 18 months in payment for my fee.

Like Howard, you may not have any cash right now. But you do have at least some of those other assets and nothing is stopping you from putting them to work. This case history is a typical example of the "creation of wealth."

The answer to the creative visualization exercise is:

S I X

Simple, isn't it? And very straightforward. A key to being creative is to look for the obvious.

You've added to your fund of Kessler's Keys to Success:

☞ Yes, you can!

☞ Creative visualization

☞ Waterway for waterhole

☞ Assume the mortgage, seller yanks the land

☞ Effort equity

☞ Create paper

9

Your Friendly Bankers

Bankers are just like anybody else, only richer.

—Ogden Nash

Some of my best friends are bankers. We play golf together, share vacation trips, discuss our families and other friends, belong to clubs together, and generally share our experiences.

Bankers are real people doing their jobs—some more creatively than others; some with more enthusiasm, and some with higher ambitions. Don't accept the common notion that all banks are institutions run by people who are old-fashioned, stodgy, and unimaginative. They are in business primarily to make money. And to do that, they will usually listen to any reasonable proposition.

This chapter illustrates different ways you can use institutions such as banks, savings and loans, thrifts, finance companies, insurance companies, and credit unions to help you creatively acquire property with their financing. For ease of reference, I will refer to all of these institutions as banks, since in effect that is what they really are—they bank money.

Although some of the larger, old-line banks are conservative, they are not the only ones in the banking business. Neither are they the only source of funds. Look for newly opened banks, small local banks, and aggressive banks that advertise extensively. They are more likely to listen favorably to creative financing propositions and to recognize that the risks are perhaps different but no greater if you've structured the transaction well.

DO YOUR HOMEWORK

My reference to newly opened banks brings back an unhappy memory. The incident taught me a lesson I have never forgotten. I'll share it with you, both for the value of the lesson and a chuckle.

Early in my real estate career, after I discovered the secret of providing people benefits by finding, determining, and filling a need, fortune smiled on me and I accumulated some money. Because I was young and ambitious, I wanted to put that money to good use in support of my business, real estate.

By this time I had expanded my operations and was involved in developing and building. As a result of the substantial balance I kept on deposit and my scrupulous attention to meeting obligations on time or before, I had a line of credit with my local bank of $200,000. I used every penny of it to help my business grow.

In my search for a good investment, to diversify but also to be supportive of my objectives in real estate and development, I discussed my needs with my friendly banker. When I explained to him what I thought my need was, he suggested that the money business seemed to fit the description of what I sought. When I continued to question him, he told me that banks and insurance companies were making most of their income and profit from lending money to real estate developers. I immediately put two and two together and came up with five, as you will soon see. In thanking him, I said, "Jim, I shall never forget you." Little did I know how long I would remember.

Within a few days, I had gathered a group of five of my friends from school days, all of whom were successful and fairly affluent (for those days), postwar businessmen and professionals. One was a prominent young attorney who had the distinction of being the youngest lawyer to refuse an appointment as a judge. Another was an executive vice-president with the Revlon organization. Another was the inventor of a new plastic fastener and had factories at home and abroad. The fourth was an ophthalmologist, and the fifth a securities broker annually earning six figures.

I suggested to them that we could band together, pooling our knowledge and financial resources to form a bank and an insurance company. I must have made a very persuasive presentation of convincing arguments because, to a man, they agreed to commit to acquire a charter to open a state bank and to qualify for a license to start a life insurance company.

With the expertise and perseverance of the group of doers I had organized, within a year we had both our bank charter and a license from the commissioner to form a life insurance company. We did both, at breakneck speed. Not too many months later, we were proudly hosting our bank-opening party. One of the honored guests was, of course, my friendly banker, Jim. His advice had triggered all of this and I was grateful. A charming and canny Scotsman with a twinkle in his eye, Jim asked me how it felt to be a banker. I replied, "Great, but then, Jim, who would know better than you? You've been a banker for twenty years, eminently successful and loved by all." He thanked me, offered a toast to our success, and asked me to lunch the next day as a new colleague.

The next day at lunch, after our usual exchange of pleasantries and the latest jokes, Jim got down to business. He asked what my intentions were regarding my banking relations with him. I assured him that I had no intentions of making any changes, that I had always received everything I ever wanted and needed from him, and that I was looking forward to a continuing relationship. I reassured Jim that I intended to use my own bank as an additional, supplementary source for expansion of my real estate and developing operations, and not as a replacement for his services. He acknowledged my "pledge of allegiance" and we finished lunch.

The very next day, Jim called and invited me to his office. When I arrived, he got right down to business. "A.D.," he said, "what is the authorized lending limit of your bank?"

"$90,000," I replied. "That's not too bad for a new bank with a board of directors averaging twenty-eight years of age, is it?"

"No," said Jim, "as a matter of fact it is quite good."

And then he dropped not only the first shoe but both shoes at once. They were hobnailed boots, and they both landed squarely on top of my head. Or maybe it was my heart. In any event, I crumbled inside when he said, "You know, under the banking laws in this state, we have a regulation that no bank can lend any more than the limit of that party's own bank to a major stockholder-director of another bank. Your current loan balance here is $200,000. I will have to ask you to reduce that to the $90,000 limit of your bank. How soon may I expect your check?"

I remembered then Robert Frost's definition: "A bank is a place where they lend you an umbrella in fair weather and ask for it back when it begins to rain."

In the emergency meeting I called of my board of directors that afternoon, I discovered that two of them would find themselves in the same boat. Suddenly I wasn't regarded as very bright, neither was I very popular.

Throwing my creative mind into high gear, I said, "Gentlemen, I believe I have a solution to our common dilemma. Our life insurance company will be in operation within 30 days, and at that time we should be able to make arrangements to reduce our loans to the new limits with our old banks and at the same time arrange for the loans we will need from the new life insurance company."

With sighs of relief and smiles of hope, we adjourned the special meeting of the bank's board of directors in order to press on with the business of getting the life insurance company into full operation at the earliest possible moment.

Once again talent and persistence prevailed, and within the month we were all proudly hosting our opening party at the new life insurance headquarters downtown.

Life insurance companies make a lot of money. They fill a need and as a result deserve their profits. Salesmen are the key to those profits, and life insurance salesmen earn high commissions. In the first policy year, as much as 80% (and sometimes more) of the premium collected is allocated to sales costs—to pay sales commissions and for support services to build a better, larger salesforce. Any business, not just a life insurance company, has to train, support, and sustain a good salesforce in order to prevail and become profitable. But in the life insurance business, the "front-end load"—the cost of getting started—is exceedingly heavy. So heavy, we found out, that there really isn't much money left for the investors in the beginning years. Neither are there sufficient reserves of cash accumulating rapidly enough to strongly venture into the loan business, if at all! None of us had enough experience in that business to know that. It reminds me now of what Mary Tyler Moore, playing Mary Richards, said: "I'm an experienced woman; I've been around . . . well, I might not have been around, but I've been . . . nearby."

In this emergency board meeting of the life insurance company directors, I had no creative solutions, no ray of hope to offer my trusting and loyal colleagues. All I could do was to promise to make every effort to sell our banking and life insurance companies as soon as possible. Although the companies were chartered and well started, there was no other alternative if we were each to meet our primary business obligations and return to business as usual. Only by disposing of our bank could we each regain high enough lines of credit from established sources to resume the way of business that we had earned, and to which we had become accustomed. And only by disposing of the life insurance company could we avoid the hemorrhaging of cash that was usual for the first years of a new insurer.

Sell, we did. But it took the rest of that year for me to produce buyers for our bank and life insurance company. We all came out whole and wiser. The "boys" are still talking to me, even these many years later, and I am grateful to them and proud of their strength of character and the fortitude of their friendships. I am not so proud of the fact that I had to learn the simple lessons that I have related in various parts of this book the hard way.

First, had I done my homework thoroughly, we all could have been spared those traumatic experiences and worrisome times. Second, if I had truly analyzed my needs, wants, and desires, I would have known that the bank and life insurance company were desires, not needs. I wouldn't have placed myself and my colleagues in the position of the man who needs transportation but desires a Rolls Royce. (I almost had to settle for roller skates!) Third, had I thoroughly and properly examined the first two points, I would have realized that one should *stick to what one knows best!* The only consolation is that what I did know, I did well. Both companies were well organized, with a good potential market; they are both still thriving beautifully.

Wouldn't it be nice if we could sell our mistakes for what they cost us? I will always remember the lessons. I would like you to, also. Let the *lenders* lend. You can try some of the following formulas, or your own custom-made variations, with their help.

WRAP-AROUND MORTGAGE

Felix wanted to buy real estate at a time when money was extremely tight. The institutions weren't parting with a single dollar that wasn't backed by top-notch collateral and credit. Felix had no money and needed 100% financing. Every banker Felix went to with his application refused him when he suggested a nothing-down loan. Felix started thinking that a banker is someone who is willing to make a loan if you present sufficient evidence to show you don't need it.

Undaunted, Felix found a $100,000 building with a $60,000, 8% mortgage on it. The building was older but well managed. It had a positive cash-flow, more than enough to cover the payments being made on the $60,000 loan. Felix offered the owner $40,000 down on condition that he could assume the existing mortgage. The owner eagerly accepted. Now all Felix had to do was come up with $40,000.

With the tight-money situation, Felix's chances of securing a straight $40,000 second mortgage on an old building were virtually nonexistent.

One of the bankers he had previously visited suggested that Felix contact me, and he made an appointment to see me. In counseling him, I advised Felix that in the right circumstances banks will consider *wrap-around* mortgages. I worked with him on the details and we planned a presentation. He then went back to see one of the bankers who had turned him down earlier.

As a result of our discussions, Felix was aware that the prevailing interest rate on new mortgage loans was 12%, a full 4% higher than the rate on the older $60,000 first mortgage. With the knowledge he had gained during our talk, he knew that he could use this differential to his advantage.

Dressed in his best business suit, Felix approached the banker and said, "I'd like to give your bank the opportunity to collect 12% interest on a $100,000 loan, and to get it you'll only have to lend $40,000."

The banker was immediately interested. Felix continued, "First you lend me $40,000, which I will use to pay off the seller's equity in this building, thus putting the current owner out of the picture. That leaves us with the obligation of making monthly payments on the existing $60,000, 8 percent mortgage. Those payments are $500 per month.

"Next, I would like you to write this new loan *not* as a $40,000 mortgage but as a $100,000 mortgage at 12%, and wrap it around the existing loan. My payment to you on a $100,000 loan at 12% will be $1,025 per month. Since the net income on the building before debt service is $1,200 monthly, this $1,025 payment will be no problem. When I make that $1,025 payment to you, all you have to do is take $500 of it and pay the first mortgagee, then keep the rest."

The banker accepted the arrangement, and here's why: First, his bank only had to part with $40,000, which at 12% would have required a payment of about $400 per month. Yet Felix would be paying the bank $1,025 per month, as if he had borrowed the entire $100,000. After the bank collected his $1,025 and paid out the $500 on the first mortgage, it would have $525 left every month. Subtract from that the $400 that would go to pay the $40,000 loan and you see the bank would net an additional $125 monthly without substantially increasing its risk just for wrapping the old mortgage. In effect, the bank would collect 4% interest on $60,000 that it never even lent out.

When the transaction was completed, Felix had purchased a building for nothing down in a tight money market. The seller received $40,000 and went away happy. The banker scored points with his superiors by lending $40,000 and collecting interest on $100,000. Since Felix did all the work, I accepted only a nominal fee for advice and planning. He paid by giving me $75 of his $175 net every month for 10 months.

The building appreciated rapidly in an upturning market. Felix raised the rent at the end of the first year, and with the increased equity from appreciation exchanged "up" for a $275,000 building within eighteen months. In three years, we again exchanged him "up" into a $1 million strip shopping center, and today he is one of the most prominent developers of small shopping centers in the Midwest.

Persistence, creativity, leveraging people, and loyalty are still paying off handsomely for my friend Felix.

SALE AND BUY BACK

Institutions are involved in many real estate transactions, but they don't generally like to own the property. There are several reasons for this. One of the most important is covered in the next case history. For now, just remember that a bank would rather not own land—it's knowledge from which you can profit.

Jim owned a contracting firm that I'll call Quality Builders. Quality Builders owned land that was zoned for subdivision and Jim was anxious to put houses on it. But like many builders, Jim was caught in a cash bind and couldn't afford to buy a bucket of nails. Since it's hard to get a big mortgage on empty land, Jim was stuck. The only way he could raise enough cash would be to sell the land. But then where would he build?

Jim came to me with his problem and I worked out both a plan of action and a solution.

Jim went to his neighborhood banker and offered to sell the land to the bank. That seemed like the last thing to do because Jim didn't want to sell the land and the bank didn't want to buy it. But Jim's offer had a twist. He would sell the land to the bank for $90,000 and immediately buy it back for $100,000.

In actual practice it worked like this: Quality Builders sold the land to the bank, which immediately deposited $90,000 into the Quality account. Quality then bought the land back on paper (with a note) for the agreed $100,000 and subdivided it into ten lots, each proportionately valued at $10,000. The purchase had a condition that provided that no lot would be released to Quality until a house had been built on it and sold to a *bona fide* buyer.

Jim used the $90,000 in the Quality bank account and went to work. He bought materials, paid workmen, and built a house for a net cost to him of $25,000. He sold the house for $45,000. On the day of the sale, he took $10,000 of the buyer's money, went to the bank and exchanged it for a deed to the lot on which he had built. He turned this deed over to the home buyer. Jim's costs were $25,000 for the house and $10,000 for the land. His net profit was $10,000, which he deposited in the Quality bank account. He bought more materials and started building two more houses that he also sold at a profit. Eventually he sold all ten houses for a combined profit of over $100,000. The bank made $10,000 on their investment of $90,000, a profit of approximately 11% plus the interest on Jim's $100,000 note. In addition, the bank made the permanent home loans to the buyers and profited. At the time that was more than the bank could have made just lending the money to Quality, and the transaction involved less risk to the bank than an unsecured loan.

Jim had no problem paying me a fee from his profits for the solution, plan, and advice, and he willingly did so. Recently he paid me a substantial commission for the profitable sale of one of his multi-million dollar developments.

Keep another point in mind: bankers abhor risk. Show them a way to make more money with reduced risk and they'll go out of their way to deal with you.

REO (REAL ESTATE OWNED)

REO is one of the reasons bankers shy away from property ownership. REO is an acronym for real estate owned, and under banking regulations, institutions are restricted as to how much real estate they can own. When they own too much property, they have to divest themselves of it in a hurry.

Institutions acquire most of their excess real estate through foreclosure. When someone borrows from a bank and then defaults on a mortgage, the bank forecloses on the loan and takes ownership of the property. Banks don't really want the property, but they have no alternative. They are obligated to take back the real estate and to try to find a new buyer as quickly as possible.

Sylvia had worked in a bank mortgage department and was familiar with REO. She had inherited vacant land worth $100,000 and was anxious to realize some benefit from it. The land was producing no income and Sylvia needed income. One answer was to build an apartment building on the land, but Sylvia had no money to build with. Rather than try to borrow on the land and wait the year or so that it would take to build and rent a building, she came to me for advice.

I discussed the possibility of working with her former bank on their REO portfolio and suggested some alternatives to explore. In checking, she found out that the bank had recently foreclosed on an apartment building that was generating income. The building was worth $100,000 and the bank, of course, now owned it free and clear. We structured a transaction wherein Sylvia offered to exchange her $100,000 worth of vacant land for the bank's $100,000 building and have the bank immediately lend her $80,000 on the building.

At this point, Sylvia would have the income from a fully rented building plus $80,000 in cash. But the bank would still be holding $100,000 worth of REO Everybody has to win, remember? I did, and I had Sylvia offer to buy her vacant land right back using $30,000 as a down payment and borrowing the rest from the same bank.

Now the situation is different. Sylvia owns a productive apartment building, owns $100,000 worth of land, and has $50,000 cash to begin construction on another building. The bank no longer has its unwanted REO and it has lent a total of $150,000—$80,000 on the building and $70,000 on the land. And lending money is what banks are in business to do.

Sylvia paid me in cash for my assistance and the bank contacts me regularly, to this day, for assistance in disposing of their REO.

We have acquired two more properties for Sylvia from the same bank, and in less than four years Sylvia has a financial statement that shows over $1,800,000 in real estate. Banks (all financial institutions, remember) are in business to make money on money. They usually have plenty of money and lending it out is their prime source of income. All you have to do is to establish credibility with them as a responsible "renter" of their money. Let them win as you win, and allow the people benefits of your transactions to make everyone wealthier in the process.

If you wondered, as you read it, why the bank had to foreclose on the $100,000 apartment building that was generating income, here's why. The owner had overfinanced (with 2nd and 3rd mortgages) to pyramid. Unfortunately his pyramid collapsed, and the loan on this building was only one of a number that he couldn't make payments on. Another illustration of our maxim, there are no problem properties, merely problem ownerships.

Add to your creative arsenal of Kessler's Keys to Success:

🔑 Do your homework

🔑 Wraparound mortgage

🔑 Sale and buy back

🔑 REO (real estate owned)

10

Other People's Money (OPM)

> *. . . money is Aladdin's lamp.*
>
> —Byron

Some banks won't get involved in certain transactions and sometimes you don't want them to. Often it is possible to establish situations where private individuals play banker and lend money themselves. This is called private financing and is a bonanza for the Creative Real Estater.

This is a limitless source of available money. Because of natural greed and the never-ending increase in individual wealth, it is a source that by its very nature will never dry up. Therefore, it is the one source with which you should become thoroughly familiar. Since you will be dealing with individuals, all with similar motivations and objectives, you should be able to specialize in this area with less experience and knowledge than might be required elsewhere. Many of the most successful real estate fortune-builders have used OPM (other people's money) as a basis for their wealth. It is an alternative to partnerships and syndications that can be very desirable. The lion's share of profits rightfully will belong to you; with a good performance record, you will establish sources eager to continue the relationship. Your responsibility is to be fair in providing adequate people benefits and to be loyal to your proven "suppliers."

MY FIRST EXPERIENCE

My first experience with other people's money was in 1946. By then my World War II injuries were mending and I had graduated from a wheelchair to crutches to occasionally using canes. I no longer wore my Air Force uniform, so I was just a civilian who didn't walk too well without help. Since my mobility was limited, my time off was usually spent rather quietly. On one particular Sunday in August, I was visiting with my parents at the seashore resort hotel where they were staying for the summer. With the hustle and bustle of resort activity going on around me, I was glad to be able to sit in a rocking chair on the lawn, sharing the Sunday edition of the *New York Times* with my dad. Quite naturally, my attention focused on the advertising section and in particular the classified pages containing real estate and business opportunities. As I scanned the "Business Opportunities" section, one item caught my eye. "Manufacturer-user wants plants in Northeast for expansion program. Call Ben at Skyloft 3-1751 Elmira."

There was nothing unusual about this particular advertisement, but I wondered why they were not more descriptive about the type of plants they wanted. Were they referring to factory buildings or to the entire manufacturing operation? Why hadn't they stated what they manufactured? Without spending too much time pondering these questions, I moved along to the real estate section of the classifieds. As I scanned columns, I came to the "Real Estate Wanted" section. This was a category of advertisement that I always paid strict attention to, and still do. I recommend that you make it a practice to give this particular category, "Real Estate Wanted," careful scrutiny in any advertising section you read. It is a never-ending source of prospective transactions. I found a familiar-looking ad leader: "Manufacturer-user wants plants . . ." I read the rest of the ad and compared it to the one I had previously read in "Business Opportunities." They were identical. Now my curiosity was aroused. Was the duplication of the advertisement intentional or had the newspaper made a mistake? If the newspaper had not made a mistake, why did this particular advertiser put the ad in two places?

I called the situation to my dad's attention and asked him what he thought. He responded in his simple, direct style, "It could be an error by the newspaper; on the other hand, it could be someone who is highly motivated. Why don't you contact him?"

I did. Early the very next morning—so early, in fact, that I really did not expect anyone to answer the phone. (Perhaps I was going through those paces because I really hadn't done any "homework.") To my surprise, the phone was answered within the first two rings with, "Good morning, this is Ben Blank, may I help you?"

Since I hadn't expected the call to be answered, I was sitting at my desk adding up a column of figures. Taken aback, I took a moment to muster my wits and in my very best businesslike manner, stuttered, "Uh, I'm, uh, adding on your call." There was a pause, a good-natured chuckle, and Ben said, "Would you please repeat what you just said?"

By now I had put down my pencil and was concentrating on what I should have been concentrating on when I first made the call. I apologized and said, "I read your advertisement in the Sunday *Times* and I am responding to it. I am involved in the real estate business as a broker and consultant and have some experience in site location. If you will describe to me what your requirements are, perhaps I can be of service."

Ben then told me the name of his company, adding that he was the founder and that they were among the top three companies in the greeting card industry. He said that during the war, since they were not a "necessary" industry, they had been unable to continue their growth pattern that had been progressing nicely since the mid-1930s. Now they wanted to accelerate their expansion plans in order to make up for lost time and were looking for several plants in the Northeast that would be suitable for their type of operation. I asked whether their policy was to buy the plants or lease them. He responded that they preferred long-term leases so that they could use their capital in their manufacturing operation. He sounded friendly, yet was succinct.

In the next few minutes Ben described to me exactly what their requirements were, including preferred locations and price ranges they were willing to entertain. I asked him whether he would be willing to sign an exclusive employment agreement with me to locate the sites he wanted. He replied, "No, but I will personally guarantee that you will receive your fee or commission for whatever site or sites you make available to us."

One of the first rules in the real estate business is to refrain from spending your time and effort spinning wheels without an exclusive agreement. A second rule is to use judgment in applying the first rule. Applying the second rule with some caution, I told Ben that I would be in touch with him as soon as possible.

With that, he asked me for my name, address, and telephone number. In my unprepared stupor, I had neglected to give them earlier in the conversation.

As we hung up, I vowed to show Ben that I was not the idiot I appeared to be in our initial telephone conversation. I spent the next several hours on the telephone locating some potential sites for Ben. One, in Middletown, New York, presented a particularly good opportunity involving the settlement of an estate by the court on Wednesday of that week. If the physical inspection of that plant verified the description I had received, it would be ideal. I called Ben back that afternoon and discreetly described what I had learned concerning the fine details except for the precise location. I told him that I would be inspecting the plant the next day, Tuesday, since we had to act on Wednesday. I was really applying the second rule I mentioned above, with caution. The total amount of time I would waste in this effort would be two days and with that investment, I might have found a marvelous client. I was betting on it.

Ben said he was interested and asked how I proposed to show the plant to him and his operations people before I acquired it. Did I intend to buy it whether or not he was the user?

I replied that I really wouldn't have considered buying the plant if not for his need. As a matter of fact, I told him I would have to work out some prepayment on the long-term lease from him before I could come up with the necessary money for the court to award me the building. I learned early in my career that busy, successful people make quick decisions.

Ben asked me when I planned to inspect the plant, to which I replied, "At noon tomorrow, Tuesday." Ben said, "We'll meet you for breakfast at the Red Apple Restaurant on the highway just outside of Middletown at 8:30 tomorrow morning. We can discuss the entire opportunity in detail at that time, before you make your site inspection."

I told him that would be just fine, and he said, "Would you mind giving me the name of your banker so that I can call him for reference about you?" I told him I wouldn't mind at all and proceeded to give him the name and telephone number of Jim, my friendly banker, whom you read about in the last chapter.

Ben asked one more question: how much money would I have to put down to have the court award me the building on Wednesday? I answered him that as far as I knew, it would take between $20,000 and $22,000 paid either in cash or by certified check.

We exchanged descriptions of cars as well as physical descriptions, gave license plate numbers, and agreed to meet for breakfast the next morning.

On Tuesday morning I arrived early at the Red Apple Restaurant. This time I was going to do my homework as thoroughly as possible. I reviewed the description of the plant and all the financial details. As I sat there analyzing the feasibility of the situation, the blue Buick that I was expecting pulled into the parking lot alongside of me. Two distinguished looking gentlemen with marked family resemblance got out of the car. The one on the passenger's side, about 15 years older than the driver, seemed to fit Ben's description of himself. They were fashionably dressed in quiet good taste, wearing homburgs and velvet-collared, chesterfield overcoats. As the driver came around the car, my eye was immediately caught by the brown paper bag he was carrying. It seemed incongruous to me. Here were two very distinguished looking gentlemen who were meeting me for breakfast, carrying a brown paper bag?

Ben and I exchanged greetings, shook hands, and he introduced his younger brother, Dobbs, who was the corporate attorney. We entered the restaurant, were seated, and ordered breakfast.

Graciously, but in a very businesslike manner, Ben got right down to brass tacks. He asked me to tell Dobbs exactly what I had told him about the building in Middletown. When I finished, Ben added, "And you want us to put up the money for you to buy the building to lease to us, is that correct?"

I responded, "Yes, as a security deposit and prepaid rent against your lease."

Dobbs said, "As an attorney I know that the court will not accept anything other than cash or a cashier's check made out to the appropriate party. What arrangements have you made to take care of this when you go into court tomorrow?"

I told him that I was hoping to go into court with cash, so that if the deal was as good as it appeared to be I could consummate it then and there.

Once again, Ben demonstrated to me his remarkable acumen. He asked me, "What is your physical condition?" I told him that my war experience had left me in a wheelchair, that I graduated to crutches and now the canes he was looking at. I added that before long I wouldn't be using those either.

He smiled and said, "A.D., I admire your attitude. And I like your style." With that, he reached over for the brown paper bag that Dobbs had brought into the restaurant. He handed it to me saying, "Your banker friend, Jim, says he trusts you with as much money as his bank can lend. I have always operated on the basis of trust and I like you and believe you, A.D. The fact that I trust you will be proven when you open this brown paper bag. In it, you will find $22,000 in $20 bills. It's good clean money, not black market money. We drew it out of the bank yesterday afternoon. After our telephone discussion yesterday, we anticipated this meeting. It's time for you to get over to Middletown, so we'll be leaving. We expect to hear from you tomorrow when you get out of court."

I honestly can't remember what I answered, if I answered anything. I know that I took the bag with the money without opening it then. The next day I used that money to buy the building from the court. It was just right for their purpose.

When I called Ben and Dobbs and told them, they were delighted. They moved in and started operations within a week.

The rest of the story reveals more of the benefits of using other people's money. I found two more buildings and we went through very much the same procedure as in the first case. We put together two more leases. The interesting fact was (and I don't recommend that you use this as a business practice) that we never had a scrap of paper between us until a year and a half later. There was never a signed receipt for any of the money. Neither was there a lease. This was indeed the exception to Samuel Goldwyn's observation, "a verbal contract isn't worth the paper it isn't written on." There wasn't a moment that any of us had any doubts or fears about the other's performance. They continued to advance me the money for acquisition of plants, and we built a fast and deep friendship.

I met the rest of his family, and learned from them that Ben was the eldest of seven children. His parents had a difficult time feeding them all during the Great Depression. Ben left school in the eighth grade to do odd jobs full time in order to help support the family. He insisted that all of his brothers and sisters complete high school—which he never attended—and college, and provided the funds. He also vowed that someday he would get the high school he missed.

When I first visited his corporate headquarters in upstate New York, I was impressed with the academic style of the building. No wonder. I later learned that Ben had bought the high school he never attended (when it became surplus) and installed his headquarters operations there. He did indeed *get* the high school he missed.

A year and a half later, I was gathering together all my resources to prepare for my bank and life insurance company ventures. I called Ben and Dobbs from my office in New Jersey and asked them if they would meet me the next day at Ben's favorite place in New York, the Hotel Pierre. They agreed and we met as scheduled. At that meeting, I disclosed my future plans and told them that I would be grateful if they would assist me by purchasing the buildings they were leasing from me, three in all. Beautiful Ben did it again. He said, "A.D., you've done very well for us and we really hate to lose the business association with you. But we certainly wish you well in your planned ventures and will do everything we can to help you. Leave it to me and I will find out the current market value of the buildings, since you have a good long-term tenant," at which remark we all chuckled, "and you will have our check within a week."

No more than five days later a messenger delivered a very large envelope to my office containing all the paperwork we should have been doing over the last eighteen months. Also enclosed for signing were the deeds from me to them for the three buildings they leased from me. Attached was a check in the amount of $165,000, which represented over 300% profit on my investment of *their* money in the buildings. There was a small envelope from which I took a little card. On it, in Ben's handwriting, was: "A.D., you walk straight and tall. I am proud to call you friend. Good luck. Sincerely, Ben."

Ben died of cancer a few years later. I am sure you can understand why there were over 600 people at his funeral. I don't know how many people like Ben we are privileged to meet in our life, but one is certainly enough to leave a lifetime impression.

People benefits? Needs, wants, and desires? People are more important than property? Leverage people? There are no problem properties, only problem ownerships? Find the need and fill it? Win/win? Is there any one of these that is absent from my business dealings with Ben and his company? Believe in these concepts, adopt them, practice them, and you, too, may be blessed with the privilege and good fortune of knowing a person like Ben, as I was. In any event, practicing these concepts will make it possible for you to use other people's money in some of the additional ways I will describe in the case histories that follow.

SUBORDINATING DEBT SERVICE TO CASH FLOW

Neil hates to work, so he only invests in real estate that generates heavy positive cash flows—lots of income. To get the kind of income he wants, he often has to buy depressed properties that are in such bad shape that no bank will lend on them, requiring sellers to carry the debt themselves.

When he buys these depressed properties, Neil likes to have them fixed up so he can make a profit when he sells. But since he's basically lazy, he hires expensive repairmen to do the work. Neil doesn't mind sweat equity as long as it's somebody else's sweat.

Here's one example of how I advised him to protect himself in handling such a transaction. Neil found a 45-unit rat-trap that he "stole" for $90,000, with 10% down. The cash flow on it was $1,000 a month after expenses, but it needed a lot of work. Many of the apartments would soon become unlivable if they were not drastically repaired. So we put the following stipulation into Neil's purchase agreement: he would pay the seller the principal and interest on the debt only if the building generated at least $500 per month positive cash flow after expenses and repairs. If Neil had less than this minimum positive amount, he would have the right to defer paying the debt service. Since the seller wanted to avoid the headaches of the rat-trap and no bank would lend money on it, he was satisfied to agree to Neil's terms. Neil solved a problem for the seller and he also solved the big repair-bill problem for himself.

With the assurance that he had the seller/mortgagee's cooperation in being able to continue to finance the project, Neil upgraded the rat-trap to a cat's castle. He did an excellent job of supervising the rehabilitation and had no difficulty paying the contracting workmen.

Additional people benefits from this are that Neil's income from the building is almost guaranteed, and his sweat equity is being built up without his own sweat. A few handymen about town are delighted with Neil's laziness, too.

REAL ESTATE CONTRACT

A woman I know named Marlene is a whiz at managing apartment buildings. When she first consulted me, I counseled her to realize her greatest potential. We then devised a plan of operation that utilized her best abilities. Now she can take the biggest losers and turn them into money-makers as if by magic.

When Marlene buys a building, she makes daring offers that people don't believe she can consummate. For instance, she'll ask the seller to carry a debt requiring $1,000 a month in payments, when the cash flow from the building is only $600. Marlene knows she can bring the income to over $1,000 a month, but the sellers don't. So Marlene uses the real estate contract.

This is an agreement to own the property at some later date. Marlene agrees to buy the property for a fixed price with agreed-on terms. The contract is recorded and it gives her the right to possess and operate the building. The seller executes a deed to Marlene, but the deed isn't recorded, it's put into escrow. Another deed, from Marlene to the seller, is also put into escrow.

Marlene takes over the building and starts making the payments. If she can't work her magic and defaults on the payments, the seller records her deed to him (which is being held in escrow for such an eventuality) and takes the property back. This saves him the time and expense of foreclosing.

If Marlene can work her magic and keep up the payments, the deed from the seller is taken out of escrow on a prearranged date and recorded. Marlene then owns the property outright. She continues to operate the building and make the payments until she pays the building off or sells it, whichever comes first. Usually she sells at a gigantic profit.

A real estate contract can be used without the risk Marlene takes. Sometimes the seller just doesn't want to close title at this particular time. In that instance the buyer and seller can benefit without risk. You, the buyer, can take possession, make payments and profits, and build up a cash reserve to use for the down payment by the time it is due. The seller has a sale exactly when he or she wants it, is out of management, and has minimum risk.

Marlene's special magic has made her a great deal of money. Yet she claims there's nothing supernatural about her methods. Anyone can learn the techniques of good management she has put to such profitable use. Needless to say, anyone includes you.

WALK THE MORTGAGE

When you own a property that is hard to finance and you are interested in buying a property that is easy to finance, you will be able to take advantage of a technique known as *walking the mortgage*.

Jess and Martha are a retired couple who own a home, free and clear, in an old but decent area of town. Their home is worth approximately $50,000 and they had $10,000 in savings they wanted to invest. They wanted to get some more money out of that home and use it to buy income-generating property. When they went to the banks, they were given a variety of excuses: they were too old for a lengthy mortgage, the house was too old, the neighborhood was suspect. All the excuses boiled down to a big zero for them.

One of the bankers suggested that the elderly couple talk to me for some creative suggestions. We met and worked out a plan.

Jess and Martha continued looking until they found a small apartment building in a new area of town for $50,000. The apartment building had a $40,000 mortgage against it. Rather than asking to assume that mortgage, we convinced the bank to rewrite it to encumber the house the couple lived in. We pointed out to the banker that they weren't likely to default on the mortgage and risk losing their $10,000 and their cherished home. We also explained how the income from the apartment building would help them make the mortgage payment.

The banker agreed to walk the mortgage on the apartment building and secure that indebtedness with a mortgage on the couple's "unmortgageable" house instead. This left the new building totally unencumbered.

As time went by, the new building increased in value and Jess and Martha were able to raise rents. With increased value and cash flow, the couple was able to obtain a new mortgage on the building. They used this mortgage money to buy more units. All this time, their old house stayed around $50,000 in value.

If we hadn't walked the original mortgage from the apartment building to their house, they would have had to get a more expensive second mortgage when they wanted to borrow again, or refinance the first mortgage at a higher interest rate. Walking the mortgage enabled them to borrow at low first-mortgage rates on both the old house and the new building.

Another common way of walking the mortgage is in reverse. That is, when you're selling a property, rather than having your lender erase the indebtedness, just walk it to encumber your next purchase. This is particularly good when the property you're buying is hard to finance and you doubt whether you could get a new mortgage on it. Instead of trying, just walk the old one.

The new Kessler's Keys to Success are:

- My first experience

- Subordinating debt service to cash flow

- Real estate contract

- Walk the mortgage

11

Divide and Win/Win

The ability to convert ideas . . . is the secret of success.

—Henry Ward Beecher

Remember my friend Ace whose houseboat I parlayed through exchanging into the beginning of his real estate empire? Two episodes in our relationship helped him to go from a zero financial statement in 1972 to one that showed over $3 million in real estate assets in December 1980, despite the unexpected 1972-74 real estate recession. Fortunes are made in good times and bad by those who know how. During that period, I was involved with Ace in many more business dealings and real estate transactions than the two I am about to describe. However, these two clearly illustrate the divide and win/win concept I want you to know and be ready to apply when opportunity knocks. It's easy to tell winners from losers. Winners watch for opportunity to knock. Losers knock every opportunity.

Ace was comfortable and happy in his new marriage with his new home and surroundings. And Ace liked the fact that he was a part-time success in the real estate business. He liked it so well that he looked everywhere to become more involved in real estate. His business prospered, and early in 1974 he had some extra money to invest. One of his business associates made him an offer he just couldn't refuse. Ace's "friend" permitted him to join in the purchase of a real "bargain." (The tail end of a traumatic real estate recession came in 1974. Later on in this book we'll talk about investing in bad times as well as investing in good times. We'll also address the subject of "bargains.")

Ace and Associate acquired a subdivision of residential lots in a resort area that had been lying fallow for ten years. They bought it for what they thought was 10 cents on the dollar. When Ace came to me crowing about the marvelous deal he had made, I congratulated him and asked him what plans he had for marketing the property. He said, "That's the best part. I told my partner that I would only go in with him if we let you market the lots."

I thanked him and was impressed with his consideration. When I got all the paperwork on the transaction and started to plan for marketing, I discovered some facts that I was afraid would burst Ace's balloon. The lots were not legal lots. They were undersized and the subdivision did not have adequate utilities. In addition, my site inspection revealed that almost half of the property was in a wash—a natural drainage swale that had been the course of nature for a long time. None of these details were revealed in the closing documents of the transaction. There was no way the property could be sold for building lots.

When I confronted Ace and his partner with the facts, you can imagine their consternation. Unfortunately, Ace turned on his partner like a tiger. I had my hands full restraining them from punching each other out. After calming them down, I explained the alternatives, as I saw them, to the irate partners. One was to litigate against the seller and his representatives. I told them that litigation was a luxury few people could afford, particularly when the outcome was unpredictable. The other alternative was to look for the best possible solution to "make lemonade out of lemons."

It was obvious as we conferred that the partners would no longer get along, at least when it came to that ownership. We did have a problem ownership, and how!

I suggested as a first step a divide and win/win solution. One of the partners should take over the whole responsibility for this particular problem, so there would be no further cause for disagreement and possible bloodshed. Now, the problem was determining who would bite the bullet. Since I was familiar with Ace's portfolio, I took him aside and suggested that we exchange his partner out of the property and that we try later to solve the problem for him alone. He was amenable to the following offer.

He would take over his partner's half of the problem property for a value exactly the same as the partner originally paid—$3,000. The $3,000 would be paid at the rate of $100 a month, with no interest, for 30 months. The $100 was to come from the rental income of the second condominium that Ace acquired when we exchanged his houseboat. His payments on the mortgage were $450 a month including principal, interest, and impound for property taxes. By this time, he had furnished the condominium and was renting it for $550 a month, with the tenant paying the condominium owner's fee. This meant that the $100 he would pay his partner for his half of the problem land was really not out of pocket, since all costs were covered and the condominium was continuing to appreciate. Additionally, we were facing an upswing in the economy, and the condominium rent would probably go up. In any event, during the nearby racetrack's season of several months each year, the condominium rented for three times its normal price. When I explained the details to Ace's partner and assured him that the $100 would be paid each month, guaranteed by a second mortgage on the condominium, he accepted. All that was left was to solve Ace's problem with the full ownership of the problem property.

We contacted the Flood Control Authority and discussed their plans for the next ten years. They acknowledged that the piece of property that Ace was holding was in the flood plan and that at some point in the future they would be improving it as a permanent flood canal. So I took the necessary steps to have the property condemned—to be bought and paid for by the Flood Control Authority for the public benefit—and within six months Ace recovered his full cost, including the purchase price, interest on his investment, and my fee.

Strange how so many of the unique transactions involving Ace were somehow connected with water. Because we were fortunate in arriving at successful solutions to his problems, Ace was beginning to believe that I could *walk* on water.

He asked me to find a good tax shelter for him. Shortly thereafter, at a marketing meeting, a large tract of acreage was being offered on behalf of an owner who had held it for so many years that the appreciation was sufficient motivation to dispose of it.

I structured a transaction, acting as a buyer's broker (this means that I was working with net sale and purchase figures, and that the seller had no obligation to pay me any fees since they would be paid by the buyer). We offered the seller prepaid interest only, annually, for five years with the entire principal due and payable at the end of the sixth year. The advantages to both sides were obvious. The seller was receiving income from the property without having to pay a large tax on his very large profit all at once. In making the offer, I indicated to the seller—with his broker's permission— that we could work with him in the future and perhaps structure an exchange that would let him keep all of his profits tax-free. He liked this idea. The advantages to Ace, the buyer, were that he paid little cash out of pocket to acquire control of 44 rapidly appreciating acres of land in the path of progress. The cash that he did pay was in the form of prepaid interest that at that time was a deductible item against personal income tax. In effect, it was costing Ace nothing to own the 44 acres.

The transaction was consummated and Ace made me a proposition. He said that he was so grateful for my advice and handling of his real estate investment portfolio that he would like me to share in one-half of the profits at the time this property was sold or exchanged rather than pay me the fee for this transaction.

I broke several longstanding rules in accepting his offer. Those rules are:

1. Never proceed with a transaction without a clear-cut understanding of everybody's role.

2. Never proceed with a transaction without a clear-cut idea of what the fee will be.

3. Never participate in ownership with a client unless it is in a new venture, with agreement in advance regarding that participation. (In such an instance I would never take a fee for my services. My belief is that one should either be a principal or a broker when involved with other parties. Never profit from both ends.)

So who's perfect? I deviated from my longstanding principles and policies and accepted Ace's generous offer.

Four and a half years passed and the petro-dollars were pouring in to our part of the world. Without ever offering the property, Ace was contacted by foreign purchasers and offered $18,500 per acre for the 44 acres that he had purchased at $1,700 per acre. And he hadn't even paid for them yet! This amounted to a selling price of $814,000. Ace's cost at that time was zero, since his prepaid interest payments annually were tax deductible. My share, for breaking my own rules, would be $407,000.

Ace never bothered to tell me the facts I'm relating to you. I found out that the property was sold because I subscribe to what is known as a "follow-up" service with a local title insurance company. They inform me of every transaction that occurs involving any property that I have ever worked with.

You can imagine my surprise on the morning that I received the notice of this sale pending. I called Ace and asked him about it. Without a moment's hesitation, he said, "I was going to surprise you." I replied that he certainly had surprised me already. I reminded him that I had a document, signed by him, that entitled me to half of the profits of the sale. With that I asked him to send me copies of the papers that were involved in the transaction. He promised to do so, but after two weeks the papers still hadn't arrived. I called Ace and asked him and his wife to meet me for dinner and incidentally, bring along the transaction documents. We met and he was his usual ebullient self. During the course of the meal I brought up the subject of the land sale. When I raised the subject, his wife interjected, "Ace, why don't you tell A.D. how grateful you are for his help in your real estate transactions? You know that you really never made any money in anything you've done except in the real estate transactions that he handled for you."

He said, "That's right. And I'm going to take care of him for that."

At that point I asked him to show me the papers involved in the land sale. (I really didn't need the papers, since I had a complete set of them from the title company already, but I felt it only proper that he should hand me copies.) He claimed he had forgotten to bring them.

He hemmed and hawed and then dropped the bombshell. "I would like to give you $10,000 for your effort, A.D., and call it square."

I had it coming! I had broken my own rules and gone against my own principles and policies.

The next day I recorded my interest in the property and filed notice with the title company that was handling the closing. It was now less than 10 days from closing time. Within 24 hours an attorney retained by Ace contacted me and asked what I would take to settle the matter. I responded that the first thing it would take would be a meeting between him, Ace, my attorney, and me. We set up the meeting for the next day.

I'll make a long story short. This is an example of divide and win/win. What I settled for in the meeting the next day, to avoid litigation and a lot of heartache that goes with it, was 10% of the sale price, the generally acceptable commission for raw land. I agreed to accept payment upon closing, but Ace had to add a little twist there. He wanted to pay me only 50% upon closing and the balance over the next six months. I accepted with the condition that the notes be interest-bearing and personally endorsed and guaranteed by Ace.

We drew up the necessary settlement papers on the spot, signed them, and issued the notes. His attorney kept the notes until closing, at which time he sent them to me with a check.

I put the notes into my bank for collection, to keep the matter at arms length, and Ace made the payments on time.

It is important that one keep one's perspective in any business transaction. My decision to settle was based on the following factors:

1. I did not want to spend any more down time on this situation, then or in the future.

2. The time I would save by quickly closing the matter would free my mind and my time for positive efforts.

3. I could take the money I settled for and (in the up-turning real estate market) invest it to make as much money as I *might* receive if and when a lawsuit would be settled in my favor three years or more in the future. (The court calendars at that time were taking three years for a case to be heard.)

4. Even if I did win the lawsuit, the cost of legal fees plus my time to prepare the case with my attorneys would take a big bite out of the sum I would receive. In addition, I would have to come up with cash out of pocket to finance the lawsuit.

5. If I did win three years hence, Ace might not have the money to pay, particularly if he was going to continue operating in the unscrupulous manner he had displayed.

Your first loss is always your best loss. Don't look back.

Whenever you have a situation that promises to rob you of time and cause worry and concern that will inhibit your ability to go on to bigger and better things, consider whether you would be better off to divide and win/win.

There are endless variations of the process. Some I have used may give you some ideas for your current and future transactions. Read them with an eye toward that benefit.

SPLITTING THE INTERESTS

To use this technique, you have to understand the various rights that accrue to you as an owner of real estate. When you buy property, you buy more than just the right to occupy a dwelling or other type of building. You buy a bundle of rights that has been attached to land by law and tradition since ancient times.

Sell the Water

Look at water rights. When most property was rural and there were no centralized water distribution systems, the right to use the water that flowed over, sat on, or ran beneath the land was extremely valuable. Many of the most significant cases in the history of real estate law involve disputes over water rights. The results of these cases vary in different parts of the country. Water rights in Arizona, where water is scarce, are governed by laws that are different from those of Michigan, where water is abundant. Before you make any kind of transaction involving water, check the laws in the area. Employ an expert.

What kind of transactions can you make involving water? A number of people I know own vacant property on the fringes of rural areas around Houston. These areas are in the path of progress, so these people are holding the land for future appreciation. But in the meantime, the vacant land isn't generating any income, is not easily mortgageable, and actually costs the owners money in annual property taxes.

The people who have water on or under this semirural land will often sell the rights to that water to nearby farmers, who need water for irrigation. Sometimes the owners will sell the water rights outright, hoping that when urbanization does come, so will water pipes. With water flowing through the pipes, the lack of water on the land itself might not bother the developers. Sometimes the owners will sell just the use of the water on a year-to-year basis to generate income from the land.

Either way, the sale of the water generates cash that the owners can use to invest in other real estate. This is just one example of splitting the interests to divide and win/win.

Sell the Minerals

When you have oil, natural gas, or bauxite under the ground, you have mineral rights that may be more valuable than the land itself. If you're not planning to go into the oil-drilling or mining business, sell the rights to someone who already is in the business and use the money to buy additional properties. Even large deposits of gravel are marketable. Look around your property. There's more to it than you might immediately notice.

Once again I call to your attention the great advantage of leveraging people—using OPB (other people's brains) in this instance. In the oil and mining areas of the country, there are lawyers and brokers who specialize in mineral rights. They know the buyers, what the market conditions are with regard to supply and demand, and consequently know how to price your product as well as whether to sell, lease, share, or joint venture.

Sell the Air

In densely populated areas, air rights can be extremely valuable. Air rights? Certainly. When you own a piece of property, you own the air above it all the way to heaven. In recent years, this has been limited by the courts to give airplanes the right to fly over your property, provided they maintain a proper altitude. But what about closer to earth, say 20 to 50 feet above your land?

If you own property where buildings are right next to one another, every cubic inch of air is valuable. Art lived in such an area, on a deep lot, the back part of which he used for parking his three cars. Next door, the owner was adding on to his apartment building. He offered to buy the back part of Art's lot so that he could put extra units there.

Art was tempted to sell but thought, "If I do, where will I park my cars?" At one of my seminars he mentioned the offer he had received and challenged my statements that creativity is learned, not inherent and that every problem brings opportunity. He said, "If you are so creative, how about a solution for that, or how about teaching me to be creative enough to solve the problem of wanting the money from the sale and at the same time wanting some place to keep my cars?"

As a quick solution, I suggested, "Why not just sell the air above that portion of the lot?" He was thrilled with the suggestion and was going to try to use it as soon as he got home. He promised to call and tell me how it worked.

The very next day Art called me, and this is what he reported. He approached his neighbor and said, "Look, I won't sell the back part of my lot for $20,000. But for $10,000 I'll sell the air above it. That way you can put one unit over that spot and I'll still have a place to park my cars."

The neighbor accepted and now he has a rent-generating apartment held up by stilts (actually solid, poured concrete walls reinforced with steel) over the back part of Art's property. And Art received $10,000 and a free carport.

The opportunities to profit from dealing in air rights are virtually limitless. For those who like to think big, Donald Trump has a skyscraper hotel "on air rights" over Grand Central Station in New York City, and the tower above Pennsylvania Station is another air rights deal. Tennis courts, gardens, restaurants, health clubs, apartments, offices, schools and dozens of other types of installations across the country are built on air rights. Perhaps dealing in air rights could be a specialty that appeals to you, either as a principal or agent. It is certainly not an overcrowded field.

Divide the Ownership According to Ability

This is a variation of the effort equity technique I previously explained. Basically, it recognizes that different people have different skills and abilities that they bring to a transaction. Each of the people involved in a transaction then gets an ownership interest based on the relative value of his or her skills to the total project.

I know four men who played poker every Thursday. All of them were involved in real estate in some way. Jack was a builder who went bankrupt in a bad market and was without cash. Bill was a real estate speculator who had done well and was sitting on a pile of cash. Carl was a real estate attorney. Lloyd was a real estate broker who was adept at finding great bargains on vacant land.

Every Thursday, after playing a few hours of poker, the four men talked about real estate. One evening, Lloyd mentioned that he had just found some commercially zoned property priced far below the market. "If I only had the money to buy it," he lamented.

"How much money?" asked Bill, the speculator.

"Fifty thousand," Lloyd answered.

"I've got it," said Bill. "Make an offer."

Lloyd wasn't impressed. "So what if we get it? It's no good without a building on it."

Jack, the builder, brightened. "I can put up a building. I haven't got any cash, but I'll contribute general building contracting and supervision for a piece of the action."

Carl, the attorney, said, "And I'll put the deal together, do the paperwork, and find the financing. I'll even kick in a little more cash."

The poker party suddenly turned into a joint effort, with each participant receiving a percentage interest in the venture according to his agreed-upon contribution. They came to me for a method of determining how much of a share each would be entitled to. I explained that there is a clear-cut way to fairly determine the percentage to which each of the parties to such an effort is entitled. Each submits an estimate, or bid, for the value of the service he or she will contribute. In first-time relationships, it is a good idea to get competitive bids for the same work from outsiders. This gives a standard of measurement. After a venture or two together, the guidelines are well set, and the percentages are usually easily agreed on between the parties.

It worked like a charm, they made a good sum of money on that first venture, and the men have done it a number of times since. They still meet on Thursdays, but they spend less and less time playing cards. They're too busy talking about their next real estate venture.

MEDICAL CENTER OFFICE CONDO

There's an area of Dallas where doctors used to love to have their offices. It was close to all major bus routes and possessed an old-world charm that kept the district safe and attractive to their patients. But because of its charm, this district became so popular that buildings started to spring up almost on top of one another.

For the doctors, the new congestion was bad business. Many of their patients became exasperated with the crowds on the buses and chose instead to drive their own cars to their appointments. This postponed the problem but did not solve it. Soon the new buildings replaced the few remaining parking lots and the parking situation became intolerable.

In addition, the medical centers these doctors had needed years ago were now technically obsolete. They didn't have the electrical and plumbing capacity to handle all the doctors' new equipment. Slowly, the doctors began to move to new buildings in outlying areas of the city. These new buildings were designed to accommodate modern equipment and were surrounded by large parking lots.

The owners of the old medical centers panicked. When a medical tenant moved out, no new doctor would move in.

Harriet was one of the few landladies in the area who refused to panic. She knew that her medical center was still in an attractive location. She came to me, as a consultant, to discuss the problem. I suggested to her that many small businesses would love to have the space (and would pay for it at a fair and profitable rent). Insurance agents, for example, have relatively few clients visit their offices, so they don't need the parking facilities that doctors do.

Instead of clutching at her doctor tenants as her neighbors were doing, she gladly let them go. When one left, she divided the medical suite into smaller offices. Eventually, all the space was converted. Then we filed the necessary papers for the legal subdivision, received approval, and put her entire building on the market as office condominiums.

Harriet sold the condominiums for huge profits. The businesspeople who bought Harriet's condos got a good DEAL because they enjoyed the benefits of ownership (Depreciation, Equity build-up, Appreciation, and Leverage) and didn't resent making her a rich woman in the process.

Incidentally, when she again sought my advice, Harriet used her profits to build a modern medical center in an outlying area, and her children live handsomely on the rents from the doctors, many of whom were tenants in their mother's old building.

This is an outstanding example of "turning a sow's ear into a silk purse," and proving once again the Creative Real Estate concept: there are no problem properties, only problem ownerships. We changed the circumstances of the ownership for Harriet and created a win/win situation for everyone.

TAP THE TRUST

Attorneys report to me that approximately one-third of the adults in our country are the beneficiaries of an inheritance or trust. For investors' purposes, those are deferred assets. Some bequests and trusts have finite amounts, but most are subject to some fluctuation and adjustment when finally disbursed.

There are people who make a business of buying *legacies*. By definition, a legacy is an inheritance that hasn't cleared probate and been disbursed, or a trust that hasn't matured and paid off. You will find advertisements in the classified section of many newspapers soliciting legacies. The usual practice is to offer a discounted amount, payable in cash in the present, for the future principal amount of the legacy.

Darwin came to me for advice and counseling about getting started on his real estate investment portfolio. He had $2,500 in cash, a good, steady job, and a trust fund that would pay him $50,000 in seven years when he reached age thirty-five. It was paying him $5,000 a year now that he did not need to live on, because of his good-paying job.

After verifying that the trust fund was intact and secure, I suggested to Darwin that he purchase an unmortgaged apartment house that was available for $100,000. In structuring the transaction, we offered the seller a 50% interest in the trust fund, amounting to $25,000. We asked her to carry back a $75,000 purchase money mortgage, payable at $2,000 per month including principal and interest, all due and payable in seven years. In addition, Darwin would pay her $5,000 against the principal balance each year, as he received it from his trust fund.

She was happy with the offer, particularly when we assured her that the national bank that was administering Darwin's trust would acknowledge a legal document dividing in half the final trust payment showing the

$25,000 due her, and would accept and acknowledge an assignment of the $5,000 annual payments. She also had a mortgage on the building.

By dividing his trust fund, we started Darwin on his real estate fortune. He loved the idea. So much, in fact, that six months later we exchanged another $10,000 of his final trust payment as the down payment for a $100,000 factory building on a sale and lease-back.

Darwin is now in his fifties. He consulted with me recently about leaving trust funds (from the income on his vast real estate holdings) for his five grandchildren, with specific instructions that the final payment could be divided or hypothecated for acquisition of real estate. He wants his heirs to be able to divide and win/win, as he did.

The Kessler's Keys to Success you now have are:

☛ Splitting the interests

☛ Sell the water

☛ Sell the minerals

☛ Sell the air

☛ Divide the ownership according to ability

☛ Medical center office condo

☛ Tap the trust

12

Exercising Your Options

A technique or style for something original does not exist . . . it is created.

—Igor Stravinsky

In real estate, an *option* is a contract in which one person, the optionor, promises to sell property at a particular price for a specified period of time. In return for this promise, the potential buyer, the optionee, gives the property owner something of value, usually money. In other words, an option is the right to acquire title at a fixed price, on fixed terms, for a fixed amount of time.

The simplest options work like this. I own land worth $10,000. You want to buy it, but not right away. Rather than risk my selling it to someone else, you give me $100 to hold the property for you for three months. Before the three months are up, you must buy the land for the $10,000 price. If you don't, the option expires and I'm free to sell to someone else. Usually, the price paid for the option, in this case the $100, is separate from the sale price and is not refundable. Should you exercise the option, the $100 may or may not be applied against the sale price, depending upon our prior agreement.

In this chapter, we will examine a few variations on that simple option.

OPTION IN THE AIR

In an attempt to save the coastline, a coastal commission had been appointed by the governor. Although I don't doubt their sincerity in fulfilling their mission, they caused considerable consternation with the methods they employed to complete their task.

One of their regulations in particular was wreaking havoc with the construction industry. They declared a moratorium on all building in the "coastal zone" (an arbitrarily established area that covered the entire coastline as far inland as 15 miles).

In Chapter 6 we discussed peoples' affinity for the water. The coastal commission was going against nature. With no new construction on the coast, there was a pent-up demand for waterfront housing.

A planned high-rise condominium complex in an established marina was stalled. Al, a wheeler-dealer developer, had gotten wind of it and worked out his own peculiar solution. Through some mysterious political connection, he had secured a tentative approval to construct the high-rise, but there were a few "small" problems:

1. He didn't own the project.
2. The owners had not agreed to do anything.
3. Al didn't have any money.

To Al, these were only small problems. He convinced the owners that he would be able to complete the project. In return, he wanted an option to buy it at a fixed price.

To accomplish his objective, Al gave my associate, David, a listing to sell options on the "to-be-built" condominiums. In that fashion he intended to raise the money.

David had worked out a marketing plan in which he would sell the options to our sales staff in multiple units. Then, in turn, they could either resell the options as the project progressed or hold them and sell the finished condominiums at what promised to be a handsome profit. He had structured a very attractive purchase price schedule with Al.

David is a gentleman of sterling character and he's an accomplished professional of substantial wealth. But considering Al's *modus operandi*, I listened to David's story skeptically. Like most good salesmen, David is an "easy mark."

Nonetheless, we, along with our sales staff, explored every aspect of the proposition, and weighing the risks, it seemed to have potential. Besides, we were all human, even though we were in the real estate business, and we had the classic, human, emotional response to prime waterfront property— go for it!

No one buying the options had any plans, at the time, to live in the completed units. It was possible that one of us might retain a deluxe waterfront condo, but that was certainly not the motivation. Profit was.

Within one week, David had collected options for all 14 floors of the proposed building excluding the penthouse, which Al had decided would provide the style of life to which he would like to become accustomed.

I "owned" the entire eleventh floor (four apartments), and after inspecting the site I was really quite elated at the prospect of my floor in the air.

Al's propensity for wheeling more than dealing prevailed throughout our involvement with the project. After much heartache he lost the project. The building got completed after two more changes of ownership of the project-in-progress.

An option on real estate, properly drawn and recorded, has legal preference similar to a lease to survive change of ownership unless that right is waived by specific prior agreement.

But our options were on Al's project, not the building. In the fast shuffling of papers during the subsequent changes of ownership, our options were not honored because they were not technically perfect. We had let our hearts and emotions prevail, and though we were professionals, we did not sufficiently examine and protect ourselves from the consequences of Al's possible loss of legal interest. To quote Sam Goldwyn: "We read part of it all the way through."

In our enthusiasm to fulfill our emotional desires, and with greed in our hearts, we did not take the necessary precautions to employ a competent attorney to examine the paperwork. He would have undoubtedly advised us of the risk of loss we subsequently suffered.

I look pensively at the completed building every time I pass it. It is a beautiful structure in a prime location. What might have been . . .

When dealing in options, be aware of the risks. There are many. Some as yet are undiscovered. The option is a valuable tool and can make a lot of money for you, as I will show you in further examples, but always remember to deal in facts, not fancy. Leverage people and employ the most competent experts you can to examine the details of every option. It doesn't cost, it pays.

"OPTION" PURCHASE CONTRACTS

A highly profitable specialty that has made money for alert buyers has been finding new housing developments built by reputable builders and "buying" in the first phase. I place quotes around *buying* because in essence, the process is one of option. My three sons, Brian, Judd, and Earl, have all used this technique and have profited handsomely.

Good times or bad, there will always be a shortage of new houses. Even when you hear of an "overbuilt" condition, such as the condominium glut on both the east and west coasts that occurred in the 1970s, there was still a shortage of new housing. The problem was not too many condominiums but too many high-priced condominiums.

The fault was with improper feasibility studies. When all those overbuilt condominiums were started, the existing supply of condominiums in resort areas was limited and selling rapidly. The new builders jumped into the market thinking they could sell all they could build at any price. How wrong they were. Those condos went through multiple foreclosures until a combination of the losses sustained and inflation brought the prices into line with what the market could support.

Judd religiously read the notices of new building plans. He and Earl visited every promising-looking tract building site before the models were completed. They examined the location, the site, and the quality of materials on the job site. If, in their studied opinion, the house plans and all other conditions had potential for filling the need for housing in that area, they would buy several of the houses to be built that would be easiest to sell. Their standards of measurement for this last requirement would depend on the type of neighborhood, the economic level of the general area, and the aesthetics of the buildings and the site, as well as on the builder/developer's track record in building and selling desirable homes. Usually, the earnest money required for each house was $500 to $2,500.

Over a seven-year period, with few exceptions, they resold their position in each of these houses at substantial profits, ranging from $5,000 to $40,000. In some instances they closed title and then resold; in others they merely assigned their contracts to purchase.

The exceptions usually occurred in cases where the builder didn't maintain the quality promised, changed the plans, or was slow in completing the buildings. In these instances the boys canceled their purchase agreements and took a refund of their earnest money.

The requirements for making this type of option work are:

1. Do your homework. Study the areas and the new offerings.

2. Be early in the game.

3. Pick the most popular houses for the area, not necessarily the one you particularly like for yourself.

4. Keep in touch with the market.

This is a simple but certain technique for applying the concept of options to making a lot of money with minimal risk. While purists may say it's not really an option, it meets the description, fills all the requirements, and best of all, it works! If it still works in your area, use it—don't fix it!

CONTINUING OPTION

Barbara wanted to buy a piece of property that she felt was skyrocketing in value. But she was broke. Not only could she not afford the land, she couldn't afford the option. All she had, besides a job that supported her needs for food, clothing, and shelter, was the income from a few bonds held for her in a trust fund. She couldn't sell the bonds because the trustee wouldn't allow it.

Every day that went by, Barbara got more upset about the property because it was right next to a parcel upon which a major bank was building a skyscraper. The land she wanted was a small corner lot that by itself was a barely profitable parking lot that the tired owner was eager to sell, so he could join his siblings in retirement in Florida. With the new bank building across the street, the lot could be a gold mine. The owner wanted $10,000 for it.

After consulting with me for an hour, Barbara believed she had a workable formula.

Armed with my advice and H.L. Hunt's—"Decide what you want, decide what you're willing to exchange for it, then go for it"—Barbara approached the lot owner with an option contract. In it, she agreed to pay him $1,200 for the right to buy the lot for $10,000 within one year. The $1,200 would be paid at the rate of $100 per month for twelve months, exactly the amount of income from her trust bonds.

When the lot owner looked down his nose at the option, she pointed out that $1,200 was as good as 12% interest on $10,000 and that the extra $100 a month would make his parking lot additionally profitable. He saw her logic.

Barbara didn't have to wait the year. In the fifth month, a major fast-food chain, eager for the anticipated lunch business from office workers in the new bank building, gave her $50,000 for the option. Not a bad return for an investment of only $500. All it took was ambition, persistence, and creativity. Barbara is using her profits to buy options wherever she sees an opportunity. She is sticking to what she knows best.

INCREASED PAYMENT OPTION

This option makes use of the thin vein of greed that runs through all of us. It's a conventional option with an unconventional provision. A friend of mine used it and made a large sum of money. All we did was write a regular option contract in which he agreed to pay $1,000 for the one-year right to buy what appeared to be a marginal piece of property. At the end of that year, he had the right to renew for another year, on payment of $2,000. At the end of that second year, he could renew again, this time for $3,000. The property owner was ecstatic. All he could see was $6,000 in income from property he planned to hold for three years anyway.

At the end of the first year, the property was worth even less than when the option was written. But my friend was an optimist. He bit the bullet, paid the $2,000, and bought himself another year. That year, things began to happen. He received an offer of $10,000 for the option. It was tempting, but at this point my friend was not interested in fast dollars. He waited. The year went by without another nibble. At the end of it he berated himself for being a fool and paid the $3,000 for a third year of option. The owner laughed at my friend's madness as he took the last of his $6,000 windfall to the bank.

As it turned out, the property was worth a fortune. An amusement park half a mile away wanted to build an expensive restaurant but had no room in the park itself. The owners decided to find a lot in the vicinity to construct a restaurant that would be connected to the park by a sky ride. Park goers could take the sky ride, eat dinner, and then glide back to the park. My friend's optioned lot was the only location that was suitable for the park owner's purpose.

My friend received $75,000 for his option, which left him a net of $69,000. Not bad for three years of doing little but waiting, worrying, and having faith. Be advised, however, that option buying is pure speculation. My friend could have lost the whole $6,000 with nothing to show for it. He had no prior knowledge of the restaurant site search. When you buy options, be prepared to lose, but think positively. A person who aims at nothing has a target he can't miss. Operate with Kessler's Law in mind: Expect *anything,* be surprised at *nothing,* and you'll be prepared for *EVERYTHING!*

EFFORT OPTION

In many cities there's land that is ripe for development but vacant. That's because municipal governments have placed many restrictions on building. Even owners who can afford to build are unwilling to go through the time-consuming effort and bureaucratic red tape of getting the necessary approvals. So they just sit and wait for the city to change the laws or for someone to come along who is willing to put up with the hassle. They agree with Will Rogers: "Be thankful we don't get all the government we pay for."

Roger had little going for him except his willingness to work, a dream, and patience. Surly bureaucrats don't bother him, and waiting in line is his idea of a good place to read war novels. Roger had his eye on a piece of property, but he had no money, not even enough for an option.

While he was adjusting the throttle on my motor scooter one day, he asked me if there was a way he could "get hold of a piece of property without putting any money down." I was aware of the difficulty many land owners had in obtaining permits and I told him that there could be an opportunity and outlined a course of action for him. He was grateful and refused to take any pay for working on the scooter.

The next day he approached the owner of the property and told him of his plans to buy the land and build a motorcycle repair shop on it. The owner just shook his head.

"The city will never go for it. You couldn't build a convent, much less a motorcycle shop here. It's against the zoning regulations," he said.

"Are you sure?" asked Roger.

"Well, not positive, but pretty sure," was the reply.

"If you give me an option on this property," Roger proposed, "I'll go through the trouble of getting architect's plans, zoning approval, and building permits. The whole shot. If I can't exercise the option at the end of the year, all the approvals and permits are yours. You'll be able to build anything you want."

The owner realized what a good deal he was getting and signed the option.

For the next year, Roger waited in lines and argued with city officials. He even had a special ordinance passed that allowed the owner to build a motorcycle repair shop on the property, provided he complied with a series of restrictions. At the end of the year, Roger was still unable to raise enough money to buy the land, so the original property owner took advantage of Roger's success in changing the zoning regulations and built a motorcycle shop that he later sold for a handsome profit.

But as I said, Roger is a patient man. After that experience, he did the same thing all over again with another piece of property. And when, at the end of his option year, he had all the necessary approvals, he also found financing—from the owner of the first piece of property who was still looking for a place to reinvest his profits. Roger built a beautifully designed motorcycle repair shop that enables him to give the best service in town, and it is thriving. Success depends on your backbone, not your wishbone. He still refuses to take any money when he does minor work on my scooter and cycles.

VARIATIONS

The *rolling option* is a standard option with the provision to either drop it without further payment or keep it open by additional payment. It is a form of the continuing option I structured for Barbara, as described earlier in this chapter.

The *equity option* is using the equity, or an option on the equity, you have in another property as the consideration for the option you are acquiring.

The *contingency option* is a good method for real estate professionals to use to acquire property. Rather than listing a prospective client's property for sale, if you would like to buy it but need some time to accumulate the funds, sell other property first, or whatever, offer to exercise an option with the seller, exchanging to-be-earned commission on the property sale as option money. The sweetener that makes this work is to agree to give the seller 20% of any profits made in the event you resell the property within a year.

FLYING OPTION

A combination of all the option techniques was utilized by a broker who would rather fly than eat. Since he spent so much time in the air he contrived a way to put the time to good use in building his real estate fortune.

Bearing in mind my PROFIT formula (Chapter 6), he flew over all the cities within his Cessna's 400-mile range. He would note the direction in which the city was moving (path of progress). He charted the properties on hillsides, and he marked the properties that were on a waterfront on his map.

Then he would visit the areas on the ground and reinspect them for easy access. While in the locale, he would gather all the information he could from the government agencies, chamber of commerce, real estate professionals, and builders. He spoke to people on properties neighboring the areas he was interested in. In short, he did his homework.

Armed with all the facts, he would return to his office and contact his title company representatives for area plat maps, legal descriptions, and names and addresses of owners of the properties he was considering.

Then he would plot the pieces of property that had all the potential for future development and met the criteria of my PROFIT formula.

His next step was to contact the owners and negotiate for any of the many options we are discussing in this chapter that filled their needs.

Remarkably, his batting average was .500. He actually optioned half of all the properties he contemplated. As a result, that became his only specialty, besides flying. And the profits provided him with a Lear jet after six years of doing his homework.

The option is an easy way to build wealth starting from scratch (other peoples' scratch). Don't get carried away by emotion (remember my option in the air). Do your homework, and always provide people benefits by structuring win/win situations that will keep your options open.

Your additional Kessler's Keys to Success now include:

🔑 Option in the air

🔑 "Option" purchase contracts

🔑 Continuing option

🔑 Increased payment option

🔑 Effort option

🔑 Rolling option

🔑 Equity option

🔑 Contingency option

🔑 Flying option

13

All in the Family

My job is to build the future.

—Senator Charles Percy (when he was Chairman of Bell & Howell)

Building an estate should be the ultimate consideration in acquiring wealth, not merely to leave a large amount to heirs but to enjoy the benefits during your lifetime. Estate building is the *investor's* prime objective, rather than the speculator's. It also reminds one to look ahead, and planning is an essential ingredient for living a good life. It is not so much doing the thing we like as liking the thing we have to do that makes life happy. The Constitution guarantees the right to *pursue* happiness; you have to *catch* it yourself.

THE BEST-LAID PLANS

My father was 14 years older than my mother. He was a good provider and was adept at making large amounts of money. They had a good marriage, and he was concerned about providing for Mother in her later years so that she could continue to live the lifestyle they enjoyed together.

Because of their age difference, Dad was realistic in considering that he would die before Mother. As a result, after he retired in his mid-fifties, he concentrated on planning his estate so that Mother would inherit her rightful share with a minimum of legal service and the least possible tax consequences. Within a short period after Dad's retirement, Mother was the majority owner of all of their fixed assets. She was the legal owner of both her car and his. He did his job well, and leveraged people—employing the services of the most talented tax and legal authorities. My parents were secure in the knowledge that their estate was well planned and in good order.

In October of 1962, having had no prior indication of any problem, Mother was diagnosed as a victim of lymphatic leukemia. She entered the hospital for treatment, and after six painful weeks she passed away.

The loss left us all in a state of shock. After a bewildering mourning period, there were legal details to attend to.

To our dismay, we realized that Dad would have to inherit all of the assets he had so carefully and legally made Mother's, including his own automobile.

The tax consequences were considerable. Bereaved as he was over losing Mother, he had the additional problem of paying substantial state and federal inheritance taxes. To meet this obligation, he was obliged to divest the estate of some rather large assets. The estate was considerably diminished, and much of his hard work and planning had been for naught.

Always a man of admirable stature and determination, he rose to the task and dispatched his duties promptly and well. He then set about the task of making better plans for the balance of his estate. Dad lived until 1971, missing his companion of 47 years.

It was a terribly hard lesson to learn, but it left a lasting impression on my two sisters and me. This experience made us aware of the fragility of life and concerned about planning the best we could for eventualities we may not have considered. And I sincerely hope this illustration will make a point for you. Once again, remember Kessler's Law: "Expect *anything,* be surprised at *nothing,* and you will be prepared for *EVERYTHING!*"

WHAT A WAY TO GO

C.P. was a genius. In almost everything he tried, he did exceptionally well. His oil paintings were beautiful. His writing was intriguing. When he spoke, listeners were spellbound. His ideas about the subjects he concentrated on were inspired and inspiring. He taught unique, innovative, and creative methods for making money in real estate. He was a funny man, too. He made points in his seminars memorable by the injection of his original humor.

After several years of teaching many people how to get rich and continuing to practice real estate, he changed his direction because of an unexpected incident. A real estate professional in C.P.'s home town died. The man had been a pillar of the community and had been the compelling reason for C.P. to go into real estate professionally. He was respected for his wisdom as well as his apparent wealth. His family grieved over his loss. They also grieved when they discovered that he had made no provisions for an orderly transition of his wealth. They grieved even more when they realized his wealth had only been apparent. He left very little of substance as a result of mismanagement, not minding the store, and living to the hilt by spending every dime that came in to maintain the "front" that the community observed.

C.P. was appalled and he vowed to help prevent that situation from happening to anyone he became involved with.

He wrote a new course. It was specifically oriented to estate building. As with everything he did, he did it well. The research and techniques were brilliant. His presentation left indelible marks and changed the lives of many who were privileged to be his students.

In the mid-1970s, when C.P. was in his late thirties, he gave the ultimate seminar. One hundred specially selected students accompanied him to exotic Tahiti for a five-day seminar on advanced techniques and planning in building their own estates. The seminar was outstanding and was acclaimed as a benchmark in the industry.

C.P., ever his ebullient self, taught eight hours each day, later answered questions for the students, and played until the wee hours every morning.

On the fifth evening, at the conclusion of the seminar, he exuberantly ran to the beach, donned mask and fins, and dove into the surf to snorkel for two hours. The rest of the group was pleased to see him so relaxed and deservedly enjoying himself as they watched from the beach.

At sunset he returned to shore, physically spent. As he walked from the surf, he suddenly tore off his mask, gasped and dropped to the sand. Ever the practical joker, the onlookers watched, expecting him to finish the prank. When he didn't rise, they went to him and soon realized the horrible truth. He was dead.

The tragedy traumatized the group. When they recovered sufficiently, they notified his wife and father in the States, and made the sad return trip.

C.P.'s many good friends came forth to assist in the details after his death. Several of his former partners and associates became involved in the settlement of the estate. They discovered the paradox of the "cobbler who was too busy fixing others' shoes to repair his own," for C.P. had been so deeply involved in and dedicated to helping others avoid "estate shock" that at his young age he hadn't quite put his own affairs in order. The good news was that he had taught his friends so well that they did an exemplary job of quickly setting things in C.P.'s estate in the best possible order for his family's benefit.

The lesson for you is to plan your work and work your plan, particularly in building your own estate and keeping it all in the family. Do it now, as you go, and keep updating.

A good illustration of Kessler's Law and the fact that one can truly expect the unexpected is the story of little Louise. She was eight years old and very dutiful. Pleasant, obliging, and never missed saying her bedtime prayers. Her parents proudly watched and listened many evenings when Louise was preparing to retire. On one particular evening, they noted with interest that she closed her bedtime prayer differently than usual. After saying: "God bless Mommy and Daddy, Aunt Ann and Uncle Allen, Aunt Rose," she added, "and *bye bye* Uncle Ralph."

It wasn't particularly noteworthy and no mention of it was made until the next afternoon, when they received word that Uncle Ralph had been killed instantly in an industrial accident. Putting the episode aside as a coincidence, they heard Louise say her prayers for the next week in her usual manner. Then one night, she closed by saying "God bless Mommy and Daddy, Aunt Ann and Uncle Allen and bye bye Aunt Rose." The next day Mommy and Daddy were somewhat trepidatious until the suspense was broken mid-day with news of Aunt Rose's fatal heart attack. By now, the parents were quite concerned about Louise's apparent special insight, and paid close attention to her nightly vespers. Several weeks went by incident free, until one night Louise prayed: "God bless Mommy, Aunt Ann and Uncle Allen and bye bye Daddy."

Well, the next day Daddy did not want to get out of bed, to avoid any danger. He would not get into the shower, refused to shave—even with a dull razor—and certainly did not want to negotiate the stairs. He drank slowly through a straw, chewed each mouthful 100 times and swallowed carefully. He was taking no chances and avoiding all risks and exposure to accidents of any kind. By late afternoon he was feeling a little calmer, when suddenly he heard, from the kitchen, his wife's loud scream. Reflexing, he immediately started to run down the steps, but remembering the hazard, checked himself. Instead he called down to Louise—who was doing her homework in the breakfast room—to ask what happened.

Little Louise came running up the steps and reported: "The milk man just dropped dead in the kitchen."

Some things cannot be anticipated; however, good planning can provide alternatives for various circumstances and occurrences. It pays to know how to handle as many eventualities as possible. The alternatives are many.

BUY PAPER AT A DISCOUNT AND TRADE AT FACE

One fascinating aspect of real estate relates to the phenomenon of paper. By paper I mean notes, mortgages, options (as we've just seen), and various negotiable and nonnegotiable instruments.

What's fascinating about paper is that it isn't necessarily worth what it says it's worth. In other words, the face value may or may not be equal to its real value. In the continuing option example, Barbara had a piece of paper that was worth $1,200 on its face. When she sold the paper, it was obviously worth more than that.

This works the other way, too. A mortgage note is a promise to pay a specific sum of money over a specific period of time. The note is secured by a lien on the property. But because the note says on its face that it's worth $20,000 doesn't mean it's necessarily worth $20,000 in the open market today. It's only worth $20,000 eventually, that is, by the expiration date, if all the payments are met.

A client named Lynda earns her living using the leverage she created with an investment stake of $5,000. That sum may seem small, but what she's done with it is formidable.

Looking in the newspaper under "Money Wanted," she found a person who had a $10,000 mortgage note, second in line behind a large first mortgage, secured by a questionable piece of property. She called the note holder and offered to buy the paper at a 50% discount, for $5,000. When the holder balked, she pointed out that the note was second in line and that the property's value might not be able to cover both mortgages in case of default and foreclosure. Desiring the immediate cash, the holder took the $5,000 and gave Lynda the note.

At that point Lynda made an offer on a house, stipulating that the $10,000 down payment would come in the form of a note secured by a mortgage that she had just acquired. The homeowner didn't like the idea. Lynda had to convince him that the note, at face value, would satisfy his needs.

First, the question of value. After having paid $5,000 for the mortgage, Lynda could hardly argue convincingly that it was worth $10,000. Clearly, it wasn't.

"I'm not saying this note and mortgage is worth $10,000 cash," Lynda explained to the homeowner. "But we're not talking about cash, we're talking about what it's worth to you, in your situation, considering all the circumstances. If you seriously question whether the property securing this mortgage can cover its face value, I'll personally guarantee the note up to $5,000. This will protect you as far as value is concerned."

The homeowner was swayed by this guarantee, but not convinced.

"In fact," she went on, "you would be better off getting what is in effect an installment down payment because it will give you income, principal, and interest for years, rather than a $10,000 lump sum. Also, even though the value of the property may be marginal, the people who occupy it are reliable and have been paying regularly for years. We have no reason to believe they will default."

In the end, Lynda's arguments were convincing and the homeowner accepted the full face value of the note as a down payment. Again, this did not happen because the paper was then worth $10,000 in cash. But under the circumstances, with the homeowner not needing immediate cash, with the prospect of a larger overall payment in time (including the interest), and with the stability of the people making the payments, the $10,000 value could be justified to that seller. It was justified, not by cash, but by increasing the other people benefits.

Lynda received additional people benefits herself. She was able to switch from a declining debt investment (the paper) to an appreciating equity investment (the house), and later sold the house at a profit, using the proceeds to buy another house. She used the amount left over to buy more paper at a discount and started the cycle again.

If you try this, be prepared to pay tax on the paper profit you gain from conveying the mortgage to the seller. In Lynda's case, she had to pay short-term capital gains tax on $5,000 profit—the difference between the $5,000 she paid for the note and the $10,000 value she received from it when it was accepted at face. Considering the profit she turned on this investment, the tax was a small price for Lynda to pay.

ASSIGN THE PAYMENTS

If you're in a tax bracket that makes Lynda's type of transaction unattractive, there's a way out for you. Use the mortgage as a down payment, as Lynda did, but deposit the mortgage into an escrow and assign the payments to the seller. Under this arrangement, when a payment is made on the mortgage, it goes to the escrow company that is holding the mortgage. The escrow company then forwards the payment to the seller.

As far as the seller is concerned, the result is the same—he receives an installment down payment just as in the example above. For your tax purposes, the result is dramatically different. Instead of paying tax on the full $5,000 at short-term capital gains rates the way Lynda did, you would only pay tax on the payments as they come in over the years. In actual dollars, the result is ultimately similar; it's the one-time impact that is different.

Once the mortgage is paid off in full, your obligation to your seller is finished and your down payment is complete.

USING PAPER PARTNERSHIPS

For many years, people have been forming investment clubs and investing in the stock market as a group. The advantages of this practice are numerous. When several people each pool a small amount of cash, they wind up with a large amount of cash collectively. When it's invested all at one time, the investors can receive quantity discounts and save a great deal of money in brokerage commissions.

These types of clubs often have difficulty dealing in real estate because, unlike a stock portfolio, real estate must be physically managed, and squabbles arise among the members as to who will be responsible for what. "That's not my job" is a familiar complaint.

The story about four people named Everybody, Somebody, Anybody, and Nobody explains it best. There was an important job to be done and

Everybody was sure that Somebody would do it. Anybody could have done it, but Nobody did it. Somebody got angry about that, because it was Everybody's job. Everybody thought Anybody could do it, but Nobody realized that Everybody wouldn't do it. It ended up that Everybody blamed Somebody when Nobody did what Anybody could have.

One solution is to hire a professional manager. Not all properties, however, have the cash flow to support that expense.

One group I advised has solved this problem by pooling their resources to buy paper instead of property. They call themselves Consolidated Mortgages. They shop the markets for mortgages, trust deeds, and other forms of indebtedness on real estate. Sometimes their combined buying power enables them to participate in investments no single person could dream of doing alone.

One of their very successful ventures was their first, involving a restaurant that was on the verge of collapse. The large, sumptuously appointed restaurant was located near a major airport. The decor and location were great, but the food and overall management were terrible. The restaurant owners wanted out but couldn't find any buyers. Finally, a brilliant young entrepreneur/chef made them an offer. The only problem with the offer was that the down payment was small and the owners would have to accept a 30-year, $100,000 mortgage at a low 10% interest rate from the young dynamo. With no other buyers in sight and disheartened at the prospect of closing down without a sale, the restaurant owners accepted the offer. Consequently they had to carry back a large mortgage of $100,000 that would be paid off over a long period at 10% interest.

The sellers had faith in the dynamic new manager but didn't want to wait 30 years for their $100,000. They wanted cash to use somewhere else. So they offered the mortgage for sale.

Consolidated Mortgages offered them $40,000 cash for the mortgage. It was a drastic discount and the mortgage holders cringed at the huge paper loss they were taking. Still, it was cash. And it was on the table then, not in 30 years.

Then Consolidated did the ultimate in leveraging. The members used their combined borrowing power to borrow the entire $40,000 from a bank at high interest. The $40,000 was a signature loan, borrowed with no collateral other than their pooled credit ratings.

The arrangement worked because the discount was so deep that the payments on the $100,000 restaurant mortgage more than covered the payments on the $40,000 signature loan. The partners had positive cash flow without investing a dime, the restaurant sellers had cash to use elsewhere, and the dynamic new restaurant owner had a great business opportunity at extremely favorable rates.

Everyone wins again. Sound familiar? Why do they win? Because when you provide people benefits to everyone, everyone has to win.

PARENT TO CHILD

One of the difficult parts of estate planning is arranging for the next generation to benefit with minimum tax erosion and at the same time having them participate in order to understand the value of the estate.

This technique was devised to establish a half-ownership for the parent and a half-ownership for the child. It distributes the tax benefits wisely to use the advantages the tax regulations provide.

John Sr. and John Jr. acquire a $200,000 property for $20,000 down with a $180,000 mortgage. Each has a 50 percent interest and agrees to share the monthly payments. In a constant-payment amortizing mortgage, the interest portion of the mortgage payments is almost the whole payment in the early years, while the payment against principal is very small. John Sr. and John Jr. agree that John Sr. will pay the interest part of each payment and John Jr. will pay the principal portion. This way, in the early years the largest part of the payment is made by the father, and it is interest that is deductible from his income tax, which is more than John Jr's. It is very likely that he will welcome the deduction. The smaller part of each payment, the principal in these years, is contributed by the son.

As time passes and the mortgage matures, the interest portion of the debt payment decreases as the portion applied to principal increases. The father pays less each month as the son pays more—a growing process as the father's income winds down to retirement as the son's cranks up with experience and tenure.

The significant advantages are that the father receives the larger tax benefits in the early years, commensurate with his larger income and tax liability. His financial strength is what the lender will look to for satisfaction, while the son has a vested interest and responsibility. In future years, the balance is equalized as the son assumes larger payments when he is financially better suited to handle them.

TRIPLE-HEADER

Before the tax laws limited the possibilities, the technique of generation-skipping was a practical way of passing on assets with minimum tax consequences.

My method is to provide similar benefits utilizing three of the creative techniques available under current laws.

Mother and father sell their real estate holdings to son and daughter. They take no money down with an unsecured personal note from son and daughter, who make payments due on the note out of the income from the property they have just acquired.

The property is unencumbered (no loans against it of record) so it is then mortgaged, providing tax-free money for son and daughter to use to acquire more income-producing property.

Mother and father will the unsecured note they originally received to grandson and granddaughter, who will then receive the payments due on it.

The original property holdings that son and daughter acquired can then be exchanged up for a larger property. This "triple-header" uses three of the major tools available to us to retain a maximum amount of profit from real estate with minimum tax erosion: the installment sale, mortgage (re)financing, and nontaxable (deferred) exchanging.

And it keeps it "all in the family."

Now that you have a way, all you need is the will.

You've added these Kessler's Keys to Success:

➤ The best-laid plans

➤ What a way to go

➤ Buy paper at a discount and trade at face

➤ Assign the payments

➤ Using paper partnerships

➤ Parent to child

➤ Triple-header

The Rewards . . .

. . . from real estate investments are monumental for one who knows how to structure win/win transactions that provide people benefits.

Here is a list of additional ideas for reflection:

1. Whenever you use a blanket mortgage, make certain you include a clause that provides for release of increments of the security (evidenced by the note and mortgage) as you make payments and the debt declines. ($5,000 increments would be appropriate.) Then all the properties under the "blanket" won't be tied up until the final payment is made.

2. Always obtain a "right of first refusal to buy" (at the price being offered) on all notes and mortgages that you issue. Many times this paper is sold at a discount and, if necessary, you could refinance to buy it if you don't have an accumulation of cash at that time.

3. In acquiring a rental property with vacancies, offer the seller a prepaid lease on the vacancies as the down payment (or part of it). That will compensate for that loss of income.

4. Don't ever give up (pay off) low-interest mortgages. Either walk the mortgage, wrap (use a wrap-around mortgage), or balance differences with new mortgages on the other side of the new transaction to keep the old mortgage in effect with its low interest rates.

5. In exchanging (Chapter 15), always consider an *overtrade*. Exchange more value than you are getting and take back a mortgage to: (1) have paper to trade, hypothecate, or sell, (2) create an income stream from the paper, and (3) acquire an easy terms loan (on the equity you are overtrading).

6. Always *take* mortgages "subject to" and *give* them with an "assume and agree to pay" clause (Chapter 4).

7. Allocate some part of the income from a new acquisition to a down payment (or series of payments for a down payment) to acquire another property.

Real estate's value is only significant or determinable as it satisfies needs. The utilization of real property establishes its character. Mankind's collective desire for real property establishes its value.

I have given you but a sampling of the many ways to acquire real estate with little or no cash. Throughout the rest of this book I will be giving you additional methods and techniques for funding down payments and for overall creative financing.

Whenever you are solving a problem ownership, refer to all of these ideas, techniques, and methods as a memory jogger for what can be done. Check the list of Kessler's Keys To Success at the close of each chapter. Send for the free book of Kessler's Keys To Success that is offered in the coupon on the back flap of this book jacket.

Examine each example as you would a formula or a recipe. Use what fits the need; improve, add, and change what you choose.

In Part Four of this book we will consider different aspects of transactions that are available to those of you who already own property. For those getting started, exchanging provides many opportunities without the use of cash. You will learn of the outstanding opportunities to build wealth by exchanging property. The exercise of creativity by Creative Real Estaters in exchanging really pays huge dividends in dollars and increased equities without the erosion of taxes.

. . . a reward added makes the pleasure twice as great.

—Euripides

PART IV

Exchange and Prosper

> . . . *the elementary basis of our economy is that* . . . *there can be no lasting profit in the exchange unless the exchange is profitable to both.*

—Walter Lippmann

14

Tax-Free Profits

There is nothing sinister in so arranging one's affairs as to keep taxes as low as possible.

—Judge Learned Hand

KEEP IT ALL

You are about to venture into one of the most profitable, complicated, and downright delightful aspects of real estate investment—exchanging. Thanks to a real bonanza for real estate investors in the tax laws, you can build your wealth in real estate without paying taxes on your profits.

Though we'll be referring to this concept as the *tax-free exchange*, I must point out that the process of exchanging is not strictly tax-free. There are, in fact, relatively few tax-free investments in the legal sense. Nearly all investments that have tax advantages merely postpone or modify the payment of taxes, rather than allowing you to avoid paying taxes altogether; and they are actually tax-*deferred*. Exchanging is in this category; however, as you will see, the limits are such that real estate exchanging is *effectively* tax-free.

There is a great deal of confusion about these distinctions, so let's look at the differences.

State and local governments borrow money for roads, hospitals, water mains, bridges, and similar projects. Much of the money for these projects comes from individual investors, who are issued the type of bonds collectively called *municipals*. When a state or local government wants to spend money on a project, it offers these municipal bonds to the investing public and promises to pay back the borrowed amount plus interest from the taxes it collects from its citizens. Because of a provision in the United States Constitution that limits the power of the federal government over the states, the interest on this type of bonds is exempt from federal taxation.

Thus, if you were to buy a municipal bond, as many wealthy people in high tax brackets do, you could collect the interest and not even have to whisper to the IRS about it. This is not tax evasion. It is a perfectly proper and legal form of tax avoidance. The income from interest on municipal bonds is tax-free.

However, if you were to buy a municipal bond for $5,000 and sell it later for $5,500, you would have realized a profit, or capital gain, of $500. This profit is subject to a capital gains tax. It is taxable.

Between the two extremes of tax-free and taxable is a designation called *tax-deferred*. There are many types of investments that fall into the tax-deferred category. When you buy an annuity and let the interest on it accumulate, you don't pay tax on that interest until you actually collect it. Similarly, the income earned in your pension plan is not taxed until you start collecting your pension. In these two cases, you don't avoid paying tax completely, you just put it off for awhile. Thus the term tax-deferred.

The general rule in reporting income requires the reporting of gain or loss on the sale of property. This means that when you sell property, you have to report the gain or loss on it for the year in which the sale occurred. That's the general rule. But Section 1031 of the Internal Revenue Code* provides an exception. It says that no gain or loss is recognized "if property held for productive use in trade or business or for investment is exchanged solely for property of a like kind to be held either for productive use in trade or business or for investment."

Translated, this means that if you have a gain or profit from disposing of a piece of property and instead of taking that gain by means of a sale you exchange that property for a like piece of property worth the same amount of money or more, you don't have to pay tax on the gain at the time of the exchange. The payment of tax is put off or deferred until you actually receive the gain. A tax may have to be paid eventually, but not at the moment of the exchange, nor in the tax year the exchange was made, nor for many years in the future, or even during your lifetime providing the transaction was properly structured as an exchange that complies with the provisions of Section 1031. *The profits from a Section 1031 exchange are tax-deferred until you sell or die.*

Now you know the legal distinction between tax-free and tax-deferred. In this book we do not use these terms in their precise legal context, but more loosely, allowing the term tax-free exchange to represent tax-deferred exchanges. This is simply because it's convenient and more accurately describes the situation at the time of the transaction. There is no limit to the length of time you are permitted to defer taxes under Section 1031 other than until you sell or die, nor is there any limit to the number of tax-deferred exchanges you can make. Therefore, the profits from your Section 1031 transactions can effectively be tax-free.

Although the tax laws are riddled with seemingly illogical regulations, occasionally they contain a principle that makes good sense to us. One of these is the principle of *realized gains*. In plain English, it means that if you

---

* Printed in its entirety as Appendix A, along with regulations for applying it as Appendix B.

make some money but can't put your hands on it to use as you choose, you haven't actually realized that gain. Therefore, it stands to reason that you shouldn't have to pay tax on the gain. You pay tax on it when you realize or actually have the unrestricted use of the gain.

Compared to other forms of investment, real estate provides unique benefits. If you buy a municipal bond for $5,000 and instead of selling it for $5,500 you traded it for another municipal bond worth $5,500, the IRS would not let you defer the tax on your $500 gain. The second bond is not of like kind, according to their definition. (We needn't go into their reasoning for this. It's one of those tax interpretations that doesn't seem to make much sense.) The trade would be regarded as a sale of the first bond and purchase of the second. In such a case, you would be considered to have had unrestricted control of the $5,500, even if for an instant, and thus have a realized gain on the first bond, resulting in the requirement for you to pay tax on gain.

Real estate is different. If as an investment you buy a vacant lot for $10,000, hold it until it appreciates in value to $100,000, and then exchange it for a high-rise (eleventh floor) rental condominium worth $100,000, you would not have to pay tax on the $90,000 gain at the time of the exchange. The two pieces of property are considered to be of like kind as long as they are both acquired for the same use—in this case, investment. It doesn't matter that the high-rise doesn't resemble the vacant lot and it doesn't matter that the high-rise is income-producing while the vacant lot is not. What matters is that they are both held for the same reason: investment.

If, however, you sell the vacant lot for $100,000 and buy the high-rise ten seconds later for $100,000, the IRS has ruled that you would have had unrestricted use—even if only for ten seconds—of the profit on your lot. Thus, you have *realized* a gain. You'd have to pay capital gains tax on $90,000. No matter what your tax bracket, this would be a lot of money to part with. The fact that you may not have put your hands on the money in the transaction doesn't matter. What matters for tax purposes is that you could have.

When you make an exchange, your money is working within the transaction the whole time. In the exchange above, the vacant lot is never really sold with cash delivered to you, so you can't put your hands on the profits. Thanks to the provisions of Section 1031, the IRS wouldn't look to you for any taxes at that time because you haven't realized the gain.

You must also learn the tax implications of losses in your real estate transactions. I hope you won't have many, but when you do, you should be prepared to handle them so that they benefit you most.

Essentially, whatever applies to gains also applies to losses as far as reporting to the IRS is concerned. If you make a "tax-free" exchange—in accordance with Section 1031—that includes a gain, you don't have to *include* that gain in your gross income for the taxable year. The gain is deferred. That is the good news. The bad news is that if you do such an exchange that involves a loss you can't *deduct* that loss from your gross income for the taxable year, either. You don't *realize* the gain or the loss. You instead carry forward the adjusted basis.

Let's say for example that you buy an ocean-front lot in Florida for $100,000 with the idea of building an income-producing apartment tower on it. A few months later a storm erodes a portion of the land, making it unfit to build the apartment tower on. The damage lowers the value of your lot to $80,000. At that price, the owner of the adjoining property would like to acquire it and offers you a duplex in Houston in exchange. Reluctantly but wisely you accept. Remember, don't look back.

Even though you're out $20,000, you can't deduct the loss on that year's tax return. Instead you just carry forward $80,000 as if it were the price for which you sold the land. Sometime later, you use this $80,000 adjusted basis as the cost of the duplex to figure the tax consequences when you sell the duplex. That's too bad, but it's one of the rules of the game.

The rules of the tax game aren't always against you. In fact, as an investor you stand to benefit from what some citizens call tax loopholes. These loopholes refer to tax laws that are designed to stimulate investment, and anyone like yourself who puts money at risk with a reasonable expectation of profit should not feel guilty about taking advantage of these laws for tax breaks. The entrepreneurial spirit that includes the willingness to take a risk is what built this country into such a powerful economic force in so short a time. To encourage you to continue to keep your money working in the real estate marketplace, Congress rewards you with favorable investment laws.

The chief stimulus for this entrepreneurial spirit is the possibility for profit. When a tax break gives additional stimulus to this spirit it shouldn't be condemned; it should be encouraged and used.

A wise old man invented a better bucket seat—reputedly the first of its type. When a multinational conglomerate offered him a large amount of cash for his business, he asked them to exchange one of their thriving plantation businesses in Hawaii instead. He always wanted to retire in Hawaii, and this is how he did it.

The plantation had a charming, vintage plantation manor situated just inside the main gate on a beautifully landscaped 10-acre plot. The growing fields, dormitories and processing plant were all on a downwind 250 acres, with separate driveways from the manor house. He leased the business operation back to the conglomerate for 30 years with a deduction for the monthly lease payments for his use of the manor house.

Thus, instead of taking a large sum of taxable cash for his business, he exchanged tax-free.

He has been happily retired in Hawaii for many years and says, "It isn't how much money you make that counts, it's how much of it you get to keep."

SHELTER ALL YOUR INCOME

Even though you may be successful in avoiding income tax or in reducing your income tax liability, the amount of what I call "layered" taxes you continue to pay for Social Security, unemployment, disability, sales taxes, gasoline taxes, utility taxes, improvement taxes, and school taxes (and this list is by no means complete) amounts to at least 15% of your income!

The first U. S. income tax, enacted in 1862 and repealed in 1872, was used by President Lincoln to finance the Civil War. In 1914, a 10% income tax was put into effect, with a surtax ranging from 1% for earnings from $20,000 to $50,000 up to 6% for earnings over $500,000. In 1919, the maximum tax rate was 77%.

Our country was founded by a group of people who revolted against much less "taxation without representation" than the average working person endures today. Since an income in the $50,000 to $55,000 range (an income level reported by the majority of two-income families today) falls in a federal income tax bracket that, together with state income taxes and "layered" taxes, amounts to as much as 50%, tax shelter becomes a concern for more people than ever before. There was a time when only the rich had to seek tax shelter, but that was before inflation forced ordinary wage earners into higher tax brackets.

Seminars, newsletters, and books that give so-called tax shelter advice are sold all over the nation. Billions of dollars of hard-earned money are wasted each year on tax-umbrella investments purporting to take advantage of legal loopholes. Conniving investors secretly transfer millions of dollars to places touted as tax havens and spend millions more to establish shaky foreign trusts and corporations.

They all overlook or are ignorant of the significant value of real estate as the most valid tax shelter. By congressional exemption, real estate remains the one investment that provides tax deduction benefits on non-recourse loans. This is the most important advantage one can have in getting maximum, safe shelter. In investments other than real estate you cannot deduct more than your investment plus the debt you are personally obligated to repay. With the special real estate tax break using non-recourse financing (where you do not have to repay personally if the project fails), you have a tax-deduction base of the investment you made plus the entire amount of the loan. For example, you invest $10,000 in cash and finance $60,000 of the purchase. Your tax deduction benefits are based on a total of $70,000, even though with a non-recourse loan you would have no personal liability for repayment of the $60,000 you borrowed should things turn sour.

With the expectation that mortgage rates will remain in the high-single-digit to low-double-digit percent range for the foreseeable future, and that property prices will increase and inflation escalate, real estate will continue to be the ideal tax shelter. Using creative financing with no money down, there simply is minimal risk. And the basic test of any investment is the security or risk of return of your investment. With a no-money-down, comparatively risk-free investment in income-producing real estate, taxable income can be effectively and safely sheltered. It's a sure way to move from job-holder to entrepreneur and to put inflation to work for you instead of against you.

Some of the advantages to keep in mind when evaluating real estate investment tax shelter are:

1. *Depreciation.* Each dollar of ordinary depreciation offsets as much as two dollars of income. This is only a bookkeeping transaction, and you could actually receive and spend the offset dollar. Also, the depreciation may exceed the taxable income, providing you with an additional tax loss that can be used to eliminate taxes on income from other real estate.

2. *Mortgage interest.* Using large amounts of borrowed money (high leverage) provides large interest deductions. Mortgage payments generally consist largely of interest in the early years, providing maximum benefits for shelter.

3. *Expenses.* Operating expenses are deductible and can offset rental income.

Some of the risks to consider are:

1. *Property type.* Existing buildings are considered least risky. Newly constructed buildings would be next. Government subsidized housing enterprises could be the highest in risk.

2. *Tax vulnerability.* While the risk is always present that Congress may change the rules, the closer you stay to what has been acceptable, the safer the consequences. Although an existing IRS ruling doesn't guarantee there will be no subsequent change and disallowance, it would certainly be more prudent to stay within accepted practices, and if possible to obtain an advance ruling from the IRS on anything innovative.

3. *Leverage.* Risk is increased with leverage, the use of other people's money. Lenders can foreclose if payments aren't met. Payments should be realistically structured in keeping with the income

stream, and debt should be non-recourse, with no deficiency liability (see Chapter 4—*deficiency judgment*).

The recession and the dramatic decline in national output in recent years have brought about a decrease in construction of new buildings. For solid growth and good shelter, I see moderate sized apartment buildings as the best investment, followed by rental condominiums and moderate sized specialty malls (children's, sports, electronics, *etc.*)

As a buying strategy I would recommend investing in two or more smaller investment shelters rather than putting all the eggs in one basket. As in any investing strategy, diversification and product mix is well advised in real estate. Spread the money among different situations, locations, and types of property.

Finally, bear in mind that it is no longer true that "a penny saved is a penny earned." With more people than ever in the 50% bracket (including state and "layered" taxes), a penny saved is two pennies earned—a 200% return for a good tax shelter. Therefore, every person should avoid, reduce, or defer taxes. That's what Creative Real Estate is all about: using safe, innovative, and practical methods to provide those people benefits.

Taxes could be worse; suppose some of us had to pay on what we *think* we're worth!

A.D. KESSLER'S SEVEN-POINT TAX COURSE

When you are exchanging or tax-sheltering your income and profits, you are engaging in tax avoidance. This is not to be confused with tax evasion. Tax avoidance is legal, moral, ethical, and from your standpoint, desirable. Tax evasion, on the other hand, is a crime. Tax avoidance makes use of the law to postpone paying taxes or to avoid paying them at all. Tax evasion is a violation of the law in which a person does not pay taxes that are legally due.

Although Congress has given us ample opportunities to avoid taxes, the IRS takes a dim view of tax avoidance and tries to limit it as much as possible. They are, after all, in the business of collecting taxes. So, if you're going to exchange, sooner or later you'll have to be ready to deal with the IRS. When that happens, remember:

1. No matter what you think, the IRS is the ultimate authority on taxes.

2. If you are ever in a situation that is even slightly out of the ordinary from a tax standpoint, the IRS will interpret it as negatively as possible in terms of your tax liability no matter how logical, correct, or legal you believe your arguments to be.

3. The IRS makes all the rules in the game.
4. Don't try test cases.
5. Keep your visibility as low as possible.
6. Use methods that have worked in the past.
7. Employ the services of an expert who has an excellent track record in handling tax matters.

We have seen that in real estate, the best transaction is the win/win transaction. This is true in politics and in our economy as a whole. When one person can take advantage of favorable tax treatment to increase his or her wealth, and in the process provide shelter, jobs, and increased wealth for other people, that's the essence of a system that works for everybody. That's win/win!

BE TAX WISE

Why do you suppose Congress was so benevolent in writing the tax laws on real estate exchanging? Because exchanging real estate is good for the economy. We have already seen how real estate forms the basis of a sound economy by fulfilling all four of people's most basic needs: food, water, clothing and shelter. Investment capital only stimulates the economy when it's circulating. As long as it's not more advantageous and profitable to withdraw your money or, as they say, to take your profit and run, you are encouraged to leave it invested in the economy, where it is working, appreciating, and contributing to the prosperity of this great nation. To encourage you to keep your money out there working in real estate, Congress has thoughtfully given you a tax break. You would be wise to take advantage of it.

There are three kinds of people. Those who make things happen, those who watch things happen and those who don't know anything happened. Which kind are you?

Your Kessler's Keys to Success have expanded with:

☞ Keep it all

☞ Shelter all your income

☞ A. D. Kessler's seven-point tax course

☞ Be tax wise

Author's Note: Congress continually considers tax reforms that may change the percentages discussed in this chapter.

15

Who, What, Why, How . . .
and Where

It is not the possessions, but the desires of mankind which require to be equalized.

—Aristotle

WHO

This book will not make you an exchangor. No book, seminar, or mentor can make you an exchangor. Don't lose hope, though. You *can* become an exchangor. I can motivate and inspire—*you* have to activate and perspire! Earlier in this book I told you we had a contract, you and I. I will supply the information, you have to supply the effort. And commitment. You'll then have the wherewithal to become wealthy rapidly.

I hope you will agree I've kept my contract so far, and I intend to continue to . . . giving you all the *hows*. I'm giving you information on things that happened to me—how I handled them—things that happened to people around me, how they handled them. Case studies, incidents, stories, solutions, formulas, methods, techniques—all the history you need so as not to repeat the mistakes. Remember the old adage, "Those who don't study history are doomed to repeat it."

The purpose of the case studies, the formulas, the stories and the rest is to show you what has been done. What has been done once, certainly can be done again, and improved on. That's where you come in. Pick up from there. See what has been done and can be done, let your mind soar and improve on it. Remember the creative visualization we did in Chapter 8? Get into the mood, then let your mind soar when you read these case histories. See how much better you could have done or could do, and in the future will do. By all means, read everything you can on the subjects you are interested in, go to every seminar you can afford on the subjects you are interested in; get there somehow. Read, and go, and do with the knowledge that with all you hear, all you see, and all you're told it's still up to *you* to take action to make it happen. Ideas don't work unless you do.

Do you want to be successful in Creative Real Estate? Do you have to be successful in Creative Real Estate? Hearing all the fine stories about those who have done it before and are doing it today will not put any money in your pocket nor give you one more ounce of satisfaction until you do it for yourself. That is the purpose of this book, to show you that you can do it for yourself; to give you all the reasons, all the methods, all the solutions that I know of to the problems that people constantly confront, and show you how much fun, how much reward there is in solving those problems.

In this chapter I am going to give you a number of actual examples of exchanges and people involved in exchanges, and reasons for that exchange in each instance. The purpose is again to show you how it can be done, why it can be done, where and when it can be done. You're not going to find the same people and go out and exactly replicate the examples. What I did a week ago, two weeks ago, ten years ago isn't going to make a deal for you today. Or is it? It is if you can internalize the information and apply it. I mean take from the example the points basic and important to any transaction: peoples' motivations, benefits for the people, situations, problems that have to be solved, methods of solving the problems. Numbers are relatively insignificant. I made that point several times throughout this book. You can work a transaction whether it's for a thousand dollars or a million dollars or more. Believe me, they are similar with one exception: the big ones are usually easier. People dealing in those numbers usually have more experience and don't sweat the little things. They have more confidence in making decisions. Whether you deal in small numbers or large numbers, the idea is to deal. Do something. Do it now.

Rather than give you long lists of people who should exchange and reasons people should exchange and properties that should be exchanged, I think you'll get more from reading case histories and examples together with explanations of what happened.

Who Should Exchange?

Virtually anyone now owning, wanting to own, or waiting to sell real estate should closely examine the many benefits exchanging can provide. While most people dealing in real estate are aware there may be some tax benefits in exchanging, comparatively few realize that tax deferment is only one of dozens of advantages to be had.

Personal objectives can be fulfilled through exchanging because the primary benefit of exchanging is solving problems for people. That being the case, let's look at some of the people problems that would be solved through exchanging. The common chord in all of these problems is money. The root cause(s) of the money problem to the owner could be any one or several of the following: the need for income, now rather than in the future, or for deferring income now and having it in the future (notice how those two needs would make an ideal exchange); relief from management responsibilities; diversification of holdings; consolidation of holdings; (these two previous owners could exchange); capital appreciation rather than income; capital appreciation rather than benefits of depreciation; more depreciation; preserving appreciated buying power; divisibility of holdings; continuous income stream (rather than selling one and then searching for another); liquidation of hard-to-sell property.

I could fill this entire chapter with additional objectives of all types of people. Exchanging works as well as it does because it solves problems for people. In fact, as long as it's honest, there can rarely be a bad exchange. A basic precept is that *no one will give up what they have unless they get something for it that they want more.* People will only exchange property they already own for property they find more desirable. Since everyone involved in an exchange winds up with something more desirable to him than whatever it was he started with, everyone comes out a winner. The key, of course, is full disclosure by all parties so that all can make informed decisions.

Always keep in mind the principle that there are no problem properties, only problem ownerships, and you will have no difficulty spotting candidates and situations for profitable exchanges. Dealing in exchanges is one of the most exciting challenges for a Creative Real Estate Practitioner. Structuring a mutually beneficial exchange is also one of the most gratifying experiences for all parties involved. There is no better asset-building technique. The participants will prosper from the benefits and be candidates for more exchanges in the future. They will recommend new prospects to the caring, competent professional who will deserve and earn handsome fees for structuring win/win transactions.

WHAT

In order to complete profitable transactions, you must also learn to identify properties with exchange potential as well as the people who are prime prospects for exchanges.

What Properties Have Exchange Potential?

1. Vacant property that has been held by one owner for a long time and is worth many times its original cost.
2. A piece of property requiring minimum management; some examples are shopping centers, leased warehouses, and vacant land.
3. Property with the principal value in the land, with little or no depreciation value allotted to improvements.
4. Investment properties with good income streams. Those that don't require management would be net-leased department stores, net-

leased industrials, and franchised service locations; those that require management and produce large cash flow would be shopping
centers, apartment houses, office buildings, hotels/motels, and
parking garages.

5.   Investment properties with high depreciation potential, like properties with a high ratio of improvement-to-land value.

6.   Investment properties with high appreciation potential such as vacant land in the path of progress, rental property in an improving
location, and strategically located property suitable for conversion
to higher profit use.

7.   Properties that have a large equity build-up, lend themselves to
refinancing and to combination transactions involving paper and
cash, vacant lots and paper, or multiple-legged transactions.

8.   Properties with low interest rates on existing mortgages, providing
fast equity build-ups and large cash flow.

This is only a sampling of the types of properties that lend themselves
to exchanging in order to improve the circumstances of ownership for the
current owner. Using this list as a pattern, you will easily find dozens more.
The key to selecting properties with potential for exchanging is to determine
whether a change of ownership through exchanging will provide the benefits
the current owner needs.

To demonstrate the win/win concept of providing people benefits to all
the parties involved in a transaction, I have prepared the Exchange Obective
Analysis chart (on the next page) which illustrates the benefits of acquisition
and disposition in each of seven different types of properties. All that has to
be done to make a successful exchange in each instance would be to match
up the people having those particular objectives that would mesh into a
win/win exchange.

This charting technique is a variation of the Benjamin Franklin method
of analyzing any given situation by drawing a T-shaped form on a blank
sheet of paper, then listing all the positives in one column and all the negatives in the other. In our chart, we might say that we list all the positives in
one column and all the other positives in the other. Win/win!

Watch Your Language

The process of exchanging real estate for real estate, or real estate for real
estate and cash, or real estate for real estate paper, or any combination, is
specifically referred to by those in the know as *exchanging*. On the other
hand, *trade* or *trading* specifically refers to accepting personal property such
as jewelry, furs, cars, or other chattels—goods in exchange for like goods, or

Exchange Objective Analysis		
Property type	**Acquisition benefits**	**Disposition benefits**
Fixer-uppers	High appreciation (on conversions) Increased cash flow Excellent tax benefits	Freedom from heavy repair costs/time Pride of ownership Improved investment quality
Residential rentals	Income Appreciation Cash flow	No tenant contract No maintenance duties
Commercial rentals (financed)	Cash flow Appreciation Tax shelter	Debt free Out of management
Investment land (free and clear)	No management Appreciation Pride of ownership	No leverage return of equity Tax benefits
Commercial rentals (free and clear)	Cash flow Appreciation Depreciation	No leverage Return of equity
Improved properties with small mortgages	Moderate cash flow Tax benefits Equity build-up Low interest rate (if old loan)	Increase rate of retusn and tax benefits Can wrap-around loan for high yield
Leased properties (minimum management)	Secure income Inflation hedge Minimum management cost	Higher rate of return Increased cash flow

goods as total payments in exchange for real estate. To recap: *real estate is exchanged; personal property is traded.*

Just as a native of San Francisco flinches when he hears his home town called "Frisco" by the outsider, the exchangor flinches when he hears a real estate exchange called a trade.

WHY

Most real estate transactions can be improved by exchanging rather than selling. In the process of exchanging, the counseling and problem-solving phases provide opportunities to examine aspects of the overall situation that never come to light in the traditional sale for cash. The concept of people benefits, inherent in exchanging, facilitates stress-free closing of transactions.

Although exchanging real estate provides many benefits in addition to tax savings, nontaxable real estate exchanging provides various opportunities for profit that are not otherwise available.

Exchanging requires specialized knowledge and effort. Because the process can be complicated, it necessarily requires the cooperation of all participants for a successful conclusion.

Lack of information often leads to fear of the difficulty of properly structuring a 1031 exchange transaction, and will deter many people from deriving the benefits of a tax-free exchange. This is an unnecessary sacrifice because the requirements of Section 1031 of the Internal Revenue Code are clearly defined, and successful tax-free exchanging requires only two ingredients: (1) the knowledge to comply with Section 1031, and (2) provision of people benefits.

A key to putting together transactions that appear to be difficult is the willingness and ability to look beyond the situation involving the property and to take practical action in innovative ways to fulfill the objectives of the people.

With proper planning, an exchange can be structured in almost any circumstance. In many cases an exchange can be the only practical way a transaction could take place. Any planned real estate sale should first be analyzed for the added benefits of an exchange.

The Inherent Benefits of Exchanging

1. You can preserve your equity by not being required to pay tax on gains. Let's look at vacant land that you bought as an investment for $10,000 and that has appreciated in value to $100,000. You're getting close to retirement and would like some income-producing property instead. Looking around, you see that there are no apartment buildings you would like for less than $150,000—a figure you just can't afford. But there are duplexes available in the $80,000 range. The trouble is, if you sell the land for $100,000 and buy a duplex for $80,000, you have a tax problem. You would have to pay capital gains tax on your $90,000 profit. Knowing of the benefits of Section 1031, you realize that an exchange might be the answer. Yet, if you exchange a $100,000 piece of land for the $80,000 duplex and $20,000 cash, you have to pay tax on the $20,000 cash. For obvious reasons, both of these alternatives are unacceptable.

There is another alternative that depends on whether the owner of the duplex has other exchangeable property. If he does and it is worth about $20,000, he could trade you two-for-one.

But if he doesn't own any other exchangeable property, what should you do? Shop around for a piece of investment property that's worth $20,000.

Suppose you do that and find a parking lot that is producing income. The owner is willing to sell for $20,000 cash. The price is right. What do you do next?

You start by getting a $20,000 loan from a bank, putting up your vacant land as collateral. You put the tax-free loan of $20,000 in your pocket, for the moment. Now, you have a $100,000 property with $20,000 owed on it, leaving you an equity in the land of $80,000. Next, you and the owner of the duplex approach the parking lot owner and make the following offer. The duplex owner will buy the parking lot for $20,000, with nothing down. He will sign a note making the entire amount due in 30 days or less. The parking lot owner agrees and the man with the duplex buys the lot. He now owns a duplex worth $80,000 with nothing owed on it and a parking lot worth $20,000 with $20,000 owed on it. Total value of both properties— $100,000. His total equity in both properties—$80,000. The duplex owner now exchanges these two properties for your vacant land worth $100,000 with $20,000 owing on it. Equities balance at $80,000 each; loans balance at $20,000 each.

Once the exchange is made, all you have to do is to pay the former parking lot owner the $20,000 before the thirtieth day. That's no problem because, if you remember, you have $20,000 from the loan on your land in your pocket.

Graphically, it looks like the diagram on the next page.

However, a practical variation to this transaction might involve offering the parking lot owner something other than cash in 30 days. An installment sale wouldn't change the nature of the transaction and wouldn't require you to part with your cash right away. You could offer the parking lot owner a blanket mortgage to include the lot and your newly acquired duplex to assure him that he will get his installment payments promptly, as you receive the income from the parking lot. Be sure in these exchanges that everything is clearly spelled out in advance so that the exchange is a *bona fide* exchange, not a sale.

You have just exchanged your appreciated, non-income-producing land for two properties with income streams, and you didn't use cash or pay tax on your gain.

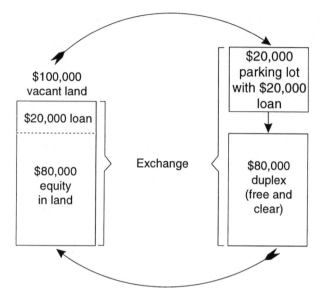

This is where the help of an experienced Creative Real Estate Professional and a tax expert will be especially beneficial. The time to consult such experts is before you close the transaction. Afterward may be too late. I have seen people put together a seemingly tax-free deal only to find out later that it wasn't. Unfortunately, the IRS won't let you go back to correct your mistakes. They'll only let you pay the tax.

Be certain, too, that you don't come out of a transaction with something extra that will destroy the nature of the transaction. This something extra is called "boot." It enters the picture in the above example in this way: if the duplex were worth only $75,000 and the owner put in $5,000 cash to make up the difference, that $5,000 difference is boot. It's not real estate, it's not property of like kind, and it's trouble for you, because that boot is taxable as ordinary income.

2. Suppose you own an old building against which no bank will lend money. It is in a special-purpose neighborhood—a garment manufacturing district—and can be easily sold to manufacturers within the district who are expanding. With a sale you would incur a very substantial tax liability. So find a newer building out of the district that is mortgageable, have the garment manufacturer who wants your building buy the newer one and exchange it, tax-free, for yours. You refinance the new building after the exchange to get cash out, tax-free. Without the exchange, your only access to cash might have been to sell the older building and pay tax on the gains.

3. You have another property valued at $100,000, which consists of a building worth $60,000 and land worth $40,000. If you exchange it for a $100,000 property consisting of land worth $10,000 and a building worth $90,000, you can take a total of $30,000 additional depreciation for more tax shelter. Land is not depreciable, only the buildings on it.

4. When you acquire property that qualifies for depreciation (improved property does, vacant—raw—land does not), you start taking that depreciation based on the value of the improvements (not the land). If you acquire a property worth $100,000 with a building worth $80,000 on a lot worth $20,000, you would start with $80,000 as your depreciable basis. If you took $2,540 depreciation each year (the 1986 Tax Act establishes 31.5 years as the "cost recovery period" for non-residential property), at the end of one year your remaining depreciable basis would be $77,460; at the end of two years, your remaining basis would be $74,920; and so on. At the end of 31.5 years, your remaining depreciable basis would be zero.

For example, suppose you bought a $100,000 property consisting of an $80,000 building and $20,000 lot and depreciated it at $2,540 per year for 10 years until your remaining depreciable basis was $54,600. Meanwhile, the property has been appreciating in value and is now worth $200,000.

A $2,540 per year depreciation on a $200,000 property doesn't provide a very substantial tax shelter, especially considering that the income from the property has probably doubled in the last 10 years. You would like to own another piece of property worth $200,000 or more to begin depreciating all over again with the new, higher value as your depreciable basis. If the new property were depreciable over 31.5 years and the improvements were worth $160,000, your annual tax write-off for depreciation would be $5,079 ($160,000 divided by 31.5 years), which is much better. If you find such a property, you could buy it for cash or you could acquire it through an exchange. You have to be careful, though, because the tax law requires you to carry forward your old, remaining depreciable basis. The only way to acquire an increase in your depreciable basis when exchanging is to move into a property with a larger loan on it than the property you are exchanging, because the tax law permits you to add the increased mortgage amount to your old, remaining depreciable basis.

For example, if your property is now worth $200,000, has no loans on it, and has a remaining depreciable basis of $54,600, you could exchange it for a $400,000 property with a $200,000 loan against it. Your new increased depreciable basis would be $254,600 (your $54,600 remaining depreciable basis carried forward from the old property plus the $200,000 loan on the newly acquired property.)

5. If it's increased cash flow you want, you can exchange a building with a high mortgage on it for one with a smaller mortgage at a lower interest rate. Depending on the value of the equities exchanged, this might have a tax consequence. Check with a tax advisor before committing yourself.

Another method of acquiring increased cash flow without the tax consequence is to exchange for a property with the same size mortgage but a smaller mortgage payment. This can be found in mortgages that have: (a) a lower interest rate, (b) a longer amortization term, (c) the same rate and term with a balloon payment at some future date, or (d) a shared appreciation loan that gives you a rate of interest approximately one-third below the current rate in return for one-third of the profit from appreciation going to the lender when you sell.

The following figures show how these would look:

a. $80,000 at 12% for 20 years would call for approximately $880 per month. The same $80,000 at 8% for 20 years would only call for $669 per month.

b. While $80,000 at 12% for 20 years demands a monthly $880, the same amount at the same rate of interest for 40 years demands only $806.

c. Again, the principal and interest payment for $80,000 at 12% for 20 years requires $880 per month. The same terms for interest alone requires only $800 per month. The principal can be paid in a lump sum (or balloon payment) after an agreed-upon number of years have elapsed.

d. The same $80,000 at 9% for 20 years would only require a payment of $720 per month.

6. Sometimes taxes make a transaction virtually impossible. For instance, if a vacant lot you paid $10,000 for is now worth $100,000, and you want to buy property requiring $100,000 cash down, selling the lot would kill any possibility of using the proceeds for the new transaction. The reason: after paying taxes, you would not have $100,000 cash. Taxes would take $30,000 of it or more. Instead, you should make the land a part of a multiple-legged exchange, with one of the other legs supplying the cash so that you would be able to use your full $100,000 worth of value to meet the down payment requirement. With a multi-legged exchange, the transaction would work.

7. If you want to cut down on property management problems, you can exchange your headache property for property that is management-free or can be managed easily by professionals. You would not necessarily be doing anyone a disservice by letting him take over your headache property. Many people will gladly assume increased management problems in return for bigger cash flow or other benefits. Remember, there are really no problem properties, only problem ownerships. What's a problem for you may be an exciting challenge for someone else.

8. If you're in business and want to relocate, instead of selling you can exchange your existing facilities for facilities in the new location without depleting your appreciated profit, as you would in a sale which required you to pay capital gains tax on the profit.

Additionally, you can build your assets by exchanging up—that is, for properties with more dollar value—using the appreciated value of your property without any loss for taxation. This gives you substantially increased buying power.

Whether you decide to diversify at one point in your life or consolidate at another time, you can accomplish both objectives most efficiently, and with proper planning, tax-free through exchanging.

By exchanging, you can keep all of your profits gained from appreciation and the equity build-up from the principal payments made against loans.

Since taxes are deferred until you sell or die, you can increase your assets and retain them all in your estate throughout your lifetime by continuing to exchange, avoiding tax on the appreciation.

The benefits are never-ending. The opportunities for profitable transactions using exchanges are countless and vary with the circumstances of each situation.

In essence, the points about exchanges that are illuminated by the examples can be summarized in two fundamental questions. Why pay tax if you don't have to? Why use money to buy property when real estate buys so much more?

HOW

The rules for non-taxable exchanging under Section 1031 apply to some types of property other than real estate, in certain circumstances. However, since real estate is what we are primarily concerned with here, let's look at another important example of real estate exchanging in action.

You buy a house for $30,000, live in it for three years, sell it, and immediately buy another for $50,000. Thanks to another provision of the tax law that lets you defer paying taxes on the profits from the sale of your residence, the $20,000 profit on the first house is yours to keep—for a while. You live in the $50,000 house for several years and sell it for $75,000. This time you buy a smaller house that costs only $65,000. A section of the tax laws lets you sell your residence for profit yet pay no tax, even if you don't buy a more expensive residence. Under the present laws, you can only do this once in your lifetime. So you live in the third house while it appreciates in value to $100,000. By this time you're tired of home ownership and want to move into an apartment. But now you're facing the prospect of paying taxes on $35,000 worth of capital gain on your house if you sell it. You decide that an exchange is the way to go, so you trade your $100,000 house for a $100,000 office building and once again avoid the tax, right?

Wrong. Sure, both of the properties are real estate and the price of the office building is no less than the price of the house. But the house was used as a residence and the office building is not going to be. It will be used for investment. Therefore, the properties are not of like kind and the transaction would not fall under the tax-deferred provision of Section 1031.

I bring this up to show you that exchanging can be a complicated business and you must be very careful what you do in order to comply with the provisions of Section 1031 for a tax-deferred exchange, especially in the more involved transactions.

If you're the principal or initiator of an exchange, you want something that you don't have now. The property you own is not fully meeting your needs, wants, or desires. Perhaps some other property will. When you want something another property has to offer, you're what I call a *taker*. Once you realize that you're a taker, do the following in this order.

STEPS OF THE EXCHANGE

1. Decide What You're a Taker Of. Figure out what you want. Take a pencil and a sheet of paper and write down your needs, wants, and desires. What location are you after? What kind of property? What kind of terms? What features are important to you? What are your price range, cash flow requirements, and desired depreciation? Be as creative in deciding what you want as you are in working out a transaction. Treat the whole process as if you were shopping. Make your list and decide exactly what you want before you go to the store.

2. Find a Don't Wanter. Once you've decided what you are a taker of, look around for properties that fit your requirements. The key here is finding people who own such properties but don't want them. Remember, the purpose of Creative Real Estate is to solve problems for people—to provide people benefits. In finding people who want out of what you want into, you have a chance to solve two problems, yours and theirs. You can find don't-wanters by looking in the classified ads, by putting your own ad in the "Real Estate Wanted" section, by working through a traditional real estate broker, or by working through one of the members of the more than 125 groups of Licensed Exchangors who meet weekly all across the country.*

If you can't find a don't-wanter who is holding the kind of property you want, don't give up. You might find a piece of property that can be an interim step to what you ultimately desire. Should you want to exchange an apartment building for a parking lot, you might have to first settle for a farm that you can later exchange for a parking lot. If the situation is right, it might be worth doing. Or, you might become part of a multi-legged exchange, coming out with what you want.

Don't-wanters will be even more open to exchanges when their particular circumstances of ownership are difficult. In fact, when mortgage payments are due and a property owner can't meet the payments, that don't-wanter will be open to any reasonable exchange you suggest.

3. Structure a Win/Win Transaction. The best transactions are the transactions that benefit everyone involved. If you plan to win by making other people lose, you might make a lot of money, but you'll also make enemies. You'll get sued a lot. Transactions will fall through at the last minute. The going will be slow and rough. When you finally do get what you want at someone else's expense, he probably won't rest until he takes it away from you. And you won't rest because you'll be worrying about it.

On the other hand, when you help people get what they want, they will help you get what you want. That's the win/win formula. It's not about winning through intimidation or sharp dealing or dishonesty. Those kinds of victories are short-lived and unstable at best. "Give and you shall receive."

When you provide people with what they want while getting what you want, you've got a win/win situation. This is what riches are made of. Henry Ford became rich by providing people with what they wanted—affordable cars. Edison did the same with electricity. Getty did it with oil. You can do it with real estate.

In your enthusiasm to provide people with what they want, don't neglect yourself. Win/win implies that you win, too. If you don't provide yourself with ample people benefits of your own, you'll find yourself on the short end of the transaction. Don't let this happen. Not only will you lose money, you'll lose your enthusiasm for Creative Real Estate. In fact, you won't be practicing Creative Real Estate at all, because if you were you would know that you must profit in every exchange, or there are no people benefits for you.

---

* To learn how to find these groups refer to the section in Chapter 16, "How to Find a Creative Real Estate Professional."

4. Close All Legs. When you have structured an exchange, no matter how complicated and multi-legged, close all the legs simultaneously if you can. Recent additions to the regulations provide for the use of a Qualified Intermediary in the event all legs will not close at the same time. Be certain to employ a Qualified Intermediary (see Appendix C, "Resources") to comply with all of the requirements. The law doesn't require a simultaneous close, but transactions are cleaner and easier to understand when closed out at a single meeting. Such close-outs also prevent the whole exchange from falling apart if a single leg reneges or pulls out, giving you the opportunity to restructure the transaction on the spot. You can also safeguard this opportunity by using a Qualified Intermediary.

There are several unpleasant ramifications when an exchange is not performed properly. Chief among these are tax consequences, but there are more, such as implied warranties, money damages, and other legal liabilities. Unless you have specialized training and experience, you would be well advised to employ professionals who do. A good, exchange-knowledgeable C.P.A., attorney, or Creative Real Estate Professional will be happy to advise you. Whomever you choose, be certain of his or her qualifications and be certain that the two of you are able to communicate to your complete satisfaction. Never close an exchange transaction until you are satisfied that you understand all the consequences from financial, legal, and tax perspectives.

A Typical Exchange

It is often said that a two-legged exchange has only two chances of closing: slim and none. The reason is quite simple. It requires each of the parties to need exactly what the other has. Since the odds of that occurring frequently are not the greatest, the multi-party exchange consisting of three or more legs is the most widely used. You can readily see the increased flexibility and potential of making more transactions possible under Section 1031.

A specific advantage is the fact that the multi-party exchange permits a taxpayer with a ready buyer to benefit from a tax-free exchange, while at the same time allowing a seller who doesn't want to exchange to participate in the exchange and end up with a sale. Section 1031 does not require *all* parties to the exchange to qualify for tax deferment.

The following example is a case history of one of my exchanges. The numbers have been rounded off to simplify the arithmetic, and the names have been changed to protect the privacy of the parties.

Mr. Farmer owns a farm worth $200,000, with a $100,000 mortgage. It's a profitable business, but he's tired of farming and wants to move to the city and acquire an income-producing business there. Mr. Ware owns a warehouse in the city. He paid $150,000 for it five years ago and still owes $100,000 on it, but it's now worth $250,000. Mr. Ware has retired and closed the warehouse because he doesn't want to run a business anymore. He wants effortless income. However, he likes living in the city and wouldn't dream of moving to a farm.

Mrs. Widow sold her house recently after having rented it out for three years. As part of the sale price of the house, she received a $50,000 note to secure a first mortgage—a note that the new owners are paying on regularly. After three years of city apartment dwelling, she would now love to move to an income-producing farm in the country.

Here we have the ingredients for a classic three-legged exchange.

Mr. Farmer's problem is that he wants to trade his farm for a business like the warehouse, in the city, but Mr. Ware, who owns the warehouse, doesn't want the farm. So Mr. Farmer needs someone who does want a farm and is willing to pay for it with property or paper (like a note) that produces effort-free income, which is what Mr. Ware (the warehouse owner) wants.

Mr. Farmer exchanges his $200,000 farm for Mrs. Widow's $50,000 note and her new promissory note to pay the remaining $50,000 due him as a down payment. To secure that new promissory note, Mr. Farmer takes back a second mortgage on the farm, and Mrs. Widow assumes payments and responsibility for the $100,000 first mortgage.

At this stage of the exchange, Mr. Farmer has disposed of the farm and has two pieces of paper with a face value of $100,000 (the $50,000 note on Mrs. Widow's old house and the $50,000 new note and mortgage against the farm). Mr. Farmer now uses that $100,000 worth of income-generating paper as a down payment on the warehouse. He gives Mr. Ware the $50,000 note on the farm from Mrs. Widow and assigns to him the $50,000 note and mortgage from Mrs. Widow's old house. The payments on both pieces of paper provide Mr. Ware with the effortless income he wants.

This leaves just one loose end. Since the price of the warehouse is $250,000 and Mr. Farmer has given Mr. Ware only a $100,000 down payment, $150,000 is still owed. There is a $100,000 mortgage that Farmer could assume, but he would still have to raise an additional $50,000. This would be a problem for Mr. Farmer, but Mr. Ware would have an even greater problem if he accepted the cash.

In all exchanges there must be a balancing of the equities. If Mr. Ware accepts $50,000 in cash, the equities are thrown out of balance and the $50,000 would become boot and an immediately taxable capital gain. Mr. Ware would have to pay a great deal of additional tax on that $50,000. The $100,000 in paper that Mr. Ware took from Mr. Farmer as a down payment was not like-kind property eligible for tax deferment under Section 1031, but since it filled his needs and provided the benefits he wanted, Mr. Ware was willing to accept it as a down payment for his warehouse. However, he certainly wanted to minimize the tax due on the profit he was making.

    To avoid paying that tax on the additional $50,000 due him, Mr. Ware does not accept the cash from Farmer but refinances the warehouse instead. Mr. Ware goes to a bank and gets a new mortgage against the warehouse for $150,000. He uses $100,000 of it to pay off the old mortgage and puts the remaining $50,000 in his pocket, tax free. Mr. Farmer then assumes this new $150,000 mortgage rather than the old one for only $100,000. He would much rather do this than assume the old one and have to come up with $50,000 cash.

    The above example, in diagram form, is illustrated below.

    Now, of course, Mrs. Widow does not actually give her payment to Mr. Ware, she exchanges it for the farm. At the same time Mr. Farmer gives Mrs. Widow's payment to Mr. Ware. Now, if Mrs. Widow gives her pay-

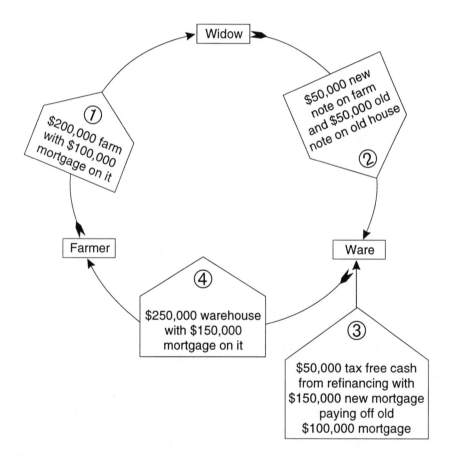

All three parties sit in a circle, each passing his/her asset (cash, warehouse, farm) to the final owner at the same time.

ment to Mr. Farmer and he gives it to Mr. Ware, it really has the same effect as Mrs. Widow giving it to Mr. Ware. They all end up with the asset they wanted: Mr. Ware with the payment, Mr. Farmer with the warehouse, and Mrs. Widow with the farm.

The actual steps taken to arrive at this simple conclusion, all parties receiving what they want are: (a) Mr. Farmer exchanges his $200,000 farm for Mrs. Widow's $50,000 new note and $50,000 old mortgage, and Mrs. Widow assumes the existing $100,000 mortgage on the farm. (b) Mr. Farmer trades Mrs. Widow's $50,000 new note and mortgage and $50,000 mortgage on her old house for $100,000 worth of equity in the warehouse. (c) Mr. Ware takes a new $150,000 mortgage on the warehouse, paying off the existing $100,000 mortgage and keeping $50,000 tax free. (d) Mr. Ware exchanges his $250,000 warehouse with the $150,000 mortgage (which Mr. Farmer assumes) for the $100,000 worth of paper tendered by Mr. Farmer in step (b). All three parties to the exchange, plus the lenders on the existing and the new mortgages and the exchange counselors in the transaction, came out with people benefits. Nine winners !

There are two important points for you to understand about these types of exchanges. First, just because there are three (or even more) legs does not mean they are unusual. On the contrary, successfully completed three-legged exchanges are much more common than two-legged ones because it's rare to find two people who each want exactly what the other has. Usually, it's easier to round out a transaction with additional property.

Second, always be sure to use actual values rather than artificially adjusting values (up or down) to fit the exchange. If, in the example above, the equity in the farm were only $90,000, it would be a mistake to value it at $100,000 merely because that's the amount of equity Mr. Ware had to be compensated for. When you play arbitrary games with the numbers, you're asking for backlash from the parties involved and from the IRS.

You now know the basics of exchanging. It is not only fun, but also can help you create "a fortune at your feet," quickly.

If you want to learn to arrange more complicated exchanges (I have been involved with some including 27 properties), take time to learn about structuring them by attending seminar workshops. For your first exchanges, I suggest that you consult an experienced Creative Real Estate Professional who will work with you step by step. It's impossible to learn all the nuances of complicated exchanges from one reading of a book or by attending a single seminar. Walking through real transactions with a seasoned professional can shorten the time and effort it takes for you to get rich. *Leverage people.*

At no time would I be so presumptuous as to say that anything I've told you about is absolutely brand-new to the world and original from me. These are concepts that have been around since commerce began, and have been used in one form or another by people in real estate as well as in other forms of transactions. All we do, time and again, is put the pieces of each puzzle together. I don't truly believe there are many original concepts in any transaction, other than the applications. What might be original about my presenting these concepts to you is the fact that I want you to know there is probably nothing original except the applications and the presentations. The applications of these concepts—when you use them—will undoubtedly be original, as were mine when I used them.

In all of these examples you should be able to clearly see that people are more important than property, and are always considered that way. People benefits always were considered first. And if you take no other message from this, let it be: if you structure all of your transactions knowing that people are more important than property and that people benefits come first, you'll have a most successful career in Creative Real Estate, whether it's for your own account or helping others. You will indeed have found how to get rich, stay rich, and enjoy being rich with Creative Real Estate in the '90s.

... AND WHERE

As I travel the world consulting, teaching seminars, lecturing, and appearing on radio and television talk shows with "Money Making Ideas" as, "The Real Estate Answer Man" and as host of "A.D. Kessler's REAL ESTATE ROUNDTABLE" television series, I am often asked, "Where is the best place to own property suitable for exchanging?" The answer is simply: "Anywhere!" That's right, anywhere.

Since real estate is only valuable as a means to an end, as a vehicle to be used to accomplish our objectives and attain our goals, what does it matter where it is situated? Location is of little consequence as long as it is a desirable piece of property to someone, an ownership that can provide people benefits. All real estate (land) has one major function: to hold the rest of the world together. Real estate has no intrinsic value. It is, by itself, worthless. However, when it serves to fulfill people's needs, wants, and desires, it's the element that provides prosperity for all.

If It Feels Good, Do It

In that context, if a beachfront property in Bali provides care-free cash flow, the security of a prudent investment, the warm glow that comes from being satisfied with your judgment, and the comfort that is associated with having done as you pleased, does it really matter if it is 8,000 miles away from you at this moment? Before you answer, consider the two aspects that affect your decision: the intellectual and the emotional. Intellectually, in your rational thought process, you may say, "A.D. is right. As long as I receive the benefits he listed, what difference does it make where the property is?"

Usually, most people have no difficulty in arriving at that conclusion intellectually. Now, examining the emotional impact, what is the situation? Some reactions might be: "I don't really want to have my money invested halfway around the world from home," or "I feel very worldly having an investment in an exotic place like Bali," or "I'll try it and see how it feels." There is no universally right emotional reaction. Be true to yourself and follow your own inclination.

CLIMB A HIGHER MOUNTAIN

I can assure you that wonderful opportunities abound to gather wealth through exchanging real estate in every part of the world. The world is your marketplace in Creative Real Estate. At our annual Creative Real Estate Exposition each spring, properties of all types, from exotic, tropical Pacific Islands to castles in Spain, have been presented for exchange by Creative Real Estaters from all corners of the globe.

An expression commonly used among experienced exchangors is "area-bound." When counseling, they will determine whether a prospective client wants to remain within a limited area, and where that area is. The most experienced and successful exchangors are not area-bound; they deal in real estate transactions anywhere that fills their needs. As a matter of fact, bearing in mind that the real property itself is only a vehicle (a form of currency), they very often don't even look at the property.

An illustration of this is the story of a reputable broker who offered a beachfront lot in an exchange as the down payment on an urban apartment building a thousand miles away. When the apartment building broker wrote to ask what the beachfront lot looked like, the beach broker sent him an envelope filled with sand.

For success in exchanging, education is important, experience is important, and skill is important. But most important are the qualities of the individual exchangor. Education, experience, and skill are significant. Honor, credibility, and good faith are *critical* to success. Without them, there will be no transactions at all, because the profession polices itself in order to maintain the integrity of the Exchange Marketplace. Anyone who embroiders the truth, overstates the positives, and understates the negatives isn't welcome for long. Few, if any, will do business with such an individual.

The ultimate compliment in Creative Real Estate's Exchange Marketplace is: "I'd go to escrow with her/him anytime." The "kiss of death" is: "I wouldn't go to escrow with him/her under any conditions." When sufficient trust and credibility is established, it becomes easy to exchange property without having to inspect it. The rationale is: "We don't physically look at all the dollars in the bank in our account, do we?" or "When we buy stock, do we go to inspect the company's factories?" Of course, this good faith dealing can only be done when you have established mutual confidence and credibility with your counterpart exchangors in other parts of the world and know they are functioning under the same set of standards as you, such as: (1) leave something for the other fellow, (2) make full disclosure, and (3) let there be no surprises.

When I founded INTEREX, the International Exchangors Association, and established the professional designation of Certified Exchangor, the Code of Ethics and Standards of Fair Practice helped to standardize and professionalize the industry world-wide, with active members successfully exchanging properties from Nigeria to New Zealand and San Francisco to the Swiss Alps.

You too can climb a higher mountain or span a wider sea, if that is your desire and if it fulfills your wants, and, most of all, your needs.

FROM SEA TO SHINING SEA

For those of you who are already experienced in exchanging, as well as for those of you who are now intrigued by it, I have included a bonus.

My friend Chester W. "Chet" Allen, SEC, CCIM, is a graduate of Stanford University. He is skilled in economics, in building and developing, and in Creative Real Estate. He has been a provider of people benefits, a skilled exchangor, and above all a gentleman and caring human being. He taught seminars under the auspices of my Professional Educational Foundation, and it was always a pleasure to work with him. His seminar, "Developing, Syndicating and Big Money Brokerage," was one that nobody in the business could afford to miss, and his "Analyzing Investment Properties," as well as "The Secrets of Successful Exchanging" seminars have been in demand nationwide. The articles he has written for *Creative Real Estate Magazine* are a wealth of information. He recently joined me as a member of the panel of experts in the premiere presentation of "A.D. Kessler's REAL ESTATE ROUNDTABLE" on national television. He has won awards for outstanding exchanges, both nationally and in his home state of California.

One award-winning exchange that he put together caused the prominent real estate attorney Marvin B. Starr to remark that he needed a can of Raid, since it had more legs than a centipede. The description of that transaction, for your edification, amusement, and wonderment follows.

It started with a phone call in late December with the client saying, "Let's exchange the fourplexes," and ended the following April 21 with the recording of 64 properties valued at over $13 million in states from coast to coast and border to border. Among the hundreds of people involved were 35 principals, 13 brokers and 14 lenders.

The clients had owned 47 fourplexes for 13 years. They were tired of the day-to-day management and wanted more passive investments. A $1,100,000 judgment in favor of a former partner and affecting some of the fourplexes was about to be handed down.

The decision was made to market the fourplexes individually to obtain the highest possible price. By early January, 200 sales books were completed and printed, at which time the clients raised their price from $4,150,000 to $4,552,000, requiring changes in the printed material. Real estate prices were increasing almost daily, and there was no telling how this would affect the salability of the fourplexes.

During the reprinting, Chet Allen, the exchange counselor (broker) who had the listing, attended a national marketing meeting searching for the next leg of the desired exchange (known as the "up" leg). He wanted leased commercial or industrial property with a value of $4,552,000 to $8,000,000. He received several preliminary offers subject to cashing out (finding someone who would pay cash for) the fourplexes. The clients were interested in three: A Rocky Mountain city office building, an east coast shopping center, and a Hawaiian Center.

Within two weeks they were on a plane, and two days, 7,000 miles, and seven airlines later, they had inspected the office building, the east coast center, and a border state center belonging to the same owner. They made offers on the two centers and made another trip to a state on the northern border where the same developer/owner had a third center. They made an offer on that center as well. After much negotiation, the clients agreed to acquire the three centers with a guaranteed 10% net return. The developer leased back the vacancies at a rental that netted Chet's clients the 10%. In the meantime, the fourplexes were selling. All sold in nine days, all at full price and many with cash payments. Some of the transactions were exchanges involving fourteen additional properties.

The next problem was the $1,100,000 judgment. Chet's clients did not have $1,100,000 cash, and their bank was too small to lend that amount on a signature loan. They could have refinanced, but the cost of refinancing the fourplexes twice (once for his clients and once for the buyer) would have been prohibitive. Armed with 47 deposit receipts and exchange agreements for the disposition of the fourplexes, they approached two of the big banks for a signature loan or a second mortgage. They were turned down because the banks refused to make loans when repayment was predicated on a future escrow closing. The solution came from the head of a big bank's real estate mortgage subsidiary. He would give a standby loan commitment that would be used only if escrow did not close. Therefore, the payoff to the permanent lender was not predicated solely on closing escrow. Another bank made the $1,100,000 loan, the judgment was paid, and a satisfaction (legal proof of payment) was recorded so that clear title to the fourplexes could be transferred to the new owners.

A table showing how the property values were balanced in the exchange follows.

Developer/Shopping Center Owner		Chet's Clients	
Market value:		Market value:	
East center	$4,350,000	47 fourplexes	$4,552,000
South center	2,377,710	less costs (legal, loan, printing,	
North center	840,000	mailing, marketing)	300,000
Total value	7,567,710	Total value	4,252,000
Minus loans:		Minus loans:	
East center	3,150,000	Fourplexes	1,052,000
South center	–0–		
North center	694,000		
Equity for exchange:	$3,723,710	Equity for exchange:	$3,200,000

The clients gave the developer/shopping center owner $523,710 to balance equities. In a separate escrow immediately following the exchange, the clients placed a new $1,664,000 loan on the free-and-clear south shopping center, and from the proceeds (the cash they received as the loan) they paid off the $1,100,000 bank loan. They had $564,000 left over. In 61 other escrows, the 47 fourplexes and 14 properties that were part of the transaction were cashed out (cash buyers acquired them) by the developer/shopping center owner.

Each of the buyers of the 47 fourplexes required termite reports and new loans. Even though the buyers were convinced of the value, the lenders were not, and they were turned down by many lenders. Eventually, eight lenders were contacted who would lend on some of the units, but by the time they had done their loan processing the contract time limit of April 5 had expired. An extension of time to April 21 was negotiated and agreed on. The developer and his attorney flew out on April 12 to sign closing papers, only to find that 13 fourplex loans had not been approved. All parties explored closing part of the exchange, but closing either the east or south centers without the other would have adverse tax consequences. The shopping center owner suggested that the participating brokers buy the $918,000 equity in the 13 fourplexes (subject to the existing sales contracts) with $178,000 down and the shopping center owner himself carrying back a $740,000 second mortgage, all due and payable in 55 days. This would allow time to obtain the loans. To have sufficient funds, Chet's clients agreed to allow the shopping center owner to leave $740,000 of an $840,000 second mortgage on the east center, to be paid from the proceeds of the second mortgage on the 13 fourplexes.

In order to close by April 21, additional title and escrow staff were called in to assist the escrow officer who had devoted the previous five weeks, full time, to this escrow. They worked every night and Saturday. At 9:00 p.m. on the night of April 21, they still weren't sure they had all of the documents, but the county manager of the title company made the decision that the paperwork was adequate. Next morning, at 11:00 a.m. Eastern time, 9:00 a.m. Mountain time, and 8:00 a.m. Pacific time, documents were recorded that concurrently transferred the 64 properties.

Benefits? Chet's clients increased their cash flow by approximately $140,000 and paid off a $1,100,000 judgment. The shopping center owner received all cash for his centers, and 33 other principals acquired income-producing investment properties.

People benefits galore! And it all happened in the Exchange Marketplace that you will read about in the next chapter.

First, adopt these Kessler's Keys to Success:

🔑 Who, what, why, how

🔑 Steps of the exchange

🔑 . . . And where

🔑 Climb a higher mountain

🔑 From sea to shining sea

16

The Exchange Marketplace

The fear that one's gain is another's loss is undoubtedly the greatest obstacle to human progress.

—Walter Lippmann

" . . . the best-kept open secret in the real estate world today" is the way Howard Ruff described the Exchange Marketplace when he first discovered it.

With the publication of the first edition of this book, it was no longer a secret. For it serves no useful purpose to keep the curtains drawn on the stage featuring the process of creating wealth quickly without the erosion of taxes. Indeed, we turned on the floods and spotlighted the Exchange Marketplace. Within a year of the publication of the first edition, attendance at exchange marketing meetings doubled. People from every one of the 50 United States, Canada, Great Britain, Mexico, Australia, New Zealand, India, Kenya, Spain, France, Hong Kong, Japan, Nigeria, Germany, Italy, and other places around the world contacted us to become involved.

WHERE IS IT?

More than 40,000 Creative Real Estate Professionals and 20,000 private investors in the United States and some more abroad meet regularly in their own areas. They have formed groups to share information, expand their education, and market real estate through tax-free exchanging and other creative means.

There are more than 125 of these local exchange groups, and over 175 investors groups called clubs or associations. Most of them operate as non-profit associations of individuals. Some form corporations for legal ease of operation in their particular areas, but the principle is the same: to establish and conduct a forum for education and marketing in local areas on a regularly scheduled basis. An educational and marketing calendar for events nationwide is published monthly in *Creative Real Estate Magazine* as a public service. A sample is illustrated on the next page.

EDUCATIONAL AND MARKETING CALENDAR

NOTE: Creative Real Estate Magazine offers this feature as a regular public service and cannot guarantee the reliability of performance or content. Any complaints or discrepancies should be communicated to the individual producer, with an information copy to Creative Real Estate Magazine.

DO YOU WANT TO ATTEND A SEMINAR AND/OR A MARKETING SESSION?

FIRST, LOOK IT UP HERE:

September 26-Oct. 1
ADVANCED NETWORKING PAPER BOOTCAMP
John D. Behle — Salt Lake City, UT
National Note, Inc.

October 10-15
ADVANCED NETWORKING PAPER BOOTCAMP
John D. Behle — Salt Lake City, UT
National Note, Inc.

October 19-23
COMMONWEALTH CONVENTION
Jack Miller — Orlando, FL
National Capital Corporation

October 28-31
PROFITS IN DISCOUNTED NOTES
Jonathan Richards — San Francisco, CA
NoteWorthy Newsletter

October 29-30
LEASE/OPTION MARATHON
Ron LeGrand — Atlanta, GA
The LeGrand Group

November 4-6
C.Y.A.
Jack Miller — Las Vegas, NV
National Capital Corporation

November 7-12
ADVANCED NETWORKING PAPER BOOTCAMP
John D. Behle — Salt Lake City, UT
National Capital Corporation

November 11-12
FINDING DISCOUNTED NOTES
Hank Harenberg — Las Vegas, NV
Capital Concepts

November 18-20
MULTIPLE LISTING SERVICE BOOT CAMP
Ron LeGrand — Tampa, FL
The LeGrand Group

November 18-20
8th Annual SUBSCRIBER CONFERENCE– East
Jimmy Napier — Orlando, FL
National Financial Marketing, Inc

December 3-4
* PAPER COURSE
Peter Fortunato — Orlando, FL
Peter Fortunato

December 9-12
OFFSHORE
Jack Miller — Cancun, Mexico
National Capital Corporation

December 10-11
LEASE/OPTION MARATHON
Ron LeGrand — Atlanta, GA
The LeGrand Group

January 18-21
SUPER REAL ESTATE MARKETING CONFERENCE
Ron LeGrand — Orlando, FL
The LeGrand Group

March 6-11
MASTERS OF SUCCESS
Ron LeGrand — Waikiki, HI
The Legrand Group

June 2-4, 1995
NOTEWORTHY CONVENTION
Jonathan Richards — San Francisco, CA
NoteWorthy Newsletter

* Approved for listing in Who's Who in Creative Real Estate Directory

THEN, REGISTER WITH THE PRODUCER LISTED HERE:
(see last line of listings above)

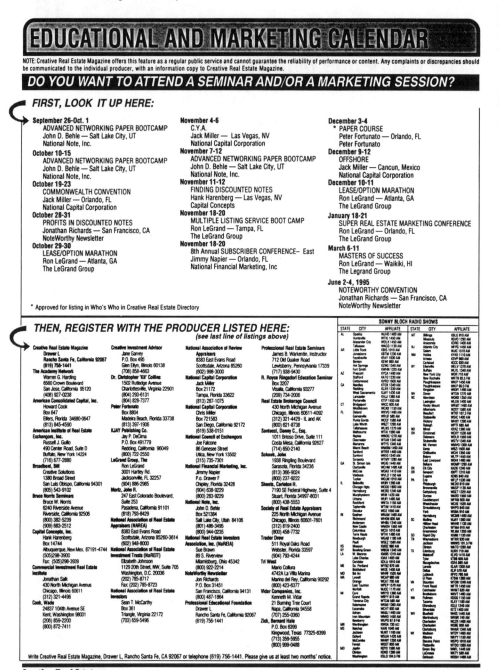

Write Creative Real Estate Magazine, Drawer L, Rancho Santa Fe, CA 92067 or telephone (619) 756-1441. Please give us at least two months' notice.

WHO PARTICIPATES?

Almost all of the groups have established membership requirements. The minimum requirements for the professional groups ("Exchange Groups," directory illustrated on page 206) generally are:

1. Possession of a real estate license as a broker or salesperson.
2. Specialization or interest in specialization in exchanging.
3. Specific transaction-making education in the basics of exchanging or commitment to acquire it within a definite period of time.
4. Commitment to meet attendance requirements.
5. Payment of annual dues (usually nominal).

The older, established groups generally have additional requirements, in the interest of advancing the state of the art and conducting more effective marketing sessions. They might require, in addition to the minimum standards:

1. Membership in the local Board of Realtors$^{®}$.
2. Participation in a national marketing session.
3. Participation in a regional marketing session.
4. Participation in a statewide marketing session.
5. Additional education in legal aspects and tax aspects and formulas.
6. Subscription to *Creative Real Estate Magazine.*

The requirements for membership in an investors' club or association are less demanding, primarily in order to encourage more novices to participate. Generally all that is required to attend meetings of an investors' club are:

1. Be, or desire to be, involved in real estate investment.
2. Attend scheduled meetings.
3. Share information about local market conditions.
4. Nominal annual dues or one-time meeting fees.

The older, established clubs might have additional requirements such as:

1. Participation in committees on various assignments.
2. Sharing special vocational or avocational expertise by lecturing.
3. Subscription to *Creative Real Estate Magazine.*
4. Membership in *Creative Real Estate Magazine's* TAPE-OF-THE-MONTH CLUB.

WHAT HAPPENS?

Most of the professional groups (licensed brokers and agents) meet weekly for at least four hours. A typical meeting would include an instructor speaking on exchanging or some other aspect of Creative Real Estate, a "have/want" session, a "country store," a "million-dollar roundtable," and marketing presentations.

The instructor is usually a local member who, in addition to actively practicing in real estate, teaches extension college classes, or is a cooperating professional such as a lawyer, a tax accountant, a title officer, a lender, or an appraiser.

The have/want session is a rapid-fire presentation, usually limited to one minute, with each participant telling what he is looking for, what he has to dispose of, or both. Very often in this session personal property items such as boats, cars, trucks, jewelry, furs, or other non-real estate items will be offered. The have/want session is fast-moving, exciting, and sets the pace for the meeting.

The country store was first conceived by my good friend, the late Murray Sobel of Beverly Hills, California. He was a pillar of our industry and started a large number of newcomers on their careers in Creative Real Estate. He instructed them, assisted them in their initial transactions, and helped them to form new exchange groups in their areas. The country store consists of printed, written, drawn, or pictorial offerings on single sheets of paper that are hung up on the walls around the marketing meeting room. A standardized form we developed is illustrated on the next page. In a typical country store you will find offerings, in addition to real estate, of tape recorders, TV sets, pickup trucks, resort acreage, cultured marble manufacturing franchises, airplanes, time-shares, gemstones, jewelry, precious metals, coins, furniture, motorbikes, and many other items.

At the million-dollar roundtable, properties with an equity of $1 million or more are presented and brainstormed by the group to produce the best solutions and complete transactions. Often, people with properties smaller than $1 million will sit in on the session for one or both of two reasons, to: (1) learn, and (2) offer their smaller properties as increments of a "leg" of an exchange or as a catalyst to start another "leg."

The marketing presentations consist of verbal presentations of the packages (listings of the properties for exchange) to the entire group by each member. Each person in the assembled group has been given a copy of the written details so he can follow along and take notes. In the course of the presentation, a moderator (an experienced exchangor who moves the proceedings along in an interesting and orderly fashion) will question the presentor about various aspects of the people involved in the ownership, the problems associated with the ownership, and the details of the physical property. The moderator may offer a solution and ask for questions from the

COUNTRY STORE SHEET

I WANT THE FOLLOWING:

FOR THE ABOVE, I HAVE THE FOLLOWING:

CONTACT:

NAME_____   MEMBER NUMBER _____

COMPANY _____   PHONE (OFFICE) _____

ADDRESS _____   PHONE (RESIDENCE)_____

HOTEL _____   ROOM NUMBER_____

assembled group. The questions may bring forth additional solutions from the group. Then, the presentor will leave the podium and go to an adjoining room, called the "transaction table" room, where all those interested in the package will join in the brainstorming in order to structure a transaction. Many of the established exchange groups require that the presentor have an exclusive agreement with the client and, often, a limited power of attorney to act on behalf of the client. In this fashion, tentative transactions subject to the client's inspection and final approval can be quickly structured. Where the property is broker-owned, it is not unusual to complete a transaction on the spot, handing it for closing to the escrow officer, title company representative, or Qualified Intermediary who usually is present in the transaction table room.

The attendance in the groups across the country varies from six to three hundred. Often, Creative Real Estate seminars of one-, two-, three-, or four-day durations are sponsored by a group and scheduled either just before or just after their regular marketing session. This procedure tends to attract participants from other areas for both the seminar and the marketing sessions. As a result, the properties marketed receive wider exposure.

Most of the investors associations/clubs meet monthly, either in the evening or on a weekend day for three to four hours. The evening meetings are often preceded by a no-host dinner at the meeting room establishment (hotel or catering hall). The schedule customarily includes a speaker—often a nationally known authority, or a local expert who might even be a member of the group. The meeting might start with an exchange of information among the attendees about the local market activity, regulations, laws, resources and suppliers, or that session could be after the speaker's presentation. Before the close of the meeting, time is allocated to permit the attendees to network. It is then and there that many joint ventures, exchanges, sales, purchases, and partnerships become reality.

YOU CAN, TOO

Almost without exception, the groups permit guests and qualified visitors. Usually the requirement is that the guest or visitor be accompanied by a member/sponsor, but this should represent no problem if you are sincerely interested. All you would have to do is to call the president of the group you wish to visit and he or she will arrange for your visit. As a point of interest, I have observed an equal number of women and men participating in the exchange groups and investors clubs as I address them in my speaking engagements all across the country.

Many Creative Real Estate Professionals schedule themselves to attend exchange meetings wherever they are traveling around the country. Most exchangors not only attend their local group meetings regularly, but frequent

out-of-area meetings as well. Often they will find someone out-of-area looking for something in their home area, and they can fill the need.

By now I am sure you are wondering how to find out where these
exchange groups and investors' clubs meet, the days that they meet, and
how to contact the president. That's simple.

A Directory of Exchange Groups is published monthly as a public
service in *Creative Real Estate Magazine*. The name of the exchange group,
the president, the telephone number, the address, and the meeting day are
listed alphabetically by state and city. For your information a sample section
is included on the next page.

To connect with an investors club closest to you, call or write the
Public Information Service of *Creative Real Estate Magazine* at Drawer L,
Rancho Santa Fe, California 92067, phone (619)756-1441. No collect calls,
please, and include a stamped, self-addressed envelope when writing.

STARTING FROM THE TOP

A unique phenomenon of the Exchange Marketplace is the fact that it has
developed from the top down. It was at our Annual Creative Real Estate
EXPO (attended at once by as many as 2,500 people from 46 states and 5
foreign countries) that the innovations, new developments, improvements,
and changes that affected the entire industry took place. It was there that we
had the opportunity and the forum to experiment with and prove new ideas,
while improving established methods and techniques. It was an opportunity
for meeting the leading professionals and instructors in Creative Real Estate.

In 4 days there were more than 90 mini-seminar roundtable discussions, 20 educational workshops, and 24 hours of marketing with over $2
billion in property offered for sale or exchange. With a staff of over 100 of
the most experienced exchangors and instructors, it was not only "the largest
real estate marketing and educational event in the world" with the "best
education available," it was a memorable event for all participants. As I
travel the country and other parts of the world, I am inevitably compli-
mented about EXPO by someone who attended or who knew someone who
attended and benefited from the education and the marketing of properties.*

The forum allowed instructors from everywhere, teaching many different seminars, to be seen and heard by people from all over the country and
other parts of the world. This provided the instructors and educational chair-
persons the opportunity to schedule the succeeding year's seminars all at one
time and place. Many of today's prominent instructors got their first national
exposure at EXPO. The benefits to the attendees were the opportunities to be

---

* It is a tribute to all the great ladies and gentlemen of our profession who participated as
staff. As chairman, I am deeply grateful to them. I know of no other industry or profession
that can claim this outstanding *esprit de corps* and the benefits it provides for all.

NOTE: We publish this feature as a public service to our readers. If you would like to have your group listed, send us the information (as shown in listings below) together with a roster. Please advise us promptly of any changes that should be made in this directory. Mail to: Directory, Creative Real Estate Magazine, Drawer L, Rancho Santa Fe, CA 92067.

ARIZONA
Certified Arizona Exchangors
Bob Watkins — (602) 458-4388
301 North Garden Avenue
Sierra Vista, Arizona 85635
Tucson Real Estate Exchangors (TREE)
Jim Dreis — (602) 790-7319
3711 South Palo Verde
Tucson, Arizona 85713
Wednesdays
Valley of the Sun Real Estate Exchangors (VSREE)
Joe W. Morgan – (602) 488-2059
Box 1113
Carefree, Arizona 85377
Thursdays
Yuma Real Estate Marketing Group
Ken Broyles — (602) 878-0304
6649 West Sunnyside Drive
Glendale, Arizona 85304
Tuesdays

ARKANSAS
Century 21 Investment Connection
Les Shoaf — (214) 541-0221
420 Decker, Suite 200
Irving, Texas 75062

CALIFORNIA (Northern)
Associated Investment Marketing (AIM)
Donald S. Herbert — (510) 484-2211
555 Peters Avenue, Suite 200
Pleasanton, California 94566
3rd Thursday
CCIM Northern California Chapter No. 1
Nancy Hunter — (510) 938-5366
1547 Palos Verdes Mall, Suite 255
Walnut Creek, California 94596
2nd Tuesdays
California Association of Real Estate Exchangors (CARE)
Esti Barak — (209) 266-7573
1759 Fulton Street, Box 6
Fresno, California 93721-1634
Tuesdays by invitation only
Central Coast Exchangors
Marvin Cohen — (818) 988-3333
P.O. Box 7649
Van Nuys, California 91409
3rd Thursday
Northern Counties Exchangors
Bob Browning — (916) 345-6111
1215 Manorove Avenue, Suite A
Chico, California 95926
Thursday mornings
Ontario-Upland-Chino Exchangors
Thom Bohan — (909) 982-5718
9125 Archibold Avenue #AA
Rancho Cucumonga, California 91730
3rd Thursday
Placerville Exchangors
Charlene Makis — (916)626-3333
111 Main Street
Placerville, California 95667
Tuesday mornings
Sacramento Real Estate Exchange Group, Inc (SREEG)
Whit Woodward — (916) 624-7171
2020 Marconi Avenue
Sacramento, California 95821
Fridays
Sacramento Women in Commercial Real Estate (SWICRE)
Gretchen Lindemann — (916) 331-8080
1750 Howe Avenue #550
Sacramento, California 95825
2nd Thursday
San Joaquin Valley Exchangors
Susan Darsey — (209) 561-4560
P.O. Box 116
Three Rivers, California 93271
4th Friday
Santa Cruz Exchangors
Terry Reeder — (408) 688-7711
Box 928
Aptos, California 95003
2nd Wednesday
Sacramento Commercial Realtors
Bonnie Bray — (916) 922-7711
2003 Howe Avenue
Sacramento, California 95825-0176

Visalia Real Estate Marketing Group
R. Royce Ringsdorf — (209) 734-2006
P.O. Box 3207
Visalia, California 93277
2nd Friday
Yosemite Marketing and Exchange Group
Dennis Horton — (209) 658-7135
P.O. Box N
Oakhurst, California 93644
2nd Friday mornings
Yuba City Exchangors
John Messick — (916) 751-2000
P.O. Drawer 3329
Yuba City, California 95992
Wednesday mornings

CALIFORNIA (Southern)
Creative Exchangors
Bill Dunn — (619) 232-5322
Box 1904
La Mesa, California 91944
3rd Wednesday
Creative Real Estate Associated Marketors (CREAM)
A.D. Kessler — (619) 756-1441
Drawer L
Rancho Santa Fe, California 92067
By Invitation Only
Golden Circle Exchangors (NCE)
Jean Henderson — (909) 980-8829
6954 Berkshire Avenue
Alta Loma, California 91701
1st Thursday
Long Beach Exchange Counselors (NCE)
Robert Cooke — (310) 371-4446
19800 Hawthorne Boulevard #285
Torrance, California 90503
3rd Wednesday in Long Beach
Los Angeles International Exchangors
Andrew Almanza — (310) 820-3025
11663 Kiowa Avenue #410
Los Angeles, California 90049
4th Wednesday
Orange Coast Exchangors
Fred Gross — (714) 770-6067
4650 Von Karman
Newport Beach, California 92660
1st & 3rd Fridays
Real Equity Marketing Association (REMA) (NCE)
Marvin J. Hayes — (714) 676-4804
44611 La Paz Road
Temecula, California 92392
3rd Tuesday in Perris
San Diego Problem Solvers (NCE)
Ben Holden — (619) 464-2533
Box 1904
La Mesa, California 91944
2nd Tuesdays in San Diego
San Fernando Valley Exchangors (NCE)
Paul Williams — (805) 497-7236
1707 Schoolhouse Circle
Westlake Village, California 91362
2nd Monday in Van Nuys
Santa Anita Exchangors (NCE)
Mike Ludecke — (818) 445-0123
610 North Santa Anita
Arcadia, California 91416-7777
1st Tuesday
SLOMARK (A Creative Real Estate Marketing Group)
Bill Broadbent — (805) 543-9102
1380 Broad Street
San Luis Obispo, California 94301
1st & 3rd Thursdays
South Orange Coast Exchangors (SOCE)
Mike Matcham — (619) 728-1031
1442 South Mission
Fallbrook, California 92028
4th Tuesday in Dana Point
Southern California Chapter (NCE)
John Barta — (818) 708-2698
Box 17777
Encino, California 91416-7777
2nd Monday
T.R.U.S.T. Foundation
Jean Stirling — (714) 673-1611
Box 8833
Newport Beach, California 92658-8833
Last week of month

COLORADO
Colorado West Marketing
Steve Flemming – (303) 243-3322
851 Grand Avenue
Grand Junction, Colorado 81501
2nd and 4th Thursdays
Mile-Hi Exchangors
Tom VanErp — (303) 478-5947
6345 Northway Dr.
Morrison, Colorado 80465
Wednesdays in Denver
Montrose Exchangors
Del Leger — (303) 249-4200
1500 East Main
Montrose, Colorado 81401
By appointment
Summit County Exchangors
Daniel McCrerey — (303) 668-3600
619 Main Street
Frisco, Colorado 80443
Call for information
Vail Exchangors
Sue Dugan — (303) 476-0764
Box 3768
Vail, Colorado 81658
Call for information

FLORIDA
Broward County Investors Association
Sandy Wilkenson — (305) 974-6832
6972 N W Fifth Court
Margate, Florida 33063
1st Wednesday
Central Florida Realty Investors
Duane Williams — (407) 831-2235
Box 940545
Maitland, Florida 32794
1st Wednesday
Englewood Exchangors
John McCall — (813) 475-3999
1460 McCall Road, Suite 2-D
Englewood, Florida 34223
Florida Real Estate Exchangors (FREE)
Ming Toy Taylor — (407) 629-9045
1950 Lee Road Suite 125
Winter Park, Florida 32789
2nd Thursday & Friday
Ft. Walton Beach Exchangors
Tom Fugua — (904) 651-9696
Five Clifford Drive
Shalimar, Florida 32579
Last Tuesday
Gainesville Real Estate Exchangors
Ron Reeb — (904) 377-2615
727 Northeast Fifth Avenue
Gainesville, Florida 32601
2nd Wednesday
Gulf Region Exchangors and Traders
Ken Allen — (813) 923-2321
3131 Clark Road #102
Englewood, Florida 34231
Fridays
Orlando Area Real Estate Exchangors
Milton Armstrong — (407) 644-9509
P.O. Box 940365
Maitland, Florida 32794-0365
1st & 3rd Wednesdays
Real Estate Exchangors of the Bay Area (REEBA)
Trader Drew — (904) 793-4244
11303 Country Road #683-E
Webster, Florida 33597
Every three months
Sarasota Real Estate Exchangors
John McCall — (813) 475-3999
1460 McCall Road, Suite 2-D
Englewood, Florida 34223
Fridays
St Petersburg Exchangors (SPREE)
Arlen "Al" Alton — (813) 341-0077
7310 Central Avenue
St. Petersburg, Florida 33707
Wednesdays
Southwest Florida Real Estate Exchange
Chuck Bundschu — (813) 481-0300
Box 7326
Ft. Myers, Florida 33911
Wednesday mornings

Suncoast Real Estate Exchangors (SREE)
Michael Rodetsky — (813) 593-3353
12551 Indian Rocks Road, Suite 8
Largo, Florida 34644
Thursdays
Tampa Real Estate Exchangors
Martin G. James — (407) 871-6895
614 South West Lakehurst Drive
Port St. Lucie, Florida 34983
Thursdays
Treasure Coast Real Estate Exchangors (TREE)
Lon F. Parsons — (407) 464-4967
P.O. Box 3025
Fort Pierce, Florida 34948
3rd Thursday

GEORGIA
Association of Georgia Real Estate Exchangors (AGREE)
Nick Nichols – (404) 432-8266
190 Windy Hill Road S E #2
Marietta, Georgia 30060
3rd Thursday

IDAHO
Boise Exchangors
Joe Schwilling — (208) 376-9000
1070 North Cole Road
Boise, Idaho 83704
Treasure Valley Exchangors
Chet Pipkin — (208) 376-9000
1070 North Cole Road
Boise, Idaho 83704
2nd Wednesday

ILLINOIS
Chicago Area Real Estate Exchangors (CARE)
Marilee Anderson — (708) 705-0808
855 Sterling Avenue, Suite 140
Palatine, Illinois 60067
2nd & 4th Thursdays, Arlington Heights

INDIANA
Indiana Real Estate Exchangors (IREX)
Ron Richer — (800) 937-1202
1202 N. Pennsylvania Street
Indianapolis, Indiana 46202
2nd and 4th Thursdays

IOWA
Iowa Association of Realtors, Commercial Investment Division
Tom Keiser — (800) 392-1305
101 North Main
Charles City, Iowa 50616
2nd Wednesday

KENTUCKY
Kentucky Real Estate Exchangors (KREE)
Chris Dischinger — (502) 451-9000
6040 Dutchmans Lane, Suite 220
Louisville, Kentucky 40205
1st & 3rd Thursdays

LOUISIANA
Century 21 Commercial Marketing Group
M.E. "Rocky" Chatham — (713) 542-0221
10700 N.W. Freeway
Houston, Texas 77092

MARYLAND
Mid Atlantic Real Estate Marketing Association (MAREMA)
Paul C. Watson, Jr. — (703) 569-9323
P.O. Box 641
Lanham, Maryland 20703-0641
3rd Wednesday in Tyson's Corner

MICHIGAN
Grand Rapids Traders and Exchangors (GREAT)
Ron Nanzer — (616) 364-0273
2136 Lafayette Northeast
Grand Rapids, Michigan 49505
2nd Thursday
Michigan Association of Realtors Exchangors (MAREX)
Bob Lucas — (616) 889-3400
Box 27
Arcadia, Michigan 49613
2nd Friday

instructed by many outstanding educators from myriad venues, on a wide variety of topics, book them for future presentations to their local groups, and be able to network with folks of similar interests from far and wide. In addition, for those who came to market, their offerings had the widest possible targeted market exposure at the most reasonable cost. Talk about win/win!

Many exchange groups informally competed for recognition for the largest attendance from a group because they felt that participation in a national and international event such as EXPO was a vital part of the training and experience for an exchangor.

On the third and next to last day of marketing at one year's EXPO at Caesars' Palace in Las Vegas, I was called to the registration desk. It was unattended but for a hotel security guard. He was talking to a seedy-looking character in well-worn, faded denim dungarees, scuffed, high-heeled cowboy boots, a sweat-stained six-gallon sombrero, and a two-days' growth of beard. He looked like a hard-working ranch hand who'd just gotten off the range at roundup time.

He wanted to register at full price for the entire EXPO, to attend that afternoon's marketing session only. I carefully explained to him that unless he had a very specific purpose in being there for that short period of time, he would not be getting the full value for his money. He grunted his acknowledgment of what I had said, took a large roll of bills from his denim jacket, peeled off the full price in large bills, and mumbled something about "not having time to palaver." Since I was shortly due back on the platform, I asked the guard to make certain that the gentleman received his registration portfolio, name badge, all the marketing packages and materials, and was introduced to our director of marketing.

The next time I saw the cowboy was about an hour later at the transaction table. He was with five other people. Because I was curious, I walked over and asked him how he was faring. With a charming smile, he stood up, shook my hand, and said, "Sir, I want you to know that in thirty minutes I just acquired a $130 million shopping center that I've been after for 11 months!" I was astounded and almost speechless but I engaged him in further conversation. He willingly joined. I found out that he had over 72,000 acres in Texas, on which he raised high-priced cattle. He had enjoyed a good year with the increase in beef prices and was looking for tax-shelter and appreciation in real estate. The year before he had gotten wind of the shopping center he had just acquired, but his property manager hadn't completed negotiations for delivery, and his fiscal year was ending in 30 days. When he inquired back home about the property, he was told that the broker had gone to EXPO to present it. After finding out what and where EXPO was, he left the roundup, flew his own Lear jet to Las Vegas, made the $130 million acquisition in exchange for a combination of land, cattle futures, and installment cash payments. And in the same afternoon, he was Lear-jetting himself back to his Texas roundup!

During this same event, a handsome young man with a deep southern drawl, inquired about someone I knew well and had done business with. I had no reservations in answering emphatically in the affirmative. Two days later the young southern gentleman sought me out to tell me that:

1. This was his first EXPO.

2. He would never miss another as long as he could fly, drive, walk, or crawl to it.

3. He had just exchanged, on firm agreement, a $12,000,000 coal mine that had been a family estate problem for the last three years. He had acquired divisible holdings in the exchange to satisfy his mother, his two sisters and their husbands, and himself, all with separate interests.

Even after many years, EXPO remains such a unique, dynamic experience that I could write an entire book about the happenings at one five-day EXPO!

The book would recount incidents that are, at once exciting, dramatic, ecstatic, pathetic, and at times, unbelievable.

At the next level, there are the regional marketing sessions sponsored by local groups in different regions during various months of the year.

These events are patterned after EXPO. They are valuable experiences in the development of exchange counselors, in addition to being an active marketplace. Attendance has ranged from 50 to 300 people.

Next on the ladder are the statewide marketing sessions. Again, patterned after EXPO, they provide a close-to-home, valuable learning experience for the new exchangors and a viable marketplace for the "old pros." Some of the states have formed statewide exchange organizations to which each of the local groups belongs. This very practical and successful method of operating completely eliminates schedule conflicts and permits pooling of effort and resources to provide better quality events. Arizona has been a leader in this concept. Another very successful concept has been developed in the state of Florida by the statewide organization, FREE (Florida Real Estate Exchangors). A marketing session and educational event are conducted in a different location around the state each month of the year. An excellent marketing package book is printed and distributed to members (I've received mine in California like clockwork). It provides an outstandingly successful, continuing market forum between marketing sessions.

Well, now the secret is out. The Exchange Marketplace is a cooperative effort by generous professionals to establish a forum for the creative marketing of real estate. In the next section I will fill you in on the details of a marketing presentation so you too can take advantage of this "secret."

THE NITTY-GRITTY

In a formal marketing presentation the presentor distributes a package to all attendees. The package is the Exchange Marketplace listing information. Usually it is typewritten on an $8\frac{1}{2}$ x 11 sheet of paper. It provides a basic outline of the property, problems of ownership, personal information about the owner(s), and the owner/client's objectives. The format is standard, and that is a critical point. Since the package serves as a quick advertisement to all, it should be easy to read and follow in order to make notes during the presentation. An example of the standard format that we originated for our annual Creative Real Estate EXPO is illustrated, together with the instruction sheet for completing the "package form" most effectively, on the next two pages.

Deviation from the standard package format only confuses everyone and seriously hampers the potential of a transaction. Local groups often will add some information requirement that is peculiar to their area. Unfortunately, some groups have changed the form merely to exercise pride of authorship.

Scanty or incomplete information in a package is generally a forecast of an impossible exchange, or at least one that will require too much time and energy to make it feasible.

On the other hand, too much information takes too much time to read during a busy meeting. Pertinent details are important, but should be confined to the "property brief," most often called the "backup package." There *can not be too much information* in the backup package. It should contain information to familiarize one who has never seen nor heard of the property with all the necessary details to make a decision. The accuracy and completeness of the information in the backup package may determine whether or not a successful exchange will be completed.

Items that should be covered in the backup package are:

- Copy of the package
- Copy of the listing agreement
- Legal description
- Preliminary title report
- Photographs of property, exterior and interior
- Plat maps
- Area map showing location
- Road map showing location
- Aerial photos of area
- Plan showing utilities and services in area
- Copy of owner's association by-laws and rules

Assigned Package # *Leave blank*
Regular Package
Extra Package

L *Listing date*	*A catchy name that describes your package.*
	Package Title
F *Fee or commission rate*	
	Street
E *Listing expiration date*	City County State

Price $ *Listed price*

Loans $ *Total Loan Balances*

Equity $ *Price minus loans*

Picture, map, or other information (optional)	ANNUAL INCOME		ANNUAL EXPENSES	
A black and white glossy print of the property reduced to size and pasted in the box. Or paste in a plat map or area map, or any other optional information, such as your business card.	Gross Actual Rental Income	$	Taxes	$
	Plus: Other Income	$	Insurance	$
	Total Gross Income	$	Maintenance	$
	Less: Vacancy and Credit Losses	$	Management	$
	Gross Operating Income	$	Utilities	$
	Less: Total Operating Expenses	$	All other expenses	$
	Net Operating Income	$	Total Operating Expenses	$

HAVE: *A detailed description of the property you have to offer.*

BENEFITS: *What benefits does this property offer the prospective taker.*

LOANS: *Give current principal balance, monthly payment, interest rate, lender, due date, and assumption fee for each loan.*

WHY DOESN'T WANT: *Motivation — Describe why your client no longer desires this property.*

WANT/OBJECTIVE: *Describe what your client will take, and what he hopes to accomplish.*

REMARKS: *Your candid remarks that might spark a transaction or be informative for the participants, such as client's business activities, family situation, etc.*

CAN ADD: *Describe any real or personal property value and equity, and any cash your client can add to help make a transaction.*

CLIENT: *Your client's name so an offer may be written to him.*

BROKER: *Your name, address, and telephone numbers with area code.*

The above information is not guaranteed accurate, and is subject to price change, correction, error, omission, prior sale and withdrawal.

Creative Real Estate expo Las Vegas

MARKETING PACKAGE

Assigned Package #
Regular Package
Extra Package

L _____ Package Title _____   Price $ _____

F _____ Street _____   Loans $ _____

E _____ City   County   State   Equity $ _____

Picture, map, or other information (optional)

ANNUAL INCOME		ANNUAL EXPENSES	
Gross Actual Rental Income	$	Taxes	$
Plus: Other Income	$	Insurance	$
Total Gross Income	$	Maintenance	$
Less: Vacancy and Credit Losses	$	Management	$
Gross Operating Income	$	Utilities	$
Less: Total Operating Expenses	$	All other expenses	$
Net Operating Income	$	Total Operating Expenses	$

HAVE:

BENEFITS:

LOANS:

WHY DOESN'T WANT:

WANT/OBJECTIVE:

REMARKS:

CAN ADD:

CLIENT:

BROKER:

The above information is not guaranteed accurate, and is subject to price change, correction, error, omission, prior sale and withdrawal.

- Copies of trust deeds, mortgages, agreements and contracts
- Inventory of personal property included
- Copies of tax bills
- Copies of income and expense statements
- Copies of appraisals
- Comparable sales information
- Copies of leases
- List of tenants
- Copy of property management agent's agreement
- Copies of equipment leases
- Copies of equipment service contracts
- Conditional loan commitments

Despite the length of this list, it may not be complete for every purpose. Additional details are added or subtracted as required.

Excellent sources for the required information are available in every part of the world. The following is a partial list.

1. A title insurance company is the source for the preliminary title report and copies of most legal documents pertaining to the property and the area. Documents such as deeds, contracts, mortgages, recorded leases or options, restrictions, easements, zoning, plat maps, and others peculiar to specific areas and situations are usually available on request.

2. City, county, and state offices can supply tax records, surveys, zoning maps and regulations, use restrictions, master plan maps and guidelines, highway and road maps, and plans.

3. The U.S. Post Office can supply population figures, trends, growth rate, and service projections.

4. Utility companies can supply information on the cost of services, projections for the area, population figures, and growth patterns.

5. Chambers of commerce can be a wealth of information combining all the facts and figures available in the area. It is advisable to verify specific information with a number of individual sources.

6. The Boards of Realtors® (in some areas known as Realtors® Associations) maintain libraries of information about sales and building activity in the area, as well as population, commercial-industrial development, and growth rates.

7. Lending institutions are the sources for information about loan requirements, availability of money, verification of existing loans, and general area demographics.

8. Public libraries can be a deep well of all kinds of information other than the recorded legal documents that may be required.

9. Newspapers maintain archives that can reveal specific details for specific times, particularly about laws, regulations, zoning, and incidents.

In any area, there are many other indigenous sources of information. No stone should be left unturned in seeking information to prepare a complete and accurate backup package. The backup package or property brief is the substance from which solid exchanges can be properly structured to close, and thus provide the people benefits promised.

LET'S GO TO A MARKETING MEETING

Suppose we are attending a local exchange group meeting. Typically, we might expect a schedule like the one that follows:

7:15 a.m.	Enter a room set up with tables and chairs in classroom style with a lectern on a platform in front of the room
7:30 a.m.	No-host continental breakfast Put up Country Store circulars
8:15 a.m.	Meeting called to order Introduction of visitors and guests by sponsor members
8:30 a.m.	Announcements President gives agenda for the day
8:45 a.m.	Members report transactions that closed since last meeting
9:00 a.m.	Guest speaker/Instructor
9:45 a.m.	Haves/Wants
10:00 a.m.	Marketing presentations Transaction tables
12:00 p.m.	Lunch
1:00 p.m.	Marketing presentations Transaction tables
2:00 p.m.	Million-Dollar Roundtable
3:00 p.m.	Adjourn

From this agenda you can see that the presentation of marketing packages from the podium is the main feature of the marketing session. An interesting point about this is that while the presentor has only the one package he or she is presenting on the block, every package in the room is a potential taker for the presentation. As a matter of fact, when I attend marketing meetings to do business, I seldom make a formal marketing presentation from the podium. I do prepare my packages completely (together with backup packages), and distribute the packages to everyone present. But, instead of spending my time in a pre-presentation counseling session, making the actual presentation, and then going to the "transaction table," I stay in my place reading and listening to every package. I then write offers, attaching a copy of my package(s) and backup package(s) to every possible package that can meet the objectives of the packages I am marketing. In this manner, I maximize my effectiveness during that meeting by being alert and ready for every opportunity. During breakfasts, refreshment breaks, and lunches, I walk around the Country Store wall hangings with my voice-activated, micro-mini tape recorder in my breast pocket. When I observe an offering on the wall that interests me, I dictate all the details into my recorder, together with remarks concerning my interest in that offering. I move along at a brisk pace.

When I return to my office, the tapes are transcribed and typed double-spaced. I then have a written record to which I can add calculations and annotations, and from which I can take further action. If I happen to know the offeror well, I sometimes send him a photocopy of the transcribed remarks with annotations in the margin. For the rest, I send written offers to those that still interest me. I sometimes turn the entire typewritten transcript over to an associate for follow-up action.

Another use for my recorder is to record marketing presentations; during them, I overlay my remarks on the recording. This gives me an opportunity to catch up after the meeting, if I have been too busy writing offers to respond immediately to all that interested me.

For those making presentations, a moderator is generally assigned to counsel on the package before they go to the podium. During the presentation, the moderator will ask questions, promote discussions, generate ideas, and catalyze solutions.

When the moderator feels enough time has been spent, he or she will ask how many in the group are planning to make an offer. The moderator will then direct the presentor to a numbered transaction table in the adjoining room and instruct the takers to meet the presentor there.

The offers can be made using any one of several forms. The one most often used is the Preliminary Exchange Proposal, or Mini-Offer. This type of form was first developed by my good friend, the late Don Eymann, who was the marketing production director of our Annual Creative Real Estate

EXPOs. A copy of a later edition, Suggested Exchange Transaction (SET form), developed by my son, Judd, is printed on the next page for your information.

The mini-offer is a tentative proposal showing an interest in structuring a transaction and suggesting some methods. The next step would be to go firm, by meeting, resolving the questions that may be raised, carefully structuring the transaction, and reducing the agreement to writing on a "Long Form Exchange Agreement." This agreement is the formal document that is used to place the transaction in escrow or in the hands of title-passing personnel.

Sometimes when the property offered at a marketing meeting is either broker owned or controlled by power of attorney, the long form is the first and final offer. Many transactions are completed in that manner. For your observation, a Long Form Exchange Agreement Supplement to the California Association of Realtors® real estate purchase contract and receipt for deposit is reproduced later in this chapter.

There are variations in different states and countries. The proper forms should be used for each jurisdiction. The best sources for the correct forms would be Creative Real Estate Professionals practicing as Exchange Counselors in that particular area, the local Exchange Group, the local Board of Realtors®, or the appropriate State Association of Realtors®.

It is important to remain as long as possible after adjournment of the scheduled marketing meeting to distribute the offers that were written and to discuss them with the presenters along with offers that may have been received. Even if you didn't make a formal presentation from the podium, your package was distributed, and if it was properly made up, there will be offers for it. Many of the transactions generated at the meeting will be resolved and solidified by talking with the parties *after* the formal session is over.

An interesting fact is that some of the largest exchanges that I have been involved in have originated over a cup of coffee after a meeting. And the offers were written on napkins more often than not. I can remember at least five occasions when I handed the napkin to an escrow or title officer for closing. On one occasion, the agreement was on a brown paper bag. Many people believe that the only legal document is a printed one. In fact, almost the opposite is true. In the eyes of the law, the document that is considered the most valid and binding as a classic expression of the parties' intentions is the hand-written agreement. The lowest in priority of recognized legality is the printed form. So, if you have a good idea for a transaction, don't hesitate or delay. Write it—on whatever and with whatever happens to be available. If it is basically sound and clearly expressed, it could be the basis of one of the best transactions you'll ever make. One of mine was!

(**SET** FORM-1)

Suggested Exchange Transaction

"get SET to make money!"

DATE _____ MEETING _____

T
O

F
R
O
M

YOUR PACKAGE NUMBER   MY PACKAGE NUMBER

TITLE _____   TITLE _____

DESCRIPTION/COMMENTS: DESCRIPTION/COMMENTS:

To fit window envelope, fold here

To fit window envelope, fold here

PRICE	LOANS	EQUITY
$	$	$

PLUS:

PRICE	LOANS	EQUITY
$	$	$

PRICE	LOANS	EQUITY
$	$	$

PLUS:

PRICE	LOANS	EQUITY
$	$	$

TOTAL PRICE	TOTAL LOANS	TOTAL EQUITIES
$	$	$

TOTAL PRICE	TOTAL LOANS	TOTAL EQUITIES
$	$	$

BENEFITS, TERMS,
CONDITIONS, REMARKS, ETC.

_____

_____

_____

_____

This is not a formal offer, but merely a suggested way to structure a
transaction between us.   SUBMITTED BY: _____

Please reply before _____

REPLY

_____

_____

ANSWERED BY: _____

This form available exclusively from: Creative Real Estate Magazine - Drawer L - Rancho Santa Fe - CA 92067 - (619) 756-1441   Copyright © 1978 J. S. Kessler

(**SET** FORM-1)

Exchanging and problem solving have often been referred to as art. Perhaps in the early stages this might have been so, but what once was an art is now a science. It requires specific knowledge and skills that together with experience form the science of exchanging and problem solving.

In summary:

1. The objective of the Exchange Marketplace is to establish and provide a professional forum for the creative marketing of real estate.

2. The objective is fulfilled by Creative Real Estate Professionals organizing and meeting together regularly for the purposes of upgrading their specialized education, expanding their experience, and sharing their knowledge and ideas to market real estate creatively.

3. The personal integrity of the participants is critical to the successful operation of the Exchange Marketplace.

4. There is an organized Exchange Marketplace that operates in an environment of ethical faith and cooperation that you may become a part of, if you desire.

WHO CAN YOU TURN TO?

As you have seen, the Exchange Marketplace is a professional forum. Exchanging is considered a part of the transaction-making process that is regulated in all of the states. If you are not a licensed and practicing real estate professional, but are or want to be a Creative Real Estater, you should have direct access to the Exchange Marketplace.

The most effective way to gain entree to the Exchange Marketplace is through a Creative Real Estate Professional.

HOW TO FIND A CREATIVE REAL ESTATE PROFESSIONAL

As a public service, *Creative Real Estate Magazine* maintains rosters of Creative Real Estate Professionals practicing in every area of the country. These rosters are on a database and are updated at least once a month. You may request the names of professionals in your area merely by writing or calling the Public Information Service of *Creative Real Estate Magazine,* Drawer L, Rancho Santa Fe, California 92067, telephone (619) 756-1441. If you write, please include a stamped, self-addressed envelope. We cannot accept collect calls for this service.

You will have to put in time and effort to determine who you can work with most comfortably and effectively. Take the names you acquire and

☐

EXCHANGE SUPPLEMENT

THIS IS INTENDED TO BE A LEGALLY BINDING CONTRACT. READ IT CAREFULLY.
CALIFORNIA ASSOCIATION OF REALTORS® (CAR) STANDARD FORM

The following terms and conditions are hereby incorporated in and made a part of the Agreement dated _____ , 19____ , executed

on property commonly known as _____

by _____ | | Buyer, | | Seller, | | Other _____

and _____ | | Buyer, | | Seller, | | Other _____

(If this agreement is used as a modification of an existing agreement, the parties intend to modify the agreement as below. All other provisions of the existing agreement shall remain in full force.)

1. **INTENT TO EXCHANGE:** It is the intent of _____
("Exchangor") to utilize this transaction as part of an exchange of like-kind properties under Internal Revenue Code §1031 and the regulations promulgated thereunder.

2. **TERMS:** The undersigned agree to cooperate in effecting such an exchange, provided that:

   (a) Exchangor intends to exchange the property being transferred under this agreement for "Other Property" as follows:

   (Check One)

   ☐ the property described as _____
   ☐ property to be located and designated by Exchangor who shall take all steps necessary to enter into a contract and complete acquisition or transfer of such Other Property pursuant to this agreement.

   (b) Exchangor shall indemnify and hold harmless all other parties to this transaction from all costs and liabilities arising from or connected in any way with the exchange.

   (c) If Exchangor is unable to locate, designate, enter into a contract to acquire, or transfer, or complete acquisition or transfer, of such Other Property:

   (Check One)

   ☐ This transaction shall close as a sale, without extension of time for closing.
   ☐ The close of this transaction shall be extended by a maximum of _____ calendar days to enable Exchangor to complete such arrangements.
   ☐ This transaction shall be cancelled and all parties shall be released from further obligation.
   ☐ Other: _____

   _____

   _____

(d) No party to this transaction shall be required to take title to the Other Property, for any period of time, as an accommodation to Exchangor, unless agreed to in writing.

(e) All parties agree to take such actions and execute or consent to such additional documents and transactions as may be reasonably requested by Exchangor, provided that all other conditions of this agreement are met.

3. ADDITIONAL TERMS: _____

_____

_____

_____

_____

_____

4. **TAX AND LEGAL ADVICE:** The manner of structuring an exchange transaction will have significant tax and legal consequences. Parties should consult their legal and/or tax advisors regarding this important matter. Locating and designating properties pursuant to this agreement, if applicable, are the responsibility of the Exchangor, and will not occur automatically as a result of this agreement. If the exchange will be non-simultaneous, under federal tax law (a) the property to be acquired by Exchangor must be identified within 45 calendar days after transfer of Exchangor's current property, (b) the acquisition must generally be completed within 180 calendar days after transfer of Exchangor's current property, and (c) the 180 day period may be shorter under some circumstances. Receipt of a copy hereof is acknowledged.

Signature _____ Date _____   Signature _____ Date _____

Signature _____ Date _____   Signature _____ Date _____

OFFICE USE ONLY

Reviewed by Broker or Designee _____

Date _____

FORM ES-14

EQUAL HOUSING OPPORTUNITY
M-SC-OCT-91

make appointments to see each one in person. You should be concerned primarily that they are interested in you as a person, and with their desire and willingness to help you achieve your objectives. Schedule the appointments for times when you are alert and unpressured. Be punctual, supply the information requested, and be factual and honest.

Some questions you may want to ask the counselor are:

1. How long have you been practicing Creative Real Estate?
2. What professional affiliations (exchange group, state organization, designations, etc.) do you have in Creative Real Estate?
3. How extensively do you research and keep records of the market trends?
4. What are the tax consequences of the majority of your transactions?
5. May I speak with some of your recent clients?

It is very possible that you may decide that the first person you interview is the right one. Great! Remember my previous advice: don't look back. Go with your feelings, decisions, and the resulting flow. Give it your full attention.

If the first interview doesn't feel good, try another. However, don't talk to another counselor unless you have the serious intention of making a commitment. It is an unfair use of the counselor's time for you to be just "shopping." When you find the right party to work with and the right "chemistry," be ready to act.

Besides the many professional advantages a broker can provide for you, an established Creative Real Estate Professional can often provide significant additional benefits for the starting Creative Real Estater.

In the course of their regular dealings, Creative Real Estate Professionals complete many transactions by acquiring "can adds" (see Chapter 4) for themselves or clients. They usually receive these in large, multiple-exchange transactions to balance equities for tax purposes. They have no other real use or purpose for these small properties and are very often more than willing to sell them for nothing down on extended terms with soft paper (Chapter 4) to someone who will perform.

This could be a good starting opportunity for the new Creative Real Estater.

To summarize, your purpose in interviewing is to find someone with whom you can work for as long a time as it takes to build your estate rapidly and comfortably.

When you do, I will see you in the Creative Real Estate Marketplace.

Your new Kessler's Keys to Success are:

🔑 Where is it?

🔑 Who participates?

🔑 What happens?

🔑 You can, too

🔑 Starting from the top

🔑 The nitty-gritty

🔑 Let's go to a marketing meeting

🔑 Who can you turn to?

🔑 How to find a creative real estate professional

PART V

Keeping and Enjoying Your Wealth

Seek not proud riches but such as thou mayest get justly, use soberly, distribute cheerfully, and leave contentedly.

—Francis Bacon

What's Ahead?

As I write this in the second half of 1994, many trends and occurrences are setting a pattern for the balance of the decade. The waning recession, impending inflation, and continuing high unemployment require that conditions and opportunities be given thorough scrutiny in order to plan for the financial future.

Interest rates are now increasing almost daily. Financial institutions are seizing the opportunity to make up for their past misdeeds. The depository institutions, when they were deregulated, were permitted to share in equity profits with their borrowers in return for a lower interest rate and easier payment schedules on the loans. As a result, when the real estate marketplace took its recent nosedive, many of the greediest, and resultingly careless, financial institutions became insolvent. This resulted in the largest government bailout in history, by the then newly formed Resolution Trust Corporation (RTC).

The RTC was formed by the federal government to salvage the failing and failed banking institutions (savings and loans), and dispose of the enormous volume of loan-defaulted and foreclosed real estate held by these institutions.

Contrary to justifiably cynical expectations, the RTC did a reasonably credible job of liquidating a large volume of loan-defaulted properties in less time than predicted. This served to help clear the decks for what should be a steady, though slow, recovery over the next several years.

However, the continuing high unemployment rate, the ongoing downsizing of industrial and commercial giants, plus the replacement of humans with electronic and other high technology must be considered threatening to a resumption of the pre-recession socio-economic lifestyle.

Tallying the downsizing and closure plans of major corporations like AT&T, IBM, General Motors, Boeing, and Sears reveals a potential loss of more than a million jobs. Already over 24 million businesses are being operated at home, and the likelihood is that number will exceed 35 million in this decade.

The pattern is clear. Entrepreneurialism will become the most significant growth opportunity of the decade. With that comes the need for more application of creativity than ever before in history. Real estate has a head start, already having had to develop creativity as a survival mechanism. This decade will be recorded as the milestone in which creative financing was dignified and elevated from a skillful art to a recognized science.

In the '80s, a naive fan club of homeowners confused inflation with appreciation. Recent adjustments, in some areas more severe than others, were hard to accept. But the recession left no choice. Reluctant buyers forced prices down, wiping out the unrealized profits.

Gold fever became a widespread malady, and more speculators than ever entered the gold market. It promptly stagnated and shows little sign of dramatic price increase in the foreseeable future.

The energy crunch was dramatically emphasized as the culprit that damaged the stability of the dollar. It was a convenient scapegoat. We are consuming more power, electricity, fuel, and energy by-products than ever, with a continuing supply available.

Petro-dollars were having an increased impact in the real estate market. A decade later, the oil sheiks are still amassing fortunes and buying for cash whatever they fancy, but in the long-term they have made no significant difference in the real estate economy.

STATISTICS THAT FORECAST THE ECONOMY

We hear commentators and read columnists referring to "The Economy." How do they know? It's certainly not quite as simple as the Boy Scout trick of wetting an index finger and holding it up to see which side dries in order to determine wind direction. Or is it? Not if the government is involved. The government has established an Index of Leading Indicators which is designed to predict the economy's course six to nine months into the future. However, like weather forecasting, it has a spotty record. To arrive at a predicted percentage of growth or decline, the Commerce Department uses these statistics to establish the Index of Leading Indicators.

- Manufacturing Labor Hours—average hours employees work per week
- Unemployment Claims—weekly claims on unemployment insurance
- New Consumer Goods Orders—orders for manufactured consumer goods and materials
- Delayed Deliveries—percent of firms getting delayed deliveries
- New Plants, Equipment—contracts and orders for new plants and equipment
- Building Permits—monthly total building permits issued
- Unfilled Orders for Durables—change in manufacturers' orders for durable goods

- Commodity Prices—change in sensitive materials prices
- Stock Prices—500 common stocks
- Money Supply (M2)—real money supply average for the month
- Consumer Confidence—consumer expectations of economy's health

Isn't it interesting that those 11 indices all have equal weight, including Consumer Confidence, which has to be as qualitative as it is quantitative? And what about a margin of error, for reporting, sampling, tallying?

But most importantly, all the figures the Commerce Department releases are *at least 18 months old,* so how can these statistics be used to predict the economy's course six to nine months into the future?

Your guess is as good as mine. It's certainly more current than their guess!

With the current proliferation of investment opportunities, vehicles, and styles, the signs I read are foretelling:

A mixed bull/bear market for real estate. Many investors can't afford to invest utilizing traditional methods, but with the cost low compared to what it will be at the end of this decade and beyond, they can't afford not to invest now. The obvious solution is the employment of Creative Real Estate techniques to leverage purchases and build assets quickly.

Full recovery from the recession we started in this era will not come until late 1995, making an investment strategy geared to bad times the safest bet for the short term for those in the real estate market.

No dramatic change of long- or short-term rates is indicated, just a slow, steady, Fed-directed upward trend. Tax adjustments to provide the capital required for investment to revitalize the economy will not particularly get priority treatment by Congress. Faster writeoffs in the form of accelerated depreciation, liberal investment tax credits, and reduced capital gains tax would all be particularly beneficial to real estate investors. However, the prospect of such legislation is not in the near-term foreseeable future. As a result, the most important consideration in investment will be the one that has been most frequently overlooked outside of Creative Real Estate: the ability to reduce, defer, or avoid income taxes.

While continuing government controls and the attempt to socialize the real estate market along with the rest of the economy have eroded some of its potential, real estate continues to present some of the safest opportunities to multiply money using leverage. Anyone, regardless of age, education, personal characteristics, or background can do it, with commitment.

Consider those among the *Forbes* 400 richest men and women in America. Their estimated net worth is $220 billion.

- 15 are in their thirties, 118 are in their sixties.
- 10 never graduated from high school.
- 47 have an M.B.A.
- 55 are women.
- 106 have been divorced at least once.
- 214 had no significant inheritance.
- 11 have, at one time, filed for bankruptcy.
- 4 are survivors of Nazi concentration camps.

Economies are not static systems. Causes and effects forever change. In the next two chapters, I offer suggestions for investment strategy in both bad times and good. While no list of ideas or techniques can be all-inclusive, nor can individual results be guaranteed, following these steps can enhance your opportunities to make, keep, and enjoy your wealth.

Your dreams come true when you act to turn them into realities.

We are such stuff as dreams are made of.

—Shakespeare

17

Making Money in Bad Times

*People find riches in fields, buildings, veins, river beds, and pockets.
Whichever, it takes work to get.*

—Art Linkletter

By now you know that I am not a pessimist. The pessimist looks at a twelve-gallon bucket with six gallons of water in it and says, "My bucket is half empty." The optimist, observing the same situation, says, "My bucket is half full." Technically, both are correct.

As a realistic idealist, I look at every situation as a challenge. I say, "How can we make more effective use of this situation? What can we do with the water, and the remaining, unused capacity of the bucket?"

And that is my outlook on our economy. Make the best use of what we have under existing conditions, and plan for the most effective use of the unused capacity. The only constant is change. We can count on that. Therefore, there's one thing you can say for sure about good times or bad times: they *will* come to an end. A capitalistic economy is, by its nature, cyclical, and the very events that take place in one swing of the cycle set the stage for the next.

It is important to realize that, as cycles change, markets change. During the '80s, Denver was in the throes of a real estate depression. In 1993, Denver's housing market was the hottest in the United States. According to a survey of 25 major areas by Runzheimer International, a consulting firm based in Wisconsin, Denver housing appreciated 15.5% in 1993. A typical 2,000 square-foot, four-bedroom suburban house averaged $131,383 in January 1993. By January 1994 that average had increased to $151,813. Other appreciating areas are Salt Lake City—by 14.4%; Kansas City, Missouri—8.8% rise; Cincinnati—up 6.5%; and Milwaukee—gaining 6%. During that same period, California prices continued to decline: San Francisco, traditionally price-stable—down 1.7%; and Los Angeles, the largest market—decreased 7.3%. It is interesting to note the relationship between those figures and employment in those areas. The appreciating areas have the lowest unemployment numbers, the depreciating areas the highest.

The heavy buying and rising prices of the upswing lead to overpricing, overextension, and market saturation, all of which signal the start of a downswing. Boom is followed by recession, which is followed by boom.

Each time a recession hits, people view it with amazement and a "how could that have happened?" attitude. Yet recessions are nothing new. According to the National Bureau of Economic Research, since 1854 there have been 29 periods of economic expansion and 29 recessions. The average expansion lasted 33 months, while the average recession lasted 19 months.

Overall, this is encouraging. If history remains an accurate forecaster, we can expect more good times than bad. Nevertheless, to mind our store we should have a strategy and plan for each environment. And the "ostrich theory" (putting your head in the sand until trouble goes away) doesn't work effectively in commerce, real estate, or other crises.

Interestingly enough, the longest recession in America's history was not the Great Depression of 1929, which lasted 50 months, but the doldrums of 1873 to 1879, which prevailed for 65 months. The shortest recession was the one following World War I, a 7-month dip. Not yet counting the recession that was in force until this year, the next most recent trough—in 1980— was 21 months long, and the 1973 decline lasted a little less than the average—16 months. The length of the period of decline or rise does not necessarily correlate with the severity or boom of each.

Recessions are simply a fact of economic life, and cannot be ignored any more than sun-worshippers can ignore the rain. As you venture into Creative Real Estate, you will encounter recessions as they occur, and may even begin your career right in the middle of one. They are unavoidable, but predictable, and should be built into your investment planning.

The essential point that you must recognize is that bad economic times will not necessarily cause you to lose money. They may slow you down, but they will not break you if you follow a sound, conservative approach to investment. A baker's dozen of the proven elements of such an approach follows.

1. During Recessionary Eras, Proceed with Caution. In a difficult real estate market you must broaden the range of your watchfulness. In addition to watching prices and cash flows, you need to watch interest rates, the availability of money, the condition of the general economy in your area, and any social, economic, or political event that can possibly affect the status of your investment.

You must continue to use the "worst possible situation" philosophy. Suppose you find an investment opportunity that because of the recession looks like a true bargain—a building selling at 50% below the price it should be. A temptation even during the worst of times. But before you jump to buy it, consider what would happen if the entire market dropped another 20%.

Could you stand it? Could you afford to keep it at those levels? Could you afford to sell it at that price? These questions must be answered before you make an offer.

In bad times, it's better to be out of the action and safe on the sidelines for awhile, than in the fray and sorry.

2. Keep an Eye on Unemployment Levels. The unemployment level is the single most significant factor that indicates who is going to be buying real estate. This holds just as true for commercial and industrial property as it does for residential.

When people are out of work, they hold on to their cash rather than spend it to make down payments on homes. They force themselves to be satisfied with a $350 monthly rental payment rather than obligate themselves to a $500 monthly house payment. When times are really bad, families double up in apartments to share the rent among two unemployed or partially employed breadwinners.

During periods of high unemployment, factories not only stop expansion, they close down and wait or sell off. In a recession, everyone and every organization wants to keep costs at a minimum. People with small offices start doing business at home. People in large offices squeeze the desks together and manage with less square footage. The unemployment rate is directly related to it all. You must watch that figure constantly during recessionary times.

Many people put great emphasis on housing starts as an indicator. The number of housing starts is misleading and all it shows is the state of activity in a particular, relatively small industry. Housing starts depend on the availability of land, money, government subsidies, and other factors—factors that are traditionally out of phase with general real estate cycles. Builders usually start building when times are good, and finish their projects in time to try to sell during the next downturn.

Unemployment levels are the indicators most closely linked to real estate use. Direct your attention to these signals at all times, but in bad times watch them as if your investments depended on them. They do.

3. When Selling, Start Earlier. As a seller, you must be aware that in bad times buyers are going to be following our first point of advice: they are going to "proceed with caution." They will take longer to make up their minds on a purchase. No matter how tempting your price and terms, they will analyze and re-analyze every aspect of a transaction. All this boils down to is delay, and if you're in a hurry to sell, it can be maddening as well as costly.

If under ordinary circumstances it would take 90 days to sell a property, in depressed circumstances allow 150 to 180 days or more. That's up to six months, which is a long time to wait for something to happen. Yet it won't seem so long if you put your property on the market that long before the date you actually need or want to sell.

Bad times create a buyer's market. The prospective purchaser has more to choose from, more people after his money, and time on his side. He cannot be pushed. If you're pressured by time to sell in such a market, you have to make your offering sweeter and sweeter, giving up more and more to generate action from reluctant buyers. You can wind up being your own worst enemy, just by having waited too long. So, when selling in down times, don't wait. Put your property on the market six months earlier than usual.

4. Invest for the Longer Haul. At best, speculation for quick profits is a calculated risk. In bad times, speculation is nothing more than a gamble, and a risky one. Don't speculate. There are always those who succumb to the temptation of the great bargain, the "steal" that just "has to skyrocket" as soon as the market turns around. And almost always their fate is sad.

Besides the normal risks surrounding speculation at any time, in bad times there are two additional pitfalls: (1) you don't know exactly how long it will be before the market turns around, and (2) when it finally does, there will be prudent investors in addition to many other speculators trying to unload their properties as well. Unless you are a seasoned speculator, and unless you can handle losing, both financially and psychologically, unless you can go into a game *knowing* you're going to get clobbered and handle it well, then don't speculate in bad times.

Yet bad times can be a fine time to invest. Prices are low, sellers are willing to concede to favorable terms, and cash is king. A judiciously chosen investment, with enough security to weather the storm if the recession deepens, could be the best move you will ever make. But don't expect results tomorrow. Be willing to wait a long, long time. Dramatic moves, according to historical charts, take six to eight years to happen in real estate. If you're set in your mind and in your bank account to wait that long, you'll make money.

5. When Buying, Offer 5% Less. If in normal circumstances you make it a practice to initially offer 10% less than the asking price, in bad times offer 15% less. This is not to suggest that when things are rough, you are going to take advantage of people's misfortune and try to steal their property. Not at all. It's simply sound business strategy that makes use of conditions in the marketplace.

Despite the old saw, opportunity does not knock but once. In fact, opportunities are like streetcars. Another one is always coming. If you miss one, you merely have to be ready to catch the next one that comes along.

In slow times, there are more properties to choose from. The negotiation time is longer. There are more factors to consider. By making the offer 5% lower, you are setting up a longer negotiation period, you are opening up the space for the seller to concede to other terms, and you are giving yourself more time to act. The offer is not ridiculously low. It still sets the stage for a win/win situation. And it shows that you're an informed buyer in a buyer's market. You will have extended your opportunity time and find yourself closer to the upturn.

6. Confine Your Activities to Areas You Know Well. Bad times are not the times to learn a new game. Not when everybody's hungry. Not when everybody's running scared. Not when people are tempted to be less truthful and less ethical than they might be if times were good.

If you venture into an unfamiliar arena of lions that have just been fed, you may get out of it alive. If you venture into it when the lions are hungry, you can imagine the result.

When the market is tight and dealings are sharp, you had better be talking a language you know. You'd better know every aspect, every pitfall, and every possible mistake. That means stay close to what you know and do best. Put off entering new markets for the good times. You will be better able to afford that kind of education when money is flowing more freely. Experience may be the best education, but the tuition is always too high.

7. Be Prepared to Pay High Interest Rates. Despite all its efforts to legislate and regulate the money supply, the government has never succeeded in changing the law of supply and demand. When times are tough money is scarce, and when money is scarce it costs more.

People (and this includes institutions) who have money when money supplies are low are simply not willing to lend without charging heavily. They have many options open to them, and can maximize profits by taking advantage of depressed prices. They can choose to deal with only the most highly qualified borrowers. Also, they are in a position to wait out the market.

The government, in releasing more cash into the system or in lowering the banks' reserve requirements, is only putting a Band-Aid on a severe wound. After more than 60 years of the government playing with our money supply, we find our monetary system in worse shape than ever. Furthermore, despite all of this manipulation, we still find that in bad times, when it is sorely needed, money costs more, while in good times it costs less. According to Ludwig Von Mises, "Government is the only agency that can take a useful commodity like paper, slap some ink on it, and make it totally worthless."

Lamenting or arguing with the situation doesn't serve any useful purpose. Accept it. Work with it. Be prepared to usually pay more for money in a depressed market and allow for that in your negotiations. Recessions eventually turn around, and when interest rates go down, you can refinance. It may not always be easy, but it is possible and is another factor to build into your structuring of transactions in a recessionary economy. High interest rates, along with high unemployment and unstable prices, are part of the down cycle. The most recent recession has been "the exception that proves the rule." With its low interest rates it validated Kessler's Law and provided exceptional opportunities to refinance. There is nothing *you* can do about lowering the high rates. At those times, make the best deal you can and refinance in better times.

8. Be Skeptical of Bargains. When people are hungry, their particular way of exercising creativity may include elements of dishonesty. They are more likely to dress up a deal or a property to make it look like something it's not. Or they might embroider the truth and neglect to address the negatives.

Should you encounter a seemingly terrific "bargain," investigate thoroughly. Ask yourself, "If this deal is so good, why hasn't someone snapped it up already?" Real estate is a complicated business and there are many factors that lurk below the surface—factors that you cannot see without thorough investigation.

Try to determine the real reason the property is for sale. Since there are no problem properties, only problem ownerships, try to learn the specific problem you would be solving for the owner by buying this particular piece of real estate. If you cannot determine a legitimate ownership problem, watch out. There must be factors the owner is neglecting to mention in discussion of the transaction.

If you are interested, even knowing that you cannot rely upon the seller's representations, investigate more thoroughly. If you still cannot determine the real reason for the problem ownership, pass. "One swallow does not a summer make." There will be many more problem ownerships for you to solve both safely and profitably.

9. Make Offers with Low Cash Outlays. In depressed periods, cash is king. As a wise investor, you must conserve your cash in every way you can. If an emergency strikes and you need cash, where will you go? To the banks who "aren't lending at this time," or pay exorbitant interest rates elsewhere? Or will you go to your pocket and get through the crisis on your own?

Remember, as a bad-times buyer, you're doing the seller a favor by taking the property off his hands. His biggest concern may not be cash, but getting out of a deteriorating situation. So go easy on the cash. Besides, if the soft market continues, you may need your cash to pay other debts.

If a seller cannot agree to your terms, offer non-cash inducements: increased collateral, a slightly higher price with a carryback mortgage, an attractive leaseback, an option to buy back, or anything reasonable, short of cash.

10. Seek Expert Counsel from Local Brokers, Lawyers, and Accountants. In times of economic distress, your real estate transactions aren't going to have as much margin for error as they would in good times. It would take less to turn a good transaction into a marginal or bad one. The social and political climate in the locale of your prospective purchase takes on greater significance. Minor events in politics and in the economy of the area could seriously alter the value of your purchase. Though your own attorney may be the most renowned expert on tax shelters in New Jersey, if he doesn't know that the people in Fictitious Valley, Arkansas, are planning to assess the cost of a sewer program that would cost you a small fortune, his tax advice won't do you much good. A member of the Fictitious Valley Bar Association would be aware of that situation and would point it out to you as soon as you retained him. With that information, the bargain you found in Fictitious Valley wouldn't look as good. Similarly, a local broker would be able to advise you about occupancy rates, comparable sales, market trends, and projections based on personal experience. So, leverage people; and be careful about using the "lever" in the right place.

11. Get a Handle on Area Politics and Attitudes. Real estate is sometimes a game of politics, most often local politics. Local zoning boards, town councils, and bureaucrats have control over the operation and the future of property in their town.

While talking with an elderly gentleman in a section of the affluent suburb of Bloomfield Hills, Michigan, he told me that before anyone could put up a fence, it had to be approved as decorative by the local fence committee. A decorative fence may cost thousands of dollars more to construct than one that is not decorative by the fence committee's definition.

"Who is the fence committee?" I asked.

"I am," he replied.

In this area, one man's opinion determines whether a property owner would spend a few hundred dollars on an ordinary fence or a few thousand on a decorative one.

This is a minor example. But in the same vein, if your only reason for buying a 40-unit building in a distant town is to convert it to condominiums, and the local mayor was elected on the strength of a platform of holding down condominium conversions, you are in for an expensive fight. And very probably a losing one.

Rent control can hurt the real estate market even without being in force. During 1980, a rent control measure was drafted onto the San Diego city ballot and almost immediately, large investors started to pull out of the apartment market—just in case it passed, which it didn't. But if it had, and you were buying an apartment house in San Diego with a plan to increase rents to cover payments and you didn't know the measure was slated to go to a vote, you might have found yourself in a no-win situation with no way out.

You must be conversant with the details of politics and government in the area where you are contemplating a purchase. This is especially true in bad times when there's no rising market to cover your mistakes.

12. Shop the Money Market Carefully. When the real estate market is hurting, you'll have more properties to choose from, but you'll have fewer money outlets available. The availability of money will not follow any recognizable pattern. By and large it will be more expensive, and the motivations of the lenders will vary more widely. Some will be looking to make a killing with loan fees. Some will actually plan to put you in the position of being unable to make payments so that they can foreclose and take the property for a fraction of its value. The money markets will be ruthless. You must pick your way through them with care.

Bad times demand that you seek an expert's advice. Many people think that getting a loan is a simple matter of filling out an application and signing a note. It's more complicated than that, and an expert who knows the financial market can not only save you money, he can save you from disaster. This is a most desirable and sensible area in which to leverage people. Employ the services of a reputable loan broker who specializes in the type of loan you seek.

13. Sharpen Your Sense of Timing. When in Doubt, Wait 10 More Days Before Acting. First, when is it appropriate to have doubts? Any one of the elements previously mentioned would be ample justification: a great bargain, a fantastic opportunity in another area of the country, a seemingly cheap loan, or any kind of unusual circumstance. In bad times, these exceptional offerings are highly suspect and warrant increased vigilance. Double-check terms and double-check the market. Play out the worst possible situation in your mind. Assess every aspect of your transaction. Prepare an offer only if you are absolutely certain of terms, conditions, and timing.

Then wait. Give it 10 days. Chances are it won't run away. If it does, don't worry. There will be others. In hard times, there are always more offerings than you can possibly become involved with. If it doesn't run away, the wait hasn't cost you a dime. You will have, in that period, sharpened your timing, reassured yourself once again, and cleared up any remaining doubts. The only risk you've run is the risk of being too safe.

If forewarned is indeed forearmed, you are now ready to do battle not only in ordinary times but in the worst of times. But before we carry the military analogy too far, let's step back. Real estate is not really a war, it's a game. To enjoy it and to ultimately win, you must continue to regard it as a sophisticated game, played by adults, for high stakes, and for keeps, with both sides winning.

To survive the game with your sanity intact, you must be ready to lose a round or two. If winning each step of the way becomes the *only* thing for you, the game will cease to be fun. So lighten up and remember that it's only money. Remember the cycles: what goes up must come down and *vice versa*. And, be it good times or bad, *your* real estate fortune will always be at your feet.

Some more Kessler's Keys to Success:

☛ *"Smooth seas do not make skillful sailors."*

—African Proverb

☛ *"To act is easy, to think is hard."*

—Goethe

18

Making Money in Good Times

Money is power, freedom, a cushion, the root of all evil, the sum of blessings.

—Carl Sandburg

Who doesn't love prosperity? Everybody's working, making money, and buying like mad. Property values are going up and the rising market covers a multitude of mistakes.

Real estate brokers are buying Rolls Royces and repaneling their offices in wood. Dentists are spending more time looking at property than at teeth. Waiters are becoming real estate experts.

At the resort real estate development I was brokering, I spent every working day in the dining room with clients, for lunch and usually dinner. One of the bus boys was always particularly interested in my presentations, listening carefully as I explained to my clients the benefits of using leverage to build assets quickly. Often he would manage to encounter me between appointments—perhaps when I was entering or departing the dining room or my office—and seek clarification of something he had heard me discussing.

Carlos had immigrated from Mexico, and was a diligent worker. He was ambitious and intent upon getting ahead in his chosen country. It was a pleasure for me to share my knowledge with him. When he advanced to a waiter's position, he made his first leveraged real estate purchase. Since then, he has become the *maitre'd* at the resort (which was recently acclaimed as the world's best spa) and he has acquired houses for his entire family—parents, married children, and other relatives—in addition to other rental properties. Whenever I see Carlos at the restaurant, we reminisce and discuss his latest transactions. He reminds me that he actually began his active Creative Real Estate career when he read the first edition of this book, and uses it as a continuing guide.

As a Creative Real Estate Practitioner, you too will benefit from an upturn in the cycle. It would almost be difficult *not* to. However, to achieve long-lasting success you must maximize upcycle benefits and use good times to build protection against future bad times. This chapter will help you achieve these goals. Here is a baker's dozen checklist for good-times investing.

1. Remember: What Goes Up Must Come Down. By this I do not mean that property that is rising in value during good times necessarily will fall in value during bad times. Too many factors are at work affecting real estate values to be able to make such a statement. As I write this book, there is a severe reorganization and consolidation of manufacturing facilities in the automotive industry. Cities with a heavy concentration of auto workers are experiencing unemployment levels as severe as those during the Great Depression of 1929. Yet housing prices have not fallen. In many of the stricken cities, housing prices have remained level during the recent recession, while in others they have actually increased!

In real estate, the saying "what goes up must come down" has a significance beyond the simple rising and falling of prices. It has to do with the type of property that can give you the best return on your investment.

When the real estate market begins an upturn, one type of property might be most attractive for investment. Let's say, for example, that during a previous slump, apartment vacancies were high and apartment buildings, having become unprofitable, began selling on temptingly favorable terms. Aware investors start buying apartment buildings and instantly their investments appreciate rapidly. You, too, may be tempted to cash in on the apartment boom.

But remember our first rule: what goes up must come down. As investors move into this rising market, prices go up, cash flows get thinner, and terms get tighter. In a short time, apartment buildings will no longer be yielding the best return on investment capital.

If you know this, you'll take a step ahead of the other investors. You'll start looking at commercial property which tends to start its upsurge later than residential property. As yields in the apartment market are going down, yields in the commercial market may be going up. Later in the cycle, commercial may be on its way down while industrial is going up.

Shop the *entire* real estate market looking one step ahead of the cycle, and you will get the maximum possible return during good times.

2. Real Estate Cycles—Major and Minor. Two to three years for small changes and six to eight years for dramatic changes are established patterns. No matter how active the real estate market appears, major market changes take time. It's the nature of the business.

Small changes are caused by fluctuations in interest rates and the temporary over-supply or under-supply of buildings. These changes stir up the market, keep people guessing, and generally move in one direction for only a couple of years.

Major changes are caused by more dramatic events, such as the recession we had during 1973 and 1974. It was a long time coming, and when we pulled out of it, the real estate market was strong until another downturn began in 1979 and 1980, followed by the 1983 upturn and the 1989 down.

As an investor, you must use this knowledge of cycles to your advantage. At the beginning of a good cycle, be optimistic. But don't expect to get rich within 12 or 18 months. Dramatic changes simply do not happen that fast.

Yet because you know that cycles do not change suddenly, you can make your move into real estate with confidence and ride the upward tide. Almost any purchase will be a sound investment for at least a year or two. This means you should:

3. Act Early in the Good Cycle. It's ironic, but people are often apprehensive of or paralyzed by rising prices. After the real estate market breaks out of a doldrum and prices start to rise, most of the investing public turns into a society of "watchers." They see housing being rented at higher prices. They see buildings snapped up in a few days at the listed prices. They see optimism starting to build all around them. What do they do? They watch and wait. They say, "Gee, I'm going to keep an eye on this trend and see if it's for real, to see if it will continue."

As they watch, the trend is playing itself out. The really good transactions are going by and being replaced by the not-so-good deals. Soon the not-so-good deals are replaced by the marginal deals, which are replaced by the shaky deals, which are replaced by the downright bad deals. By the time they act, it's too late.

In good times real estate is not for watching and waiting. It's for investing. The earlier you invest during good times, the better off you'll be. Do your waiting *after* you invest. Robert G. "Bob" Allen, in his book *Nothing Down*, quotes our favorite saying in this regard: "Don't wait to buy real estate, buy real estate and wait." Do your waiting during bad times. Don't wait while the good times are rolling—they'll roll right by.

4. Speculate for Quick Profits; Invest for the Long Haul. The speculator is someone who hopes to make money *only* from a rise in price. A speculator is a gambler. He bets on the moves in the market. By necessity, his strategy must be a short-term one.

When market conditions take an upturn, the speculator must jump in, ride his fortunes up, and sell at the first sign of a downturn. Generally he can't sit through even minor downturns. He's leveraged out too far. His purchases are speculative and any bad break can literally break him.

If you're going to speculate at all, you must do it in good times. You must be nimble. Time is not on your side.

The investor considers many factors besides price. He considers long-term appreciation, cash flow, tax shelter, and total return. He stands ready to hold onto the property during downturns in the market. He is willing to put additional money into repairs, additions, and non-cosmetic improvements. He is in for the long haul.

5. Consider the Next Downturn When Buying and Have Enough "Cushion" to Weather It. As investors, we know there are cycles in the market. Knowing this, we must always be thinking one cycle ahead when we make an investment. When times are good, it's hard to think about them being bad, but to survive, to make money, and to prosper, we can't just look at the up side.

As a buyer during good times, you know that sooner or later the trend will turn and times will get bad. Unfortunately, you don't know exactly when. You can guess, but you might guess wrong. The market may shift just at the time you want to sell. If that happens, you can either sell and take a loss or you can ride out the storm and sell at a profit when the downturn is over. You know the downturn itself will turn around. Downturns always do.

But you won't be able to ride out that storm unless you have a cushion. A cushion is enough money to take you through six to eight months of owning property when nothing is happening in the market. Six to eight months is the approximate length of time between the end of a downtrend and the beginning of the next uptrend. It's a dead spot, a time when you can sell only by taking terrific losses, if indeed you can sell at all.

For example, if during good times a building will be 100% rented, during bad times it will be 90% rented and during dead times it may be only 80% rented. If you can earn $200 a month net at 100% occupancy, break even at 90% and lose $200 a month at 80%, then you ought to have a cash reserve of $1,200 to $1,600. That is the sum you will need to take you through six to eight months of losing $200 a month. By then the downturn should have played itself out.

The investor who drops his last nickel into a piece of property is extremely vulnerable to having that property taken away some day. You'll never get rich on the receiving end of a foreclosure notice, but you will if you can weather a downturn without financial hardship.

6. Buy What Everyone Else Ignores. Earl Nightingale, the radio commentator, once said, "If you look at what everybody is doing and do the exact opposite, you may never make another mistake as long as you live." While this is an exaggeration, it holds some truth for the good-times real estate investor.

When times are good and people see profitable opportunities wherever they turn, they tend to ignore the "ugly ducklings." After all, who wants to bother with falling plaster and wheezing furnaces when there are good returns to be had on modern garden apartments?

You do if you realize that when the cycle turns, the ugly duckling you buy can't get any uglier. It will continue to plug along, while the vacancy factor mounts in those flashy garden apartments.

In good times, as in bad times, pay particular attention to our abiding principle: there are no problem properties, only problem ownerships. Seek out problem ownerships and begin converting them to their highest and best use.

While everyone else is suffering through the bad times, you're building, improving, and turning your ugly duckling into a swan. In the next good cycle, you can sell your swan at an appropriate price. Because predictably, during the next good period, everyone will again be looking for swans. And you, wiser and wealthier, will be looking for more ugly ducklings.

7. Exercise Options Early. You know the market is going to turn, but you don't know exactly when. With an option in your pocket and the market on the rise, you are tempted to sit back and let the property appreciate while your investment is limited to the money you paid for the option.

If you paid $1,000 for a two-year option to buy land at $50,000, and the good market takes its value to $60,000 in a year, you might say, "Well, I'll wait until it hits $70,000, then exercise and sell for a cool $20,000 profit. Not bad for a $1,000 investment."

But the market could go flat or even turn down in the next year. If you don't exercise, you may find yourself holding a worthless piece of paper a year later. If you do exercise, you can participate in a long-term rise and earn significant profits four years from now. A short-term dip might hurt you in the meantime, but it won't hurt you nearly as much as an expired option would have.

Remember, options expire. Land doesn't.

8. Extend Options Only with a Declining Price Formula. Using the above example, suppose the second year goes by and you don't exercise the option. It expires and is worthless. If you still believe in the long-term outlook for the property, you may want to buy yourself another year. But if immediate conditions have made the land temporarily sink in value to $48,000, you don't renew your option to buy at $50,000.

You may believe that the land will be worth $100,000 one day, and you may be right. You just don't know when that day will be. In the next year, it may turn around and head back up in a general uptrend, but then again, it might sink in a temporary lull. So if you want to renew, go ahead—but write the option so that you can exercise at $45,000. If the seller goes for it, you're in the game for another year. If he doesn't, don't chase him. Take your loss on the first option and forget about it.

You will be a wise investor indeed when you learn to admit a mistake, take a small loss, and move on to something else. You will be an eternal fool if you continually chase your original idea, trying to make up a small loss just to prove yourself right. Even the smartest market analysts know they are going to be wrong occasionally. They build that margin for error into their calculations and take enough profit when they're right to make up for the times they are wrong. But they don't brood about the errors and try to make them right. They just chalk it up to experience and move on.

9. Buy Out Partners with Profits. When times are good and property seems to be worth more every day, you will think, "My partners and I have $20,000 profit in this building already. If I buy them out now, I get to keep all, rather than just part of the appreciation that's sure to build up on it."

This is especially tempting when you have a store of cash that's not being used. Don't give in to the temptation.

Don't use your cash to buy out partners. Use your profits. If you and a partner had bought a building for $50,000 that appreciated to $70,000, your share of the paper profit is $10,000. Rather than paying $10,000 out of your pocket to buy out your partner, borrow against or use the accumulation of the $10,000 profit you have in the building. Times are good, money is available, and banks are willing to lend. If the uptrend continues, you will have the future appreciation all to yourself. If it doesn't you will still have $10,000 in your pocket to get you through the rough times.

10. Move In and Out Quickly in Speculative Opportunities. Speculation is a risky business. In bad times, you want to avoid it entirely. In good times, you want to do it carefully, if at all.

If the gambler in you won't sit still, then yield to temptation, but keep the rules of the game in mind. One rule is that speculation is not a long-term affair. When you take a position that becomes profitable, get out. Take the money and run. Go on to the next venture. You'll never go broke taking profits.

The fatal mistake of the speculator is waiting too long, hanging on, and trying to squeeze additional profits from a position before selling. A truly professional gambler does not try to clean everyone out before getting up and moving along. He always leaves something on the table for someone else to win. He knows his luck can always go bad. Someone who's better than he is can sit down and take all his profits away.

As a speculator, you're playing a gambler's game. If you buy a building at $50,000 and hold it until it's worth $80,000 but believe it can go to $100,000, take your $30,000 profit and leave the potential $20,000 for someone else. Don't begrudge profits to others. If the good cycle continues, you'll be making money on your next purchase anyway. Meanwhile, if the market turns down and the building never goes beyond $80,000, or falls in price, you'll be protected. Learn from the successful commodities traders (*that's* gambling!), whose motto is: "Always leave something on the table."

So remember, take the profits you have and leave the future profits for someone else. If you're ambitious and aggressive, you'll make money. In the stock market, there is a very appropriate saying: "The bulls make money and the bears make money while the pigs go broke." If you're greedy, you'll go broke. Guaranteed.

11. Consolidate Holdings and Investments for Long-Term Security. During upward cycles, people spread their money in many different places and watch it grow and grow and grow. They create pyramids by taking equity from one building and putting it into another to participate in the appreciation of both. They become heavily leveraged and appear to make huge paper profits almost by the day.

I strongly recommend that you avoid pyramiding even in good times. We saw earlier that pyramids created in this way are top-heavy and come crashing down with the first ill wind. Even if you're not pyramiding, it's dangerous to be *too* diversified in your property holdings.

As an investor, you're in for the long haul, and over the long haul security is the watchword. Security comes from consolidation immediately after the beginning of an uptrend. Sell off your widely dispersed properties. Take those profits and use them to build equity in a few solid properties. This will give you the economic strength to ride the next downtrend comfortably, and to acquire profit. You will then have more to consolidate and profit from when the next upturn comes. It's just good business.

12. Leave Something on the Table for the Next Person. This is a restatement of previous advice as it applies to investors. As an investor, you will have some positions that are more comfortable than others. In good times, you can live with a few uncomfortable positions because the generally rising prices are compensating for poor management, operating losses, or vacancy factors. Such situations are fine for a while, but eventually they will come to haunt you.

It's better to pull back, move into the comfortable positions, and leave something, not just for the next investor, but also for yourself rather than "ride it out" to what could be a bitter end. Avoid complacency; that is, preserve enough of your own profits to use another day.

13. Don't Get Carried Away in Good Times. I once met a gentleman who had been in the stock market before, during, and after the Crash of 1929. I knew he had lost everything in the Crash and I wondered why he wasn't able to see it coming. I asked, "Didn't you know that the market couldn't go up forever? Couldn't you hear the warnings of analysts who were predicting the eventual collapse?"

"Young man," he said with a smile and a shake of his head, "when you're drunk you think you'll never get sober."

So it is with good times. When everyone around you is saying "up, up, up," it's hard to think "down." When the money is coming easy today, it's difficult to imagine that the day of reckoning may come tomorrow.

In good times, this is exactly what you must think about, every day. When an opportunity is presented to you, say to yourself, "Now what's the worst result that could happen with this transaction?" And then act as if that result will occur. If it does, you're prepared. If it doesn't, you're just that much better off.

Murphy's Law says, "If something can possibly go wrong, it will." I don't subscribe to that philosophy. And I don't recommend that you believe it either. What I do recommend is that you *act* as if it were so. Do that, and you'll never go wrong in good times or bad, particularly if you follow Kessler's Law:

"Expect *anything,* be surprised at *nothing,* and you'll be prepared for *EVERYTHING!"*

Use these Kessler's Keys to Success:

☛ The only constant is change

☛ Be a bull or a bear, not a pig

☛ Don't wait to buy real estate, buy real estate and wait

19

People Benefits—Needs, Wants, and Desires Revisited

If you think you can do a thing, or if you think you can't do a thing, you're right.

—Henry Ford

By now I'm fairly certain you realize that I am grateful for the opportunities that life has afforded me. My war experience resulted in my embarking on a most rewarding and fulfilling career in real estate.

Success in that permitted me to explore what people benefits were all about. In pursuit of that knowledge I studied behavior. As a behaviorist I learned about needs, wants, desires, motivation, and activation.

So far in this book I've explained and illustrated—with case studies— the basic tenets of Creative Real Estate: win/win; people benefits; there are no problem properties, just problem ownerships; people are more important than property; define the need and fill it. I've referred to Creative Real Estate as not just a style of doing business, but a way of life. Thomas Jefferson's *A Decalogue of Canons for Observation in Practical Life* is a cogent summary of that premise:

1. *Never put off till tomorrow what you can do today.*
2. *Never trouble another for what you can do yourself.*
3. *Never spend your money before you have it.*
4. *Never buy what you do not want because it is cheap; it will be dear to you.*
5. *Pride costs us more than hunger, thirst, and cold.*
6. *We never repent of having eaten too little.*
7. *Nothing is troublesome that we do willingly.*
8. *How much pain have cost us the evils which have never happened.*
9. *Take things always by their smooth handle.*
10. *When angry, count ten before you speak; if very angry, a hundred.*

A Jeffersonian ideal was that Americans should own the land and be formed by the land. That is a timeless concept that will be as valid in the next century as it has proven to be in the last three. That ideal, and how to best attain it, is what we have been exploring in the pages you have been reading. The message is clear: it's not what happens, it's what you do. The key to your future is what you do with what you have, because life gets better not by chance but by change. The only way it gets better for you is when *you* get better. It's performance that counts—from the inside, not the outside.

Don't mistake movement for achievement. To succeed, examine these three major characteristics:

1. Your philosophy. It sets the course of your life, taking into account what you know, learn, and believe.
2. Your attitude. This is determined by your philosophy and how you feel about the past, the future, and yourself.
3. Your activity. What are you doing to achieve your goals and fulfill your objectives?

The time has come for you to make the decision about which specialty or specialties you will choose to explore. If you haven't been particularly attracted to any we have already discussed, I will be giving you some more in this chapter.

First, let's get into an open frame of mind. How often have you seen a V formation of geese or other fowl, flying south for the winter? Have you noticed that invariably one leg of the V formation is longer than the other? Do you know why? If you are not sure, remember the rule of creative thinking: look for the obvious. I'll give you the answer below. (Don't look yet, you'll shortchange yourself and short circuit your creative process!)

Next, to test your awareness, read the sentence in the box below:

FINISHED FILES ARE THE RESULT OF YEARS OF SCIENTIFIC STUDY COMBINED WITH THE EXPERIENCE OF MANY YEARS.

Now count the F's in the sentence. Count them only once and do not go back and count them again. You will find the correct answer below.

ANSWERS: One leg of the V formation is longer simply because there are more birds in it. Yes, there is a theory about the birds changing places to relieve each other from the buffeting of the air endured by the leader, and another one about the ideal aerodynamic form. Nevertheless, the reason one leg of the formation is longer is simply because there are more birds in it. Look for the obvious!

There are six Fs. Because the F in "of" sounds like a V, it seems to disappear, and most adults will count only three Fs in the sentence. It is remarkable how frequently we fail to perceive things as they actually are. Conditioned habit patterns or "mental blocks" restrict all of us from functioning as effectively as we should. Increased awareness can be developed by being consciously alert to the necessity to look for the obvious as well as the alternatives.

Now, let's look at some more alternatives so that you may select the one or more that will suit you best in your quest to get rich, stay rich, and enjoy being rich with Creative Real Estate in the '90s.

THE FINDER FUNDER FORMULA

When I was seven, we lived in the country. I attended a one-room school-house and walked to school by way of a mile-long route that lay between the highway and the railroad tracks. My mother cautioned me not to walk on the highway, but I don't recall her mentioning the railroad tracks. Obediently staying off the highway, my best friend and I would race each other along the railroad tracks, each of us on one of the rails. The tract was polished by the wheels of the trains and very slippery, making it an accomplishment to stay on at any speed, let along in a race. We both ran helter skelter, slipping off each of our tracks every few steps and getting back on again to repeat the process. Had we stopped to realize that all we had to do to stay on the tracks was to put our hands out and hold each other's arm, we could have walked or run the whole mile without slipping. I have often thought back to that period and have learned one of life's most valuable lessons from it. Working together—cooperating—can make endeavors more successful.

The Finder Funder Formula is based on the concept of cooperation. Every real estate transaction requires two basic elements:

1. Finding, which includes locating, contacting, inspecting, evaluating, selecting, and packaging.
2. Funding, which includes examining, evaluating, calculating, structuring, and timing.

Simply put, finders *find* deals and funders *fund* deals. This approach differs from the norm in that finders must *first* find funders and funders must *first* find finders before either one of them even *looks* for a deal. The way it usually works is that both parties, on their own, frantically try to connect at the wrong time—the finder looking for a funder after s/he finds a great deal with a short fuse (deadline for execution), and the funder floundering around trying to find a place to put some money after triggering an imminent penalty deadline for reinvesting. More often than not, neither the finder nor the funder can get rid of their hot potato in time and they both get burned.

What a shameful waste of potential! All for lack of preparation. And that's the way the majority of investors are operating today. As I travel around the country speaking at different investor group meetings, I ask the assembled members if they have teamed up as finders and funders. Less than 3% have ever done so. I am sure you can imagine how that changes before I leave their meetings!

You must decide what you are—a finder or a funder—and let others know. Then team up and get comfortable working together. Set goals, objectives, priorities, and procedures for mutual benefit and comfort. You can be both a finder and a funder by yourself, but you don't enjoy the synergism and leveraging of talents that is present when more than one is involved. There can also be teams of more than one finder or funder. A finder can have two or more funders and a funder can have two or more finders. However, it is essential that each pairing have its own clear-cut set of operating procedures. These may vary considerably with different pairings, which of itself is a possible reason for more than one pairing. Typically in an investor group meeting, I find 65% are finders and 35% are funders. That's a healthy mix, because generally a funder can work with at least two finders.

This system is one of the quickest and most effective ways for anyone with little or no cash to get started. The compensation should be worked out in accordance with the extent of detail the finder brings to the funder and the amount of return to the funder for the risk involved. A simple, single-family house that can be resold with no repairs in a reasonably short time should probably be a 50/50 split of the profits. You can adjust up or down with that as a starting point for a guideline. Interestingly, if the property requires fixing, the finder might be able to increase his or her share of the profit by adding sweat equity.

This formula levels the playing field, permitting anyone to play, even those who don't ever want to look for or at a house other than their own, but do want to invest.

The sheer simplicity of this concept is what sustains its success.

BUY LOW WITH THE HIGHEST BID

If the caption of this section confuses you, rest easy. It is the only confusing thing about the process I am about to describe. Auctions are a simple, straightforward method of sale and purchase. As in anything, however, not knowing the rules can make it complicated. Fortunately, there are not a lot of rules and the benefits are many.

Over the last several years, the use of auctions as a viable marketing tool for real estate has increased markedly. The dollar volume topped $48 billion last year in the United States, which represented a 44% increase since 1989. Single-family homes, condominiums, and residential lots accounted for 86% of all sales. It is important to note that the sale of real estate by auction is not limited to distressed properties. Since the process can be quick and produce an instant large volume of sales, many developers offer their products at auction at lower prices than they would be able to sell them using conventional single-piece sales methods. A survey conducted by the National Association of Realtors® disclosed that the average price paid for a single-family home at auction was $80,100, compared to the $125,000 average price for single-family homes sold through traditional sales during the same period.

There are three basic types of public auctions:

1. An *auction with reserve* allows the seller to reserve the right to establish a minimum opening bid, to accept or reject any and all bids, and even to withdraw the property at any time prior to the completion of the auction. The Uniform Commercial Code indicates that an auction is "with reserve" unless otherwise stated. This provides the seller with total control over the sale, but is not as attractive to prospective bidders.

2. An *absolute auction* is one which is without reserve. In an absolute auction the property will be sold, regardless of price, to the highest bidder. There is no minimum price and the seller may not withdraw the property after the opening bid has been received.

3. An *absolute auction with minimum opening bid* is a combination of both of the other two types. The seller sets a minimum opening bid which is usually low enough to attract interest while setting a reasonable floor for the bidding. The seller may not withdraw the property once the opening minimum bid has been received.

The two most important pieces of advice I can offer are:

1. Before you go to the auction, inspect the property as thoroughly as you can. Ask questions of the occupants and the neighbors. Determine if there are any undisclosed reasons for the sale, such as a drug-infested neighborhood or an intolerable noise problem. Determine the amount of repairs the property will need—if any—and estimate the cost. It could be worth your while to consult a contractor for this if you are not yet able to do it yourself. Take accurate notes so that when you get to the auction, which moves at a rapid pace, you can be sure of what you are doing. This leads to the second piece of advice.

2. Guard against catching *auction fever*. In the frenzy of milling crowds, chanting auctioneers, and chattering "ring men" (assistants to the auctioneer who walk among the crowd stirring up activity in bidding), it is easy to get carried away and bid beyond what you

had originally decided. After your inspection and estimate of the property, set the top price you will pay for it *regardless* of what occurs at the auction. Also, at the auction, do not be quick to make the first bid. Watch and wait. If no one else bids, start very low. If someone else starts the bidding on a property you are interested in, raise the bids in the smallest possible increments to keep the final price as low as possible. If the bidding either starts or goes above your predetermined figure, *quit!* There will always be more property and more auctions. If you overpay in a bidding frenzy, you won't have the money to get the next bargain.

Lastly, about payment. Most auctions require either cash or a bank check. I do not recommend that you use cash. The best method I've found is to draw cashier's checks from the bank to my order, in $500 and $1,000 increments. Then I can either endorse them to the seller, or redeposit them to my account if I don't use any of them.

Interestingly, a number of the finders and funders I introduced to that concept have been in touch with me to report that they have been going to auctions together—after the finder does all the inspections—and have made some exceptional buys.

START FROM SCRATCH AND CREATE CONSTANT CASH FLOW

Many people who attend my lectures and read my magazine articles and books tell me that they are impressed with the many creative ways there are to make money in real estate, but don't have any money to get started. As one chap who came from an affluent family but was now strictly on his own put it, "I have to start from scratch, and I don't mean my old man's." If you find yourself in that position, take heart. It is really simpler than you might think. Mind you, I said simpler, not easier. Ideas don't work unless you do. Providing you are willing to put in the effort and stay with it until you succeed, here is a way to start from ground zero, generate capital and create a constant source of cash flow.

I call it the *A Bag, B Bag Concept.* Picture a pair of money bags in which you will be keeping your fortune. The *A Bag* is the one you use to accumulate that fortune, and the *B Bag* is the one you will keep it in while it provides generous cash flow.

The items to go into your A Bag must be those you can deal in without a large cash requirement. The idea is to turn a profit as quickly as possible in order to accumulate some working capital. To accomplish this, you should first deal in options, using as small an amount of cash as possible ($100 is feasible) and turning the option over as quickly as you can. At any investor group meeting you will find a number of people who will be glad to

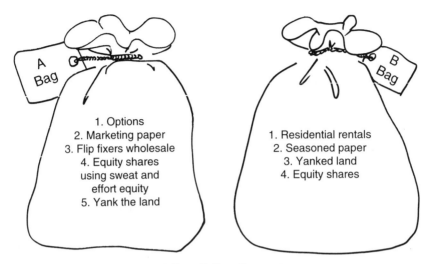

A Bag:
1. Options
2. Marketing paper
3. Flip fixers wholesale
4. Equity shares using sweat and effort equity
5. Yank the land

B Bag:
1. Residential rentals
2. Seasoned paper
3. Yanked land
4. Equity shares

A Bag, B Bag Concept

buy a well priced option from you. A small classified advertisement in your local Sunday paper can bring many prospects. So can notices on the free community bulletin boards at parks, community centers, and supermarkets. The main idea is to move quickly, without greed, sell for a small profit and go on to the next one. The key is to negotiate a good deal, with price and terms that leave room for the next buyer to make a profit. Hone your negotiating skills, because filling your A Bag will depend heavily upon them.

The second item to put in your A Bag is Paper to Market. By that I mean notes, mortgages, and trust deeds that you negotiate to buy and resell to an investor before you have to pay for them. Here again you can readily see how important it is to negotiate good deals. When you finish reading this section, it might be appropriate for you to go back to the parts of this book that address negotiating to refresh your memory of some of the techniques. The marketing process is identical to the one for options. Make the same offers to the same audiences in the same places. Now that bank savings interest rates are so low, you will be amazed at how many people are looking for good investments and don't know where or how to find them. Later in this chapter I will tell you about a never-ending source of private funds for investment that is right in your own neighborhood.

The third item for your A Bag should be fixer-upper houses to be flipped wholesale. Negotiated properly, you can tie up a property for little or no money down and offer it to the investors in the same places that I've mentioned. The difference in this situation is that the investor you are looking for is someone who is willing to fix, or have fixed, the property in order to resell it for a substantial profit. A serendipity here could be a sweat equity opportunity for you, if you are so inclined. Other than being so involved, the idea is to turn over the fixer-upper wholesale for a quick profit—without even taking title—and without spending any time or money fixing it.

Fourth, acquire Equity Shares in your A Bag. Again, locate and negotiate a good deal, tie it up and get a funder (using the same marketing methods described earlier) to put up the money, while you contribute sweat equity and effort equity (as I've explained them previously). In this instance, be sure to negotiate your equity share to be paid in cash so that you can accomplish the main purpose of this A Bag concept: to generate capital to use for creating constant cash flow from your B Bag.

The fifth "gem" to go into your A Bag is my favorite. It employs what has come to be known as my "signature formula." I call it *Yank the Land*. It involves retaining ownership of every piece of land in every real estate transaction in which you are ever involved. It is a mind-boggling concept that has been tried and proven for literally hundreds of years and is responsible for the accumulation of more wealth from real estate than any other single method. I give you all of the details in Chapter 20, so I won't take that surprise away from you now. When you do read about it, remember that it is to be used as the fifth increment in your A Bag to generate capital. For now, I will tell you this about it. It is the one item in your A Bag that you will not resell; you will generate capital from it by hypothecating, mortgaging or renting it.

Now that you have made some money on all the items in your A Bag, it is time to put that money to work creating a constant cash flow for you. The principle is to have holdings in your B Bag that will continue to appreciate while throwing off the cash flow you want. To accomplish this, you should have a time tested, diversified portfolio, consisting of the following:

First, residential rentals. Well maintained houses in middle-income neighborhoods are the most secure investment. It is best to have long-term tenants on leases, with adequate security deposits. In many instances, should you feel so inclined, you can negotiate the lease to include the tenant responsibility for repairs and maintenance. Just a word of caution about this: retain the right of frequent inspection and approval to make certain the property is being properly maintained. My preference is to take care of major repairs and have the tenant responsible for minor needs up to $200. I also recommend offering a discount for prompt and regular payment of rent. Set the rate high enough that you can afford to give them an incentive discount.

Second, have some seasoned paper in your B Bag. Acquire notes, mortgages and trust deeds that have a good payment record. Put them into the hands of a financial institution—your bank, savings and loan, or credit union—to collect and process the regular payments. This will have two beneficial effects. The bank will enjoy having a good customer who permits them to make some extra money for service and will usually treat you with additional consideration in all matters, and the payor will be more diligent in making prompt payments when a financial institution is collecting those payments.

Third, you should have all the "yanked land" from every one of your real estate transactions in your B Bag. You will not only be collecting rents on the land, but it will be continually appreciating in value. You will be able to borrow on it, "create wealth" with it, hypothecate it and, in some instances, subdivide, sell air rights, mineral rights, water rights. It will quietly make you wealthier with no effort at all on your part. In real estate, the improvements are a depreciating asset while the land continues to appreciate.

Fourth for your B Bag are the equity shares of all the property you acquire with finders. For now that you have made your fortune, you will be looking for ways to help others at the same time as you improve your own lot. You can now be the best kind of funder: one who has been a finder and knows exactly what is involved, what is possible, what to expect, and what is fair. In fact, what better training program could you institute for your children and heirs than to have them become finders whom you train and fund? That's win/win.

Before we move on, just a few tips. When negotiating to market paper (for your A Bag), be aware of the three reasons people will sell the paper they are holding at a discount. First is fear. They are afraid they may not be paid over the full life of the note. Second is greed. They feel they can do better with a lump sum of cash than with small periodic payments. Third is urgency. Either they need money right away for some unforeseen expenditure, or they feel that if they don't get a lump sum now to invest they will miss an opportunity they are perceiving.

You may have noticed that the A Bag, B Bag concept works well in conjunction with the Finder Funder formula. While this relationship optimizes both, they are not dependent upon each other. Whether or not you have a finder funder team in place, you should be working on your A Bag, B Bag concept. As a matter of fact, once you get started on either course, Finder Funder or A Bag, B Bag, one will undoubtedly lead you to the other.

TAX-FREE INVESTING

More people than ever have vested funds in retirement plans. That's the good news. The bad news is that those funds are not earning as much for their vestees as they could. Anyone with a Qualified Plan, Keogh or IRA should be taking advantage of the opportunity to invest the funds in those plans in real estate, and accumulate the profits from those investments tax free. To accomplish this, your retirement plan must be a self-directed plan.

Unfortunately, until recent years many pension administrators have kept this fact a secret. By not disclosing to the pensioner that self-directed plans are available, the administrators have been able to invest the funds as they see fit. While some have done an excellent job, others have misused those funds for pet projects of their own. There have been a number of cases exposed in the past several years of outright fraud and embezzlement. While that of itself is reason enough for you to control the investment of your retirement funds, a more important reason is the ability to invest in real estate projects that you are able to personally examine, investigate, and track first-hand.

There are very specific regulations and guidelines available to you. For details, call the Internal Revenue Service for printed materials regarding IRAs, SEP-IRAs, and Keogh plans, and the United States Department of Labor for printed materials on Qualified Plans. Armed with the knowledge you will gain from reading these materials, you should then confer with an administrator who is experienced in handling self-directed plans. In *Creative Real Estate Magazine*, you will find different articles each month discussing the many alternatives available to the holder of a self-directed plan. These are written by hands-on administrators of such plans, so you are assured of the latest information, sometimes (in the event of new rulings, regulations, or case law) before it is published by the governmental agencies. Also, to assist you in getting started, the *Resources* section of this book (Appendix C) lists the names of Retirement Plan Administrators who are experienced in the areas we have mentioned.

ARMCHAIR REAL ESTATE INVESTING

For you who have chosen and read this book for the philosophy, plus the odd chance that I would disclose a painless, no-effort way to make money in real estate, I am grateful for your support and appreciate your confidence. As it has been said, all good things come to s/he who waits. Here is your reward. There is, indeed, a way to invest in real estate without the effort of locating, inspecting, examining, negotiating, and managing property.

It is known as *real estate securitization*. In effect, securitization converts illiquid real estate assets into marketable securities that can be sold to a broad range of investors. These securities are backed by pools of commercial mortgage loans, and occasionally by a loan on a single "trophy" property. Cash flows of the underlying mortgages are segmented to create classes of securities that differ by risk profile, maturity, and various other aspects in order to satisfy the requirements of different investors. As a result, a broad selection of securities is available.

Those securities that meet their credit rating standards are rated by agencies such as Standard & Poor's, enabling investors to compare the risks of owning them with the risks of corporate bonds or other rated investments. Conservative investors can invest in triple-A securities backed by priority distribution of available cash flows. Those willing to accept more risk in return for higher yields can invest in the securities with lower ratings.

Should you choose this method of real estate investing, look for those securities that are structured so that you have even less risk than owning the underlying real estate assets. For example, issuers can use various forms of credit enhancement to guarantee payments to investors. To invest, request prospectuses from your securities broker of all the rated real estate securitization issues. Study them, and then inquire about the extra guarantees available from the issuers. You will be in good company. Pension funds, thrift institutions, mutual funds, and investment funds are all invested in real estate securities.

RIDE THE REAL ESTATE CYCLE

Intuition—familiarly referred to as a hunch—is creativity trying to tell you something. It can be wise and fruitful to pay attention to your intuition. To fine-tune your intuition about real estate investing, it would be wise to study fundamental market cycles. The best investment opportunities are available when supply and demand are out of balance.

Typically, the real estate cycle goes through four phases. The first of these is *development.* New construction is driven by strong consumer demand. Unfortunately, by the time developers are able to respond to the demand, it reaches a plateau and tapers off, leading to the second phase, *overbuilding.* Economic growth slows down at the same time as demand declines. Despite the obvious reason to stop planning new projects, those that have been in process are committed to either start or continue magnifying the growing problem.

The third phase is *adjustment.* Recognizing the severity of the overbuilding problem, lenders and developers finally act. The number of building starts screeches to a dead halt, "bottom-fishers" take up as much of the excess inventory as they can handle, and time brings about a slow cure.

The fourth phase, *acquisition,* arrives when the economic slowdown and employment begin to rebound. However, overbuilding and stagnation from the third phase have eroded both prices and rents so that new building doesn't make economic sense, yet. For the investor, this translates to opportunity time. The panic and pessimism of the stagnation from the overbuilding cycle leaves owners shell-shocked. The media and armchair experts echo Chicken Little's alarm: "The sky is falling" about real estate, shaking the general public's confidence in the strength of the economy. Those owners who have seen their overinflated values decline are anxious to sell before it gets any worse.

Every market goes through cycles, and real estate is no exception. The key to success is obviously riding the cycle advantageously—buying near the low end and selling near the top. It is important to recognize that markets are varied by locale. The cycles vary in length of time and degree of change according to conditions within the local segments of housing, retail, office, and industrial. A market tends to be darkest in its adjustment phase.

Study and understand the market trends in your area; define the phases of each real estate cycle. You will then be prepared to anticipate the coming opportunities.

TERMINAL ILLNESS . . .

. . . is prevalent in more healthy people than ever before in history. Fortunately, it is not the kind of terminal illness that results in death. It is the malady suffered by 69% of adults! According to the results of a recent poll which characterizes us as a nation of technophobes, 32% of adults are intimidated by computers, 22% don't like dealing with automated teller machines, and 15% feel uncomfortable using answering machines. A technophobe can be defined as one who has a fear and even a hatred of complex technical devices. Robert Pirsig, in his book, *Zen and the Art of Motorcycle Maintenance,* describes a view of technology as "an undefined, inhuman, mechanical blind monster. A death force."

It is time for all the techno-foes to reconcile their resistance with reality. To successfully navigate the imminent information superhighway, one will have to learn to "drive" the new "vehicles." While "The human mind is better than any machine," according to Robert Lukeman, executive director of Experienced Media, Inc., technology can speed up virtually any task, open up new avenues of productivity, enhance communication, and substantially contribute to effective time management.

So, even if one believes, as does Alan Caruba, founder of the National Anxiety Center, that "There is something buried in our archival memories that tells us machines are alien creatures," the time has come to embrace the "aliens." According to Robert Pirsig, "Flight from the hatred of technology is self-defeating . . . humanity resides as comfortably in the circuits of a digital computer as it does on the top of a mountain . . . ".

Software is very aptly named. It softens hard tasks and makes them more easily and quickly manageable. To enjoy the full benefits of creative concepts, one should conquer "terminal illness" and take advantage of the technology that can make life more productive in less time—with less effort, and overall, more enjoyable.

SOME SUGGESTIONS

Risk—a basic rule that will help you decide whether or not to take someone's financial advice is: *Don't take the risk unless the one who advises you has as much to lose as you do.*

Decisions—A great method for making a go/no-go decision is to use the old Ben Franklin or T-bar method. Draw a large T down the center of a blank sheet of paper. On the top bar to the left of the vertical, put a plus sign (+) ; to the right of the vertical, put a minus sign (–). Then, as rapidly as you can, list all the positives in favor of the decision under the + side of the T. Don't stop until you have listed all the positives you can think of.

Next, list all the negatives against the decision under the –. Again, don't stop until you've listed all you can quickly think of. Looking at the two columns you will easily be able to determine whether there are more positives or negatives to the decision, and act accordingly. One note of caution: don't list a positive and then a negative or vice versa. Complete one list before going to the other.

Where you have more than one alternative, that is, a number of choices, go with your first inclination. Scientific studies have proven that a first decision is most often the best decision. If you vacillate, you actually cripple your decision-making ability. It's like getting a teeter-totter rocking and not being able to determine where it will stop. Go with your first decision.

Take action—Anything worth doing is worth doing now. Postponement seldom enhances possibilities. More often than not it creates confusion, and oft-times the original opportunity goes away. If it feels good, do it. *Now.*

Be true to yourself—We all have a sixth sense which, if we permit it, will help guide us. How many times have you found yourself in a compromising situation as a result of doing something you felt uncomfortable about in the first place? You didn't listen to that "small inner voice." Most importantly, don't do business with people you don't like. Not because you should be a snob, but because you won't be able to give full-hearted good measure to anyone who you don't like and feel comfortable with. Chemistry of personalities has no logical explanation; recognize and accept it for how it feels. You'll be doing both of you a favor to *politely* not deal with people you don't like.

Pick a target—If you haven't already, take time right now to choose *a life objective.* Mine, which I chose at age 12, is: "To live well." With everything I do, I ask myself, is this helping me fulfill my life objective; will it help me live well?

My son Judd's life objective is: "Have fun and make money." He dropped out of high school, graduated from University of California at San Diego at age 19 with two four-year degrees, one in economics and one in computer sciences, having started and run two successful businesses while in college. Since then he has been a successful Marketing Director, Real Estate Broker, Certified Financial Planner, Software Developer/Publisher/Distributor, and Attorney. At all times, he lives his life objective. He has fun and makes money. His lovely wife Andrea and precocious son A.J. enjoy sharing his clearly defined, pleasurable lifestyle.

Picking a target reminds me of the time in Mexico we came upon a little boy holding a rifle and facing a wall 50 feet away with target circles drawn on the wall. In the center of the bullseye were a number of holes. It appeared to be remarkably accurate target shooting. I asked the young lad if he had done the shooting. "Si, senor," was his polite reply. I asked how he got all the holes in the bullseye. He replied: "I shoot the gun at the wall, then I draw the circles on the wall."

A lot of folks try to make the bullseye of their targets cover their shots after the fact. Life doesn't work that way. Choose your life objective—your target—first, and then aim at it.

Seminar junkies—To analyze the results of education in Creative Real Estate, we conducted a 12-month-long study. In selected courses, we included in the workbook free offers of valuable additional materials merely for returning a postpaid pre-addressed mailer. We placed this incentive in the first 10% of the text, so that we would increase the potential for its discovery. Of a diversified test group numbering 1,000, the total response rate was 2%. We had to conclude that the rest hadn't gotten that far into the text. Astounding, isn't it, that anyone would pay good money for a course and not use the material?

A BASKETFUL . . .

. . . of opportunities is available in the practice of real estate. Everyone serious about making real money in real estate should examine the whole lot to find which specialty is most attractive and suitable to each individual's personality.

The decision to deal in paper, rentals, fixers, options, or any of the myriad specialties should not be made on the basis of observing others making lots of money in a particular specialty. Rather, one should decide to specialize in an aspect that feels good and provides emotional satisfaction as well as monetary rewards.

In our observation over the last several decades in this business, those who are happiest at what they are doing usually prevail and succeed. Others have gone for the "quick buck," sometimes made it, but if it wasn't their cup of tea except for the money, didn't stay with it long and the "quick buck" went by the way. The best career counselors have long advised: do for a living what you would enjoy doing whether or not you get paid and the rewards will be large and lasting.*

---

* The "doers" who contribute their trade secrets in *Creative Real Estate Magazine* each month are providing a multi-million dollar basketful for you to examine, enjoy and take what suits you best. A basketful of opportunities is available to you in the mail 12 times a year. Seize yours.

Use these new Kessler's Keys to Success:

🔑 Jefferson's canons for practical life

🔑 The finder funder formula

🔑 Buy low with the highest bid

🔑 Start from scratch and create constant cash flow

🔑 Tax-free investing

🔑 Armchair real estate investing

🔑 Ride the real estate cycle

🔑 Terminal illness

🔑 Some suggestions

🔑 A basketful

20

How to Stay Rich

... there's no delight in owning anything unshared.

—Seneca

Once you get rich, you'll have an opportunity to experience first-hand one of the great ironies of American society—people generally admire, idolize and imitate the rich, but many also dislike and envy them. Even though I had been aware of this, an unexpected episode dramatically reminded me.

While planning to build a new home for our maturing family, I looked for a good builder. One who knew the crafts, was hands-on and cooperative. A stalwart Polish-American, who learned his trade literally from the ground up, seemed to fit the bill. Leo was a hard taskmaster with the tradesmen, but they respected his knowledge and gave him their best. He delivered his contracted houses on time and in excellent condition.

He met and married his wife, Eva, while he was in the Army, stationed in Germany. She was meticulous and helped him not only with his book-keeping, but in keeping his ongoing jobs clean and orderly.

While we negotiated the contract to build my home (even though I was a licensed general contractor, I didn't have time, then, to build my own home), our relationship developed into a business venture. As good a work-man as he was, Leo was not much of a businessman and he did not have any money, just his skills, to contribute. But I liked him and thought he would do well with some guidance and marketing. To give him a fresh start and motivation, I paid off his debts, bought him a new car, and gave him 50% of the new corporation.

My judgement of his skills and potential were soon validated. I con-centrated on marketing, sales, and administration, while Leo supervised con-struction. Within three months we had seven jobs in process and expanded into major concrete contracting in addition to custom residential construc-tion. At the six-month mark, we were building houses, marina condominium complexes, lifeguard stations on the beaches "where the turf meets the surf" and a library for the new University of California campus. Money was coming in and Leo and Eva were ecstatic. They had never lived so well.

When I suddenly received news that my dad was critically ill, I flew back east, leaving careful instructions and sufficient operating capital—in the form of co-signed checks in a limited operating account—for the building business with Leo and Eva. I also left telephone numbers where I could be reached, and I kept in contact with Leo every morning. Within the week, my dad passed away. After the funeral, I returned home and checked in with Leo and Eva.

To bring myself up to date, I asked for the checkbook and ledgers. They told me that the accountant had them. I asked them to retrieve them so I could work with them the next day.

The next day the books were still not available. That "little small voice" told me to check with the accountant. He told me he hadn't seen the books since last month. I then went to the bank and checked on the account balances. To my surprise, neither the operating account nor the trust account had much over one thousand dollars on deposit.

I demanded an interim statement and discovered that, even though our checks required two signatures—mine and Leo's—the bank had released close to $100,000 on Leo's signature alone! When I questioned it, the vice president told me that Leo had said it was an emergency, so he accommodated him.

Investigation later revealed that the vice president and Leo were in collusion. I won't burden you with the details of the investigations, the termination of the corporation, the firing of the bank official, and the litigation. None of it was any more fruitful than it was necessary. The lesson I did learn that I have already shared with you, is that many people irrationally envy the rich.

We had a wonderfully successful business. Leo and Eva had said they were happier than they had ever been. When I asked them why they took the money, Eva replied simply, "You're a rich man!"

When you finally hit the big time, you'll find that less fortunate friends won't want to talk to you anymore. They'll call you "stuck-up" and "filthy rich" behind your back. Political activists will give speeches denouncing you and demanding that you share the wealth. Those who don't understand wealth will join in a continuing effort to take your money away from you. And the ones who will try the hardest are the people who collect taxes.

Then there are the sycophants. This group, in order to get what you have—without working for it—will fawn over you. They will pay special attention to you, idolize and flatter you to an extent that makes you uncomfortable and, if you permit it, the laughing stock of the community.

For these reasons you need some sound advice on how to stay rich. It's no easy task, as those of you who are already rich are keenly aware. However, as you know, Creative Real Estate provides people benefits. And you are "people." So, keep the faith. Follow the specific techniques I will give you here to maintain the wealth you've earned.

YANK THE LAND

The preamble to the mission statement of the National Association of Realtors® is: "Under All Is the Land." Obviously this is true, but what it specifically means is that the basic continuing value of what we call real estate—which consists of all sizes, shapes, styles, and types of structures built upon *land*—is in the *land*. That land is what Will Rogers said "they ain't making any more of." They "make" more buildings of all kinds every day, but no one has yet figured out how to make any more land.

Considering those simple facts, if you have a mind to stay rich forever, *don't ever sell any land you own.*

Just employ what has become my "signature" technique, which I call *"Yank the Land."* Here's how it works: suppose your first real estate venture was to buy a duplex that cost $80,000 three years ago. With improvements and appreciation, it's now worth $110,000. Suppose further that at the time you bought the duplex, the land under it was worth $20,000. Now, with no more vacant land available for building in that desirable neighborhood it's worth $30,000. Eager to build your real estate empire, you decide it's time to sell and move on to something bigger.

Along comes a buyer who, like you, wants to start out with a duplex, but $110,000 is just too much for him. He offers $100,000, with a very small down payment, which is unacceptable to you. Should you reject his offer? Not outright. Instead, counter with an offer that knocks his socks off—$80,000.

How can you do it? Quite simply. Your offer is to sell him only the building. You keep the land.

Is this reasonable? Does it meet the Creative Real Estate test of providing people benefits? Let's look at it:

1. This price enables the buyer to acquire and use a property he wouldn't otherwise be able to afford. It gives him cash flow and depreciation, both of which come from the building, not the land.

2. It lets you sell the property with $30,000 of your appreciation intact.

3. It provides you with a small income from the ground rent that you'll charge the buyer for his use of the land.

4. It gives you some collateral to borrow against if you need cash for other transactions.

5. It allows you to participate in the future appreciation of the land for as long as you care to hold it.

Everybody benefits. What could be better?

Withal, there's more. According to real estate law, the owner of the land is also owner of other rights called "the bundle of rights" that go with the ownership of the land, including air rights, mineral rights, and water rights. You can sell these specific rights, individually or collectively, own the land, collect the ground rents, *and* build your "life estate." You can also borrow against the land.

The process of actually removing the land from the title when you convey the improvements is a minor subdivision. It normally requires legal documents to be drawn and filed with the planning/zoning governmental agency or agencies having jurisdiction, in order to receive approval to create the subdivision. Check with a title insurance company that operates in your area to find an attorney familiar with the process. This is not a do-it-yourself procedure, unless you happen to be an attorney specializing in subdivisions. However, it is not a major undertaking, merely a paper transaction of a minor subdivision.

There is nothing new about someone holding title to the land under improvements owned by someone else. The preponderance of "old wealth" in Hawaii is in the hands of the families who own most of the land, and lease it to builders and developers. This is referred to as leasehold land or leased land rather than fee simple. Fee simple is the term applied to holding title to the land rather than renting it.

Another example of a fortune accumulated by not selling land is the Irvine Ranch in Southern California. Grandfather Irvine made it a policy and a practice never to sell any of his $50 per acre land for any price, but to merely lease the right to use it. Because they were unable to agree on operating policies and procedures of the multimillion dollar empire, his grandchildren sold the ranch with the land leases in place for several hundred million dollars.

There are major installations on leased land throughout the world. In this country some prime examples are Rockefeller Center in New York, Stanford University in California, and L'Enfant Plaza in Washington D.C. There are many, many more in every major city as well as towns and villages across the nation.

You can make it a personal policy to yank the land on every piece of property you ever own. Buy land plus improvements and sell or exchange only the improvements. How about continually exchanging your improvements only for new land and improvements? By the time you retire, you should have substantial income from ground rents alone, and no property management headaches to contend with. Not a bad pension system.

In fact, this is better than other pension systems because both the assets and income rise in value with inflation. You can't increase your annuity from a pension but you can increase ground rents on property you own. You won't find a pension plan, public or private, that can compare with the benefits of owning leased land.

Some real estate brokers will resist your request to keep the land. They will argue that a buyer who owns a building without the land under it will have a hard time selling or refinancing the building. That may or may not be true but even if it is, it's not a major obstacle. I have always been able to explain the benefits to both buyer and seller, and when you have well matched the parties' needs, they are eager to complete the transaction.

If your buyer or your buyer's agent continues to express concern, ask a few thousand dollars more for the building. Stipulate that the extra money be paid to you in return for a long-term option to buy the land at an agreed-upon price.

Thus, you might ask $83,000 instead of asking $80,000 for the building, and include a 10-year option for the buyer to acquire the land under it for $35,000. If during the term of the option he wants to sell or refinance, you can agree to give him the right to exercise the option at any time and own both the building and the land.

As an added provision, in keeping with the yank the land philosophy, your option contract with the buyer can provide that, in the event he exercises his option, you have first refusal rights—that is, the right to buy the building and land back before he sells to anyone else. This way, you can retake the building, resell it, yank the land, and still hold the land under the ownership of the building.

AVOID THE TEMPTATION TO WANDER

Benny Goodman, the great musician, played the clarinet for more than 50 years. He might have been the best clarinetist in history, and it's probably safe to say that he mastered his instrument many, many years ago. But did he switch to the trombone after he mastered the clarinet? No! He experimented with new kinds of music, new techniques, and new challenges—all with his clarinet.

His outstanding success with the clarinet he knew so well is an object lesson.

Once you've become an expert in arranging particular types of transactions, you might be tempted to try a different formula for the sake of change and variety. Resist that temptation. Stick to what you know best and to what made you wealthy in the first place. If you don't, you'll start to waste time and lose money. You won't stay rich that way.

When you get bored with what you're doing, instead of wandering off, try a new twist or a new variation to your tried-and-true formulas. Find new challenges but stay within a structure that you know makes money.

Let's say you've amassed a small (maybe even a large) fortune using the effort equity formula discussed in Chapter 8. If you recall, that's the situation in which there is some desirable property for sale but no one is buying. You put in your effort rather than cash. You find investors, organize a partnership, get the papers drawn, negotiate the purchase, and arrange financing. In return for your efforts, you receive a percentage interest in the property with none of your cash involved.

That's the formula. Now you're at the point where you've done it so many times, there's no challenge in it for you any more. You're bored with it and tired of all that running around. How do you put new zing into your life? Stay with your successful fortune-building formula, and leverage people.

Look for other, perhaps younger people to provide the effort for you. Advertise for them, recruit them, interview them, show them the ropes, guide them through new transactions, and take a percentage as your fee. Now, not only are you in the effort equity business, you're in the people business. You're a teacher, a mentor, and a consultant. You will have to learn how to spot a real go-getter, how to interview, how to teach complicated concepts, and more.

You now have new stimulus from your additional and varied activities, and most importantly, you are still doing what you know best and make money at. If at first you find you're a poor judge of people and the youngsters (from 18 to 80) that you recruit aren't getting the job done, you can use what you already know to keep the transaction on track. At the same time you're building your skills in another area of expertise.

The general rule for staying rich is: stick to what you know best. As with any general rule there are occasional exceptions. If your tried-and-true formula isn't workable anymore, look for something else. This can happen if there's a severe turn-around in the market, if new legislation makes your formula unworkable, or if the kinds of properties you specialized in aren't available any more. If any of these conditions arise, you'll want to look for a new specialty. Even so, don't go too far afield. Use what you know well and adapt it to the new circumstances. If for some reason Benny Goodman were unable to continue to play the clarinet, nearly all of his musical knowledge could have been put to good use playing another instrument, writing music, or conducting. The point is, he'd stay in music, not switch to acting or archeology. Similarly, you should stay in Creative Real Estate, applying your experience, knowledge, and thought to any one of the myriad specialties available. Keep going, but be flexible.

The Navy Admiral's flagship was steaming along at a brisk pace when the Admiral spied a bright light dead ahead on course. He instructed his signalman to send a message: "Alter your course five degrees starboard so we may continue dead ahead." The answer came back promptly: "*You* alter *your* course five degrees starboard instead of continuing dead ahead." As the light drew ominously closer, the Admiral ordered another message sent:

"This is a four-star Admiral on an Admiral's Flagship of the United States Navy. Alter your course five degrees starboard immediately so that we may proceed dead ahead." Within moments the reply came back: "This is a civilian in the Stony Point Lighthouse; alter your course five degrees starboard immediately, or you *will be dead ahead!*"

Another exception to the stay-with-what-you-know-best rule is the fun factor. If you find a technique that is more fascinating *and* more profitable than your tried-and-true formula, then by all means switch to it. This may only rarely occur, and if it should, try to use as much of your proven formula as possible in applying the new technique.

Above all, make the change gradually. Changing formulas is equivalent to a major life change. It's perfectly fine to act quickly in making money, but it's important to go slowly when you make major changes in your life. So take one small step at a time. That way you'll progress, keep your equilibrium, and maintain your peace of mind—all at the same time.

MIND THE STORE

As Benjamin Franklin put it: "Keep thy shop and thy shop will keep thee." This is sound advice for anyone, and particularly for people who have earned enough sudden wealth to assume they are well set for life. No matter how trouble-free your property portfolio appears, no matter how highly informed you think you are, you must keep up with what's going on in your business. Your continuing success will depend upon how closely you keep an eye on things. You must mind the store.

Even the wealthiest of the world's "beautiful" people employ professional money managers to report to them regularly on their investment portfolios. Those who don't continue to monitor carefully are soon sorry. It doesn't take long to lose money. A dip in the stock market, a sudden run-up in interest rates, a change in the value of the dollar, and other sudden events can devastate even a large fortune.

After you've maximized the opportunity to make your fortune in real estate, you deserve to benefit from it. Be wise and keep an eye on the scene. Watch it carefully and keep informed of new developments in the business including new real estate legislation and new tax laws. You'll need to manage your properties, or at least monitor the activities of those who are managing them for you.

Read publications like *Creative Real Estate Magazine, The Wall Street Journal,* the local newspaper, and the information published by your local Board of Realtors® and major lenders.

Attend seminars and join clubs, groups, and associations dedicated to your objective of making money in real estate. Seek out "how-to" Creative

Real Estate seminars* for beginners and veterans that provide marketing information, transaction-making education, and the opportunity to compare notes with other professionals and investors in your field. Attend the annual Creative Real Estate Expositions to observe, participate in the real estate marketing sessions, and to meet, do business with, and learn from the top people in Creative Real Estate. Stay in touch with people with whom you've had dealings to see what they're doing and how they're doing it. You'll never know everything about your business. The quickest way to find out what you don't know is to ask someone else and listen. It's just that simple.

If you are thinking to yourself: "How can I continue to spend the time and money to keep learning?," think of the words of Derek Bok, who said, shortly after becoming President of Harvard University: "If you think education is expensive, try ignorance!"

STAY IN TOUCH WITH THE "REAL WORLD"

In my years of helping people make money, I've noticed another phenomenon that repeats itself again and again. Too often, when people become wealthy, they start to insulate themselves. This happens almost automatically when they begin associating with other rich people with whom they share common interests. This tendency is best described by the old saying, "Birds of a feather flock together."

There's nothing inherently wrong with this. It is, in fact, beneficial to associate with rich people. You have common interests and can exchange ideas that can help you become richer. This is fine to a point, but there *are* serious drawbacks to too much hobnobbing only with the wealthy. First of all, you lose touch with the real world and the everyday problems of the average, not-so-wealthy citizen. These people may not be able to tell you how to make money, but they can make you aware of other types of problems. Problems are opportunities presenting themselves. You and your rich friends only talk about what you want to hear from each other. You may be missing out on problem-solving opportunities. You may gloss over situations that appear merely annoying on the surface, but are dangerous underneath. You could easily underestimate negative factors that might be working against your holdings.

I have two friends who are exceedingly wealthy. Both started from scratch and made it on their own. There the similarity ends. One spends every day lolling around in a health spa, mingling only with the richest people he can find. After 20 years of this lifestyle, he is unmarried, ob-

---

* As a public service, *Creative Real Estate Magazine* publishes monthly a National Educational and Marketing Calendar, providing dates and places of scheduled events along with names, addresses, and telephone numbers of producers.

scenely obese, plagued with pain and illness, wears a permanently unhappy expression, and is generally bored with life.

The other is richer, trimmer, happier, and enjoys being with people in every station of society. His friends include street urchins, train conductors, chauffeurs, race car drivers, bankers, and people in many more varied endeavors, including me.

The first rich man has lost money in a number of investments and hasn't increased his fortune materially since he first accumulated it.

The second tycoon makes money with everything and everyone he touches. He's a real "people" person. He likes people of all kinds and befriends them. They keep him informed and help him in any way they can.

If you want to stay comfortably rich, avoid insulating yourself from the everyday goings-on in the real world. Ask questions of everyone. Talk with tenants in your buildings. See what they're satisfied with and what they're griping about. Are the rents unreasonably high? Is there talk of rent controls, of tenant associations, or of rent strikes?

Talk with Creative Real Estate people who are on the way up and to those who haven't yet made it. What transactions are they putting together? What new wrinkles have they discovered in your tried-and-true formulas? Can you help them? Remember, help enough other people get what they want and you'll get whatever you want. Have they found new ways that can help you?

Talk to the cleaning lady in your office, to the cab driver, and to the man who mows the lawn. All of them have intelligence, information, opinions, complaints, problems, and solutions to problems. If you think you already have the solutions, remember that most problems either have many answers, or no answer. Only a few problems have a single answer.

In the early 1970s, a major metropolitan police department received a $5 million grant to pay a management consulting firm to make the department more efficient. After spending a year studying the situation, the management consultants made recommendations that they claimed would make the police department 25% more efficient.

After it was over, one patrolman approached the Chief of Police and said, "Heck, boss, you could have made the department 25% more efficient just by spending a couple of hundred thousand dollars on electric typewriters. Nearly every cop I know wastes two hours a day pecking at a beat-up old manual typewriter that doesn't work well enough to produce a readable report."

"Why didn't you tell the management consultants that?" the Chief demanded.

"Because they never asked," the cop replied. This is not an extreme example. Often the solution to a major problem will be right under your nose, but from your exalted position you may not be able to see it. The real solution to a problem is found with the properly stated question. If you're in touch with the real world, your chances of getting the information you need will be better.

Your chances of staying rich will be better too.

KEEP LEARNING

You can never know too much, even if it's about something you believe you know very well.

You can never know too much because of the rapid rate of change in our society. New events happen all the time. New information arrives in such volume it's hard to keep track of it all. Much of what you learn could become obsolete by the time you learn it. So, even if you think you knew it all yesterday, the truth is you probably don't today. Kierkegaard told us: "Life can only be understood backwards, but it must be lived forward."

The day you assume you know everything about your field is the day that you will take your first step down the ladder you worked so hard to climb. Many people who learned a little a long time ago and made money with it think that's all it takes to keep making money. They may believe they have 30 years of experience but often they have just one year of real experience that they've repeated 30 times. Throw them a curve and they strike out. Don't rely on what you learned a long time ago. Keep learning. Look for new ways to do things. Minds are like parachutes—they only function when open.

Try variations on your established methods. Don't wait for someone to force them on you. Pay attention to how people on the other end of a transaction operate. If they're operating differently than you, find out why. Ask questions of everyone. You might learn something you don't know, but should.

Above all, learn enough so that you always have contingency plans for your contingency plans. Only by acquiring enough knowledge to find alternate ways to make your alternative plans work can you guarantee continued success.

TEACH OTHERS HOW TO GET RICH

As I travel around the world giving my seminars, appearing on TV and radio with "Money Making Ideas," as "The Real Estate Answer Man," as the host of "A.D. Kessler's REAL ESTATE ROUNDTABLE," speaking at Exchange Group and Investors Association meetings, lecturing on cruise ships spreading the word about Creative Real Estate, the question I'm most often asked is: "Why?" People all want to know why I put up with jet-lag, sometimes get stuck in flea-bag hotels, sleep on strange and often lumpy beds, and occasionally have to eat in greasy spoon restaurants. They wonder why I don't just sit by my lovely pool in sunny Southern California sipping cool refreshments, taking it easy, and enjoying my wealth. Am I eternally greedy, an insatiable egotist, or a workaholic?

No. I travel to talk about and teach Creative Real Estate for varied and rewarding reasons. I'm minding the store. I'm staying in touch with the real world and I'm constantly learning. I know that wealth is not what we have, but what we are. The *main* reason though, is contained in the moral of one of my favorite stories.

Once there was a minister who decided to ignore his pastoral duties one Sunday to play golf. He went alone to his favorite golf course and as he approached the tee on the first hole (a difficult 550-yard par five, dog-leg to the left with densely foliaged trees in the roughs on both sides of the fairway, a water hazard, and a steeply sloped green surrounded by sand traps), St. Peter spotted him.

St. Peter called the Lord's attention to the errant minister. "Lord," he said, "your servant is doing wrong by playing golf this day, when he should be tending his flock. He should be punished."

The Lord smiled and said, "Let him hit the ball." Whereupon the minister hit his drive—a bad one that sliced toward the trees along the right side of the fairway. Just as the ball seemed to be entering the trees, a bird flew out and deflected it toward the fairway, where it plopped into the water. A moment later, a frog jumped out of the water with the ball in its mouth, gasped and propelled the ball toward the green. As the ball rolled into one of the sand traps, a gopher popped out of the sand, picked up the ball in its teeth, scurried across the green to the hole, and dropped it in.

"A hole in one!" St. Peter shouted. "Lord, that's no punishment, it's a great reward. He will be delighted with his shot."

"Yes," said the Lord, smiling again, "but whom can he tell?"

Good fortune only has value when you have someone to share it with. Good news or information doesn't do much good if no one knows about it. The same holds true for the principles and techniques of Creative Real Estate.

What good would those principles and techniques do me if I kept them to myself? Whom could I deal with? Whom could I look to for understanding the win/win, people benefits concepts of the many transactions that I engage in?

People who hoard their money-making secrets are short-circuiting their ability to expand their wealth. Instead, they ought to spread the word, because in so doing, they spread the wealth.

Ultimately I know that I profit more by having both the word and the wealth in circulation. Both words and wealth multiply to create prosperity for all involved.

As financially unrewarding as teaching is, I continue to teach because I know that the teacher learns more than the student. Every time I talk or conduct a seminar, I come away knowing more than I did before. As I spread the word, other people are given the opportunity to do likewise, and they give a new message back to me. Every time I introduce someone to Creative Real Estate techniques, I have an opportunity to benefit from a transaction or to develop a new client. That's the way life works, and it's a lesson we can all learn for our mutual advantage. When you help someone up a hill, you're that much nearer the top yourself.

The wealthiest people in history became wealthy not by keeping wealth from others, but by giving many, many people the opportunity to become wealthy, too. Look at the number of people who became millionaires by supplying parts to Henry Ford, or by operating Ford dealerships, or by building Ford plants, or by selling real estate around Ford plants. Henry Ford didn't resent their prosperity; he welcomed it! He knew that he couldn't become rich by keeping others poor. He knew that the world works in just the opposite way.

I urge you to emulate this example. When you learn something, teach it to others. When you discover a new way to make money in real estate, show it to as many other people as you can. A candle loses nothing of its light by lighting another candle.

When you see an opportunity for profit, let others profit by it. A basic law of nature is "give to get." Walk your talk. This is how you multiply your wealth and stay rich.

Enjoy the benefits of these Kessler's Keys to Success:

☛ Yank the land

☛ Avoid the temptation to wander

☛ Mind the store

☛ Stay in touch with the "real world"

☛ Keep learning

☛ Teach others how to get rich

21

How to Enjoy Being Rich

When reason rules, money is a blessing.

—Publilius Syrus

The process of building wealth can be challenging, exciting, self-expressive, and genuinely worthwhile in itself, regardless of which vehicle you use to accomplish your objective. I have chosen to show you how to build wealth in real estate because that's the field I believe offers the most and best opportunities for everyone. I've enjoyed every minute of it, particularly after comparing it with making a fortune in oil, manufacturing, entertainment, or any of the other fields with which I have been involved, while keeping my main focus on Creative Real Estate.

I don't know what else I could have done all these years to be so well rewarded for having fun.

Following through on that thought, though the process of building wealth has been the main focus of this book, the key question is how much you ultimately enjoy the fruits of your labor. Great wealth, measured in dollars alone, is not enough. You aren't truly successful unless you learn how to really enjoy your wealth. "Wise are those who learn that the bottom line doesn't always have to be top priority," said William Arthur Ward.

What good does it do to go through the effort and expense of building a beautiful home for yourself if you are unable to enjoy living in it? By itself the process of building can be enjoyable, but that process is temporary. When it is complete and the enjoyment from it is over, what do you do for an encore? The most important benefit you could derive would be the on-going pleasure of living in that house. So it is with the accumulation of wealth. The challenge of making it—striving for the prize—is exciting and fun. Sometimes, for the sake of making a living, one forgets how to live. The real reward is in enjoying the prize after you win it.

FINANCIAL INDEPENDENCE

Everyone wants financial independence. Many equate financial independence with the achievement of a state of wealth and well-being. However, financial independence and wealth are not identical. Financial independence is the ability to pay your debts and to buy what you need without working. With true independence you should have additional money to buy luxuries and still retain a small financial reserve for emergencies. Wealth is more than this. Wealth implies happiness, well-being, and is generally equated with good health, good living conditions, lack of emotional stress, and positive relationships with family and friends.

The 18th century poet and essayist Joseph Addison profoundly wrote: "The great essentials for happiness in this life are something to do, someone to love, and something to hope for." Financial independence does not protect you against loneliness. Wealth does. Admittedly, financial independence can assist in the attainment of wealth, since you can easily pay for proper nourishment and travel to eliminate loneliness. Theoretically, that's sound. However, in practice we find that some of the loneliest people have lots of money, and some of the sickliest people have lots of money. If financial independence supplies wealth and well-being, why are there so many people who can pay their bills and buy what they please and still be lonely? If they are lonely, they are not in a state of well-being, and the financial independence they are supposed to have isn't enough to buy them the happiness or contentment that comes with true wealth.

THE ULTIMATE

The ultimate purpose of this book is to show you how simple it really is to achieve wealth and well-being when you have the know-how. The key to wealth and well-being is the same as the key to Creative Real Estate. I discovered both keys 48 years ago. At that time, I didn't call my business style Creative Real Estate. As a matter of fact, I didn't call it anything except making a living, achieving success, and attaining wealth and well-being. But through the years a formal practice evolved with a set of rules, formulas, techniques, and strategies that became what we now call Creative Real Estate.

In looking back, I see that all along the key has been the positive "can do" attitude. Your attitude is the control center of your life. The importance of a positive attitude is illustrated by the stories of men who succeeded *only* in making money.

In 1923, an important meeting was held at the Edgewater Beach Hotel in Chicago. Among those present were nine of the world's wealthiest and most successful financiers: the president of a mammoth steel company, the president of a major utility company, the president of a dominant gas company, the best-known wheat speculator, the president of the New York Stock Exchange, a member of the President's cabinet, a well-known Wall Street "bear," the head of a world-wide monopoly, and the president of the Bank of International Settlements.

These were men who had found the secret of making considerable sums of money. They were some of the most financially successful men alive at the time. Let's look at where those nine men were 30 years later.

Charles Schwab, president of United States Steel, died bankrupt, after living the last five years of his life on borrowed money.

Samuel Insull, president of Chicago Utilities, died penniless in a foreign country.

Howard Hopson, head of Associated Gas and Electric, lost his fortune, went to prison, and was declared insane.

Arthur Cutten, the great wheat speculator, lost more than $50 million in the crash of 1929. He later died of a heart attack.

Richard Whitney, president of the New York Stock Exchange, was released from Sing-Sing prison after serving a lengthy sentence. He was suspended from the Exchange, was forced to sell his seat, and was declared bankrupt.

Albert Fall, former Secretary of the Interior, died of ill health after having been released from prison.

Jesse Livermore, the famous Wall Street "bear," committed suicide.

Ivar Kruger, the international monopolist, also committed suicide.

Leon Fraser, head of the Bank of International Settlements, killed himself.

All of these men had learned to accumulate money and power. But none of them had learned something infinitely more important—the ability to enjoy their riches through the art of successful living.

In my 48 years in real estate, I have seen many people go through the process of becoming rich, only to find misery and unhappiness when they reached the top. And I've read many books on ways to build a fortune, without a single reflection on the dangers that such instant fortunes can create.

Money does not necessarily bring misery. Plenty of rich people are happy. Money alone does not determine how happy you are; your *attitude*, in conjunction with your financial status, determines how you go about achieving your happiness.

Before I show you how to enjoy your money and achieve true wealth, let's look at ten sure ways not to.

TEN SURE WAYS TO MAKE YOURSELF MISERABLE

1. Forget the good things and concentrate on the bad.
2. Consistently cultivate a pessimistic outlook.
3. Put excessive value and importance on money.
4. Believe that you are indispensable to your job, your company, your community, your family, or your friends.

5. Think that you are overburdened with work and that people take advantage of you.

6. Feel that you alone are exceptional and entitled to special privileges.

7. Attempt to control your nervous system with sheer willpower.

8. Ignore the feelings and rights of other people.

9. Never overlook a slight or forget a grudge.

10. Always feel sorry for yourself.

We've all heard stories about the rich and the miserable. On reflection, we'd see that those people practiced one or more of these ways to become miserable.

King Farouk overindulged in almost everything and dissipated his health and well-being with his fortune.

Late in his life, J. Paul Getty admitted to a reporter that he would gladly have given up many of his billions if he could have made just one of his many marriages work.

Howard Hughes was one of the richest men in the world, yet he died lonely and malnourished after a long, tragic illness.

These people were unhappy not because they were rich, but because of the way they *thought* about being rich, the way they *thought* about themselves, and the way they *thought* about other people. Their lifestyles validated the concept that we behave, not in accordance with reality, but in accordance with our perception of reality. The source of their misery was mental, not monetary. Misery came not from the circumstances of their lives, but from what they did with those circumstances.

I'd like to suggest that you perform an experiment, one that you may never forget. Take a piece of wax, a piece of meat, some sand, some clay, and some wood shavings and throw them, one by one, into a fire. Watch how they react.

The wax melts, the meat fries, the sand dries, the clay hardens, and the wood shavings burst into flame. There are five different reactions to the same force, in this case, fire. Obviously, it's not the outside force (or circumstance) that determines each individual reaction.

What happens in the outside world does not determine our destiny. How *we react* to those circumstances is far more important. It's not what is done to us, but what *we* do that matters. The answer is attitude. Attitude is more important than the past, education, money, circumstances, failures, successes, or what other people say or do. We cannot change any of those things. We *can* choose our attitude. In essence, you create and shape your own world; the world doesn't shape you.

This truth holds for how you make your money and it holds for how you ultimately enjoy it. Another factor that greatly affects the enjoyment of your wealth is how you treat the people around you.

REMEMBER WHO HELPED YOU UP THE LADDER

We've already seen that it is literally impossible to get rich all by yourself. As you make your way to the top in Creative Real Estate, many experts, associates, employees, friends, and relatives are going to help you. There are agents who will find properties for you. Attorneys will protect you. Accountants will save you tax money. Secretaries will transcribe your papers, take your messages and keep your records. And the people on the other side of your many successful transactions will help you become more successful.

When you "arrive," don't forget these people. Don't just shrug and say, "They were only doing their jobs." That's shallow thinking. Yes, they were doing their jobs, but in so doing they had a personal interest in seeing you succeed. They cared about you. They were pulling for you and they helped you climb the ladder of success.

When you get to the top, remember these people. Keep giving them business. Help them get ahead in their professions and in their personal lives. If you no longer do business with them, send them referrals. Help them make money in every way you can. And if you can't do any of those things, at least acknowledge them in some way, either through words or deeds. Show them that you appreciate them and care about them as people.

These simple acts of kindness will bring you as much joy in being wealthy as the money itself, maybe even more. When you look back at the times in your life that you've experienced real joy, those experiences generally came from your interaction with people—rarely from just handling money.

RECOGNIZE THE LIMITS OF MONEY

No matter how rich you are, you can only eat one meal at a time. You can only sleep in one bed at a time. You can only ride in one automobile, wear one suit, and enjoy one form of entertainment at a time.

No matter how much money you have, you can only spend so much. No matter how much of it you spend, there is a limit to how much pleasure and satisfaction money and material possessions can provide.

On the other hand, there is virtually no limit to the joy and happiness people can bring you. The satisfaction of having 10 good friends is much greater and more lasting than the pleasure of having 10 classic cars. The personal reward for helping one person get what he needs, wants, and desires in life is immeasurably greater than all the money you can possibly make from doing it.

A sure way to enjoy being rich is to be as creative in spending and using your money as you were in acquiring it. I'm not going to suggest that you become a philanthropist or give your entire fortune away, but do put it to good use by devoting a part of it to helping people. When you use part of your wealth to help others you benefit in many ways. Not only will you feel better about yourself, but those you help will help you far more fulfillingly than your money could. Eventually, spending money on things becomes a dead-end street. By comparison, using money to help people is an unending, adventuresome superhighway.

After all, what is money, really? We've all heard a lot of definitions of money, descriptions of what it can do, and advice about what you can do with it. But exactly what is it?

Money is simply a medium of exchange, nothing more. It is the basis of a system people have devised for conveniently exchanging what they don't want for what they do want. In our rush to accumulate money, we sometimes forget that it is just a means to an end. No sooner do we get it than we start exchanging it for things we want. Money in and of itself is actually worthless; it is of value only as a medium.

In assessing the value and limits of money, we are aware that it can be exchanged for land, buildings, goods, services, entertainment, shelter, food, clothing, transportation, and for different kinds of money. Few people will deny that these are necessary and desirable purchases. But what can't money be exchanged for? What can't it buy? We've already noted that money can't buy time. Both the rich and the poor have exactly the same number of hours in every day and the rich man can't buy the poor man's time, no matter what price he is willing to pay. Money can buy medical services, but it can't buy health. Money can buy attention, but it can't buy love. Money can buy pleasant sensations, but it can't buy happiness. Money can buy the accoutrements of importance, but it can't buy self-esteem, respect, or admiration.

There's an old joke that says, "Money can't buy happiness, but it can buy a Rolls Royce in which to ride around looking for it." That's true; but remember that in a Rolls Royce or on foot, you're still just looking, and attitude remains the most significant ingredient in achieving happiness

To enjoy wealth you must understand and appreciate what wealth really is. When your money buys you food, shelter, clothing, land, buildings, goods and services, be thankful. Bless your fortunate circumstances, and by all means get what you need, want, and desire with it if you can. But remember, the money is not responsible for getting you the things you want. You are responsible. Money is just the medium of exchange. It's you who deserve the credit and the responsibility for having created the money that you exchanged for those wonderful things.

Because money cannot buy you time, health, love, happiness, respect, or other intangibles that you desire, don't blame it for failing you. The money isn't responsible for not buying what it can't buy any more than it is responsible for buying what it can. You're the one who is responsible for getting or not getting the things money can or can't buy. And when you're not getting those things, don't look to money. Look to yourself. It's not what you are that holds you back, it's what you think you are not!

I made money through Creative Real Estate and I've been telling you how in this book. The fundamental principle I've emphasized is *people benefits*. Just as helping people solve their problems and satisfy their needs, wants, and desires through property ownership has made me wealthy, sticking to the basics in my personal relationships has allowed me to enjoy my wealth and my life.

If you're so caught up in money and what it can buy that you're starting to lose out on what it can't buy, you've lost touch with the basics. The basics make life happy, make life work, and make life worthwhile.

A kind word is a basic. A gentle touch on the shoulder of someone who's troubled is a basic. So is a smile, a favor, a kiss, and a hug. Consideration is a basic and caring is another.

This is not just a book about getting rich in real estate. It's a book about helping people get what they want out of life and enjoying it in the process. If you think that all life is about is getting rich, you're in for some gigantic disappointments and some unsatisfying, frustrating experiences in your relationships with others. The name of the game is people benefits, not just in real estate but in every aspect of life. By my standards I am wealthy, and I enjoy being wealthy because I created my wealth by helping people get what they want out of life. I enjoyed myself in the process—and that's what really feels good.

KNOW THAT YOU'RE DISPENSABLE

When you accumulate some money (enough to be considered rich), it's easy to acquire a distorted notion of your own importance. People often ask for your advice, kowtow to you, compliment you, and give you honors and awards you haven't earned and don't really deserve. All this attention and adulation can affect you. You may begin to think that you really are important, maybe even indispensable, and that no one can possibly know all that you know or do all that you can do. You might begin a self-satisfying ego trip and make yourself believe that you really are indispensable.

No matter how powerful or wealthy you become, you will never be indispensable. That's just an illusion. You don't have exclusive rights to information or know-how. Trying to pretend you do doesn't make you indispensable, it just makes you an egotistical fool.

Try this quick test to find out how dispensable you really are. Fill a bucket with water. Put your hand into it. Notice how the water ripples and the level rises a bit in the bucket. Now remove your hand. In just a few seconds the water is calm and there is no evidence of your hand ever having been in it, is there? Whenever you find yourself in what at first appears to be an indispensable position, think of this bucket of water experiment, and realize how little difference it would make if you were not a part of the situation you find yourself in. It works the same for anyone—rich, poor, educated, ignorant, famous, infamous, or obscure.

The only way you'll ever see a money-making technique prosper is to give it away and let other people use it, too. What's indispensable to the working of an idea is the idea itself, not the person who came up with it, and not even the person who knows it best. The more an idea is utilized and the more people that have input into it, the better that idea becomes. Its benefits become synergistic.

Another problem with considering yourself indispensable is that in so doing, you tie strings to yourself. You create needless obligations. You make it impossible for any business to go on without you. Before long, this unnecessary responsibility will drag you down. You stop enjoying your involvement with the system and you stop enjoying your wealth. Why bother getting rich if that's the way you're going to live?

So know that you're dispensable. Then relax and enjoy yourself.

BE WILLING TO GIVE IT ALL UP

I once saw a poster that showed a pair of open hands with the palms upward. Above the hands was a bird taking flight. Under this illustration was the caption, "If you love something, let it go. If it comes back it's yours. If it doesn't, it never was."

Being of a financial turn of mind, I immediately came to the conclusion that this idea, somewhat modified, can also apply to money.

When you have a lot of money and property, you can easily become quite comfortable with them. You enjoy the benefits they can buy. After a while, however, you may begin to think you can't get along without them. With that comes the feeling that if you lost them you'd somehow have less, be less, and do less. This gives rise to a fear of loss, which breeds insecurity and unhappiness.

If this is the case (unless your purpose in making your fortune was to have a lot of money to count like Silas Marner), you were better off before you had the money. You have fallen prey to the evil power of greed. You have succumbed to the greedy desire to acquire something just for the sake of having it, rather than for the benefits it can provide for you and others around you. You have forgotten the concept of providing people benefits, and you have ignored the basic rules of fulfilling needs, wants, and desires.

Our principle that people are more important than property pertains to more than just real estate. It refers to property in general, as well. Rather than acquiring money for the sake of hoarding it, use it to provide needs, comforts, and benefits for people, including yourself. Money is, in effect, property. And, since people are more important than property, be willing to give it all up. If you believe in the importance of people, you will fulfill their needs. Inevitably, because you were willing to give money away, it comes back and is yours.

YOUR FORTUNE IS AT YOUR FEET

Don't let it go to your head! The title of this book has a double meaning. It refers to two fortunes at your feet. In the first chapter when I urged you to look at what is under your feet, I was referring to real estate. The first fortune, of course, is at your feet—the opportunities in the real estate on which you walk, ride, and live. This real estate is one source of your future wealth. The second fortune starts in your head and ends at your feet. That second fortune is the control of your attitude. You are the master of your money and your life. No matter how large or important your holdings become, you must never forget that you are more important.

As long as you live, the real estate that is the source of wealth and power will be beneath you. It will always be at your feet. No matter how important it becomes, you must remain the master of it. Remain on top of it and in control of it. To give it more importance than you allot to yourself puts you in the position of letting your wealth control you. Nicholas Dandalos, the famous gambler known as Nick the Greek, puts it this way: "The secret difference between winners and losers is discipline. The winner manages his money. The loser lets his money manage him."

Henry David Thoreau said it another way: "We do not ride upon the railroad; it rides upon us." In this remark, Thoreau was talking about how we sometimes allow our possessions to possess us—how instead of owning things, we let them own us.

What good will it do you to own a real estate fortune of 20 buildings and thousands of acres of land if your life becomes a stress-filled struggle to keep from losing it? When that happens, you don't own it. It owns you. You really don't own anything unless you're willing to lose it. Remember, only when you recognize that you are the master of your possessions, that you have created them, and can create them again whenever you want, can you really own them.

Forget about losing what you have. Be willing to get along without it and you'll find you don't have to. Don't permit stress to build up. Take time out to recharge your battery. Include a generous amount of time to just stop and smell the flowers. Remember to do it regularly and often. You'll then truly enjoy your possessions, enjoy being rich, enjoy just being alive. "We work to become, not to acquire," said Eldon Hubbard. True contentment comes not from what we have but from our attitude toward life.

Keep the principles of Creative Real Estate in mind in both your business and your personal life and you will automatically develop the positive "can do" attitude that will always provide "a fortune at your feet."

> *It matters not how strait the gate,*
>   *How charged with punishments the scroll,*
> *I am the master of my fate:*
>   *I am the captain of my soul.*
>
> —William Ernest Henley

Add these Kessler's Keys to Success to all the others:

- Financial independence
- The ultimate
- Ten sure ways to make yourself miserable
- Remember who helped you up the ladder
- Recognize the limits of money
- Know that you're dispensable
- Be willing to give it all up
- Your fortune is at your feet

"Read the Instructions!"

Are you one of those people who tears open the package, pulls out the gift and tries to ride the wagon before you put the wheels on?

This reminds me of Christmas morning when the kids couldn't wait to get inside the fancy wrappings to get their 'prizes.' And all the instructions were mixed in somewhere in the flurry of the wrappings.

Naturally, Daddy had to admonish them with, "Read the instructions!"

What am I talking about? People come up to me after every speech, every seminar and at every event I appear and ask me what's the best way to make money in real estate now. There's a universal answer: Read the instructions.

And where do you find the instructions? What are the instructions?

In **Creative Real Estate Magazine** *"The How-to Journal for Anyone Who Wants to Make Money in Real Estate"* you get the inside know-how every month from a dozen different experts who have had their feet in the fire — who walk their talk. Not writers, not celebrities, but honest-to-goodness down-to-earth, real live hands-on 'doers.' They share with you their trials and tribulations and how they accomplished their successes.

As Publisher and Editor-in-Chief, I don't permit anything to be published that doesn't give the truth, the whole truth and nothing but the truth. If it happens to be entertaining, that's a plus, but I'd just as soon leave the entertainment to the entertainment magazines. Our mission is to give you how-to information that's current, complete and accurate.

Now that you've finished **A Fortune at Your Feet**. I have a Special Surprise for you. A subscription to **Creative Real Estate Magazine** for three months FREE! All you have to do is send in your payment for $60 — that's a very special low price for one year (12 monthly issues) and we will give you an additional three months absolutely free.

So, act now, while this offer still lasts and start the 'instructions' — those mind-boggling creative secrets of the experts — coming your way!

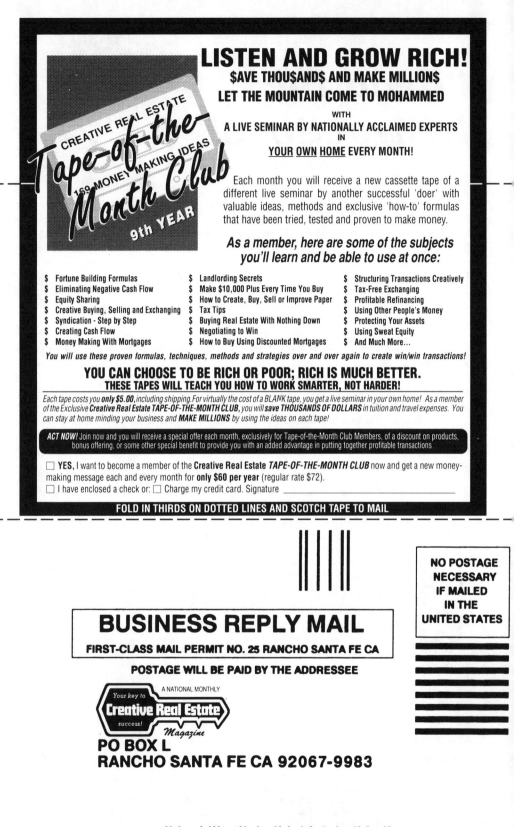

IRS Code Section 1031

HISTORY OF 1031

The concept of exchanging property without taxation first appeared in the tax system as Section 202 (c) (1) of the Revenue Act of 1921. There were various changes between 1921 and 1928, but the mechanics and definitions have remained relatively stable since that time. The earlier cases and rulings refer to these predecessor sections to Section 1031, but the principles enunciated therein are equally applicable to current law.

Section 202 (c) (1)— Revenue Act of 1921
Section 302 (b) (1)— Revenue Act of 1924
Section 203 (b)— Revenue Act of 1926
Section 112 (b) (1)— Revenue Act of 1928
Section 112 (b) (1)— Revenue Act of 1936
Section 112 (b) (1)— Internal Revenue Code of 1939
Section 1031— Internal Revenue Code of 1954

INTERNAL REVENUE CODE SECTION 1031

EXCHANGE OF PROPERTY HELD FOR
PRODUCTIVE USE OR INVESTMENT

Sec. 1031 (1954 Code). (a) NONRECOGNITION OF GAIN OR LOSS FROM EXCHANGES SOLELY IN KIND.—No gain or loss shall be recognized if property held for productive use in trade or business or for investment (not including stock in trade or other property held primarily for sale, nor stocks, bonds, notes, choses in action, certificates of trust or beneficial interest, or other securities or evidences of indebtedness or interest) is exchanged solely for property of a like kind to be held either for productive use in trade or business or for investment.

(b) GAIN FROM EXCHANGES NOT SOLELY IN KIND.—If an exchange would be within the provisions of subsection (a), of section 1035(a), of section 1036(a), or of section 1037(a), if it were not for the fact that the property received in exchange consists not only of property permitted by such provisions to be received without the recognition of gain, but also of other property or money, then the gain, if any, to the recipient shall be recognized, but in an amount not in excess of the sum of such money and the fair market value of such other property.

(c) LOSS FROM EXCHANGES NOT SOLELY IN KIND.—If an exchange would be within the provisions of subsection (a), of section 1035(a), of section 1036(a), or of section 1037(a), if it were not for the fact that the property received in exchange consists not only of property permitted by such provisions to be received without the recognition of gain or loss, but also of other property or money, then no loss from the exchange shall be recognized.

(d) BASIS.—If property was acquired on an exchange described in this section, section 1035(a), section 1036(a), or section 1037(a), then the basis shall be the same as that of the property exchanged, decreased in the amount of any money received by the taxpayer and increased in the amount of gain or decreased in the amount of loss to the taxpayer that was recognized on such exchange. If the property so acquired consisted in part of the type of property permitted by this section, section 1035(a), section 1036(a), or section 1037(a), to be received without the recognition of gain or loss, and in part of other property, the basis provided in this subsection shall be allocated between the properties (other than money) received, and for the purpose of the allocation there shall be assigned to such other property an amount equivalent to its fair market value at the date of the exchange. For purposes of this section, section 1035(a), and section 1036(a), where as part of the consideration to the taxpayer another party to the exchange assumed a liability of the taxpayer or acquired from the taxpayer property subject to a liability, such assumption or acquisition (in the amount of the liability) shall be considered as money received by the taxpayer on the exchange.

(e) EXCHANGES OF LIVESTOCK OF DIFFERENT SEXES.—For purposes of this section, livestock of different sexes are not property of like kind.

Author's Note: In 1984 and 1988, Congress added sub-sections to Section 1031. These additions deal primarily with deferred (delayed) exchanges, qualified intermediaries, and exchanges of partnership interests.

Income Tax Regulations 1.1031(a)–1

I. GENERAL REQUIREMENTS

INTERNAL REVENUE CODE SECTION 1031(a)

Sec. 1031 (1954 Code). NONRECOGNITION OF GAIN OR LOSS FROM EXCHANGES SOLELY IN KIND.—No gain or loss shall be recognized if property held for productive use in trade or business or for investment (not including stock in trade or other property held primarily for sale, nor stocks, bonds, notes, choses in action, certificates of trust or beneficial interest, or other securities or evidences of indebtedness or interest) is exchanged solely for property of a like kind to be held either for productive use or business or for investment.

INCOME TAX REGULATIONS SECTION 1.1031.(a)-1

Sec. 1.1031 (a)-1 Property held for productive use in a trade or business or for investment.

(a) *In general—(1) Exchanges of property solely for property of a like kind.* Section 1031(a)(1) provides an exception from the general rule requiring the recognition of gain or loss upon the sale or exchange of property. Under section 1031(a)(1), no gain or loss is recognized if property held for productive use in a trade or business or for investment is exchanged solely for property of a like kind to be held either for productive use in a trade or business or for investment. Under section 1031(a)(1), property held for productive use in a trade or business may be exchanged for property held for investment. Similarly, under section 1031(a)(1), property held for investment may be exchanged for property held for productive use in a trade or business. However, section 1031(a)(2) provides that section 1031(a)(1) does not apply to any exchange of—

(i)   Stock in trade or other property held primarily for sale;

(ii) Stocks, bonds, or notes;

(iii) Other securities or evidences of indebtedness or interest;

(iv) Interests in a partnership;

(v)   Certificates of trust or beneficial interests; or

(vi) Choses in action.

Section 1031(a)(1) does not apply to any exchange of interests in a partnership regardless of whether the interests exchanged are general or limited partnership interests or are interests in the same partnership or in different partnerships. An interest in a partnership which has in effect a valid election under section 761(a) to be excluded from the application of all of subchapter K shall be treated as an interest in each of the assets of the partnership and not as an interest in a partnership for purposes of section 1031(a)(2)(D) and paragraph (a)(1)(iv) of this section. An exchange of an interest in such a partnership does not qualify for nonrecognition of gain or loss under section 1031 with respect to any asset of the partnership that is described in section 1031(a)(2) or to the extent the exchange of assets of the partnership does not otherwise satisfy the requirements of section 1031(a).

(2) *Exchanges of property not solely for property of a like kind.* A transfer is not within the provisions of section 1031(a) if, as part of the consideration, the taxpayer receives money or property which does not meet the requirements of section 1031(a), but the transfer, if otherwise qualified, will be within the provisions of either section 1031(b) or (c). Similarly, a transfer is not within the provisions of section 1031(a) if, as part of the consideration, the other party to the exchange assumes a liability of the taxpayer (or acquires property from the taxpayer that is subject to a liability), but the transfer, if otherwise qualified, will be within the provisions of either section 1031(b) or (c). A transfer of property meeting the requirements of section 1031(a) may be within the provisions of section 1031(a) even though the taxpayer transfers in addition property not meeting the requirements of section 1031(a) or money. However, the nonrecognition treatment provided by section 1031(a) does not apply to the property transferred which does not meet the requirements of section 1031(a).

(b) As used in section 1031(a), the words "like kind" have reference to the nature or character of the property and not to its grade or quality. One kind or class of property may not, under that section, be exchanged for property of a different kind or class. The fact that any real estate involved is improved or unimproved is not material, for that fact relates only to the grade or quality of the property and not to its kind or class. Unproductive real estate held by one other than a dealer for future use or future realization of the increment in value is held for investment and not primarily for sale.

(c) No gain or loss is recognized if (1) a taxpayer exchanges property held for productive use in his trade or business, together with cash, for other property of like kind for the same use, such as a truck for a new truck, or a passenger automobile for a new passenger automobile to be used for a like purpose; or (2) a taxpayer who is not a dealer in real estate exchanges city real estate for a ranch or farm, or exchanges a leasehold of a fee with 30 years or more to run for real estate, or exchanges improved real estate for unimproved real estate; or (3) a taxpayer exchanges investment property and cash for investment property of a like kind.

(d) Gain or loss is recognized if, for instance, a taxpayer exchanges (1) Treasury bonds maturing March 15, 1958, for Treasury bonds maturing December 15, 1968, unless section 1037(a) (or so much section 1031 as relates to section 1037(a)) applies to such exchange, or (2) a real estate mortgage for consolidated farm loan bonds. (Reg. Sec. 1.1031(a)-1.)

Author's Note: With the additions mentioned in the Author's Note on Appendix A, questions of interpretation and qualification arose, necessitating revisions and additions to provide the public with the guidance needed to comply with the Deficit Reduction Act of 1984 and the Tax Reform Act of 1988.

On May 15th, 1990, the Federal Register published a notice of proposed rulemaking under section 1031. The Internal Revenue Service received comments from the Administrator of the Small Business Administration and the public on the proposed regulations, and held a public hearing on September 5, 1990.

On April 12, 1991, the Internal Revenue Service adopted the proposed regulations with some revisions.

Anyone contemplating qualified exchanges under Section 1031 is advised to consult competent, professional assistance for interpretation of the current Code Section and Regulations.

Resources

The following resources are listed to aid you in pursuing the real estate concepts discussed in *A Fortune at Your Feet*. They are listed as sources of information, not endorsements. Should any service or supply you receive from these organizations be less than satisfactory, please notify me so that I may update my files and remove their names from this list.

CREATIVE REAL ESTATE EDUCATION

John D. Behle
National Note, Inc.
Box 581187
Salt Lake City, Utah 84158
(800) 944-0235
FAX (801) 484-6656

Bill Broadbent
Creative Solutions
1380 Broad Street
San Luis Obispo, California 94301
(805) 543-9102
FAX (805) 543-0438

Wade Cook
United Support Association, Inc.
24837 104th Avenue S.E., #201
Kent, Washington 98031
(800) 872-7411
FAX (206) 859-6600

Jay DeCima
KJAY Publishing Co.
P.O. Box 491779
Redding, California 96049-1779
(800) 722-2550
FAX (916) 223-2834

Ron LeGrand
The LeGrand Group
3001 Hartley Road
Jacksonville, Florida 32257
(904) 886-2985
FAX (904) 886-2995

Jack Miller
National Capital Corporation
Box 21172
Tampa, Florida 33622
(813) 287-1075
FAX (813) 286-0366

Jim Napier
Drawer F
Chipley, Florida 32428
(800) 544-4488

Bruce W. Norris
Bruce Norris Seminars
2415 Piedmont Drive
Riverside, California 92506
(800) 382-5239
FAX (909) 683-0133

John W. Schaub, III
Pro Serve, Inc.
1938 Ringling Boulevard
Sarasota, Florida 34236
(800) 237-9222
FAX (813) 957-3646

Bernard Hale Zick
P.O. Box 6399
Kingwood, Texas 77325-6399
(800) 999-0488
FAX (713) 359-8501

PERIODICAL PUBLICATIONS

Creative Real Estate Magazine
A.D. Kessler, Publisher
Drawer L
Rancho Santa Fe, California 92067
(619) 756-1441
FAX (619) 756-1111
National monthly—$72 for 12 issues

Real Estate Practice Newsletter
Warren G. Harding, Editor/Publisher
6560 Crown Boulevard
San Jose, California 95120
(408) 927-0238
FAX (408) 927-0780
Monthly—$95 for 12 issues

Creative Real Estate Magazine's
TAPE-OF-THE-MONTH-CLUB
A.D. Kessler, Editor
Drawer L
Rancho Santa Fe, California 92067
(619) 756-1441
FAX (619) 756-1111
Audio Seminars—$72 for 12 monthly
tapes on different subjects

Robert Bruss Real Estate Newsletter
Robert Bruss, Editor
435 North Michigan Avenue, #1408
Chicago, Illinois 60611
(800) 788-1225
Monthly—$35 for 12 issues

NoteWorthy Newsletter
Jon Richards, Editor
P.O. Box 31451
San Francisco, California 94131
(800) 487-1864
FAX (415) 824-7720
Monthly—$89 for 12 issues

Who's Who in Creative Real Estate
George Rosenberg, Editor
Box 23275
Ventura, California 93002-3275
(800) 729-5147
FAX (805) 492-5802
Annual Directory—$25

ADVICE AND ANSWERS

A.D. Kessler
A.D. Kessler's REAL ESTATE
ROUND TABLE
Drawer L
Rancho Santa Fe, CA 92067
(619) 756-1441
FAX (619) 756-1111
Television show/
Consumer opportunities/
information from experts

H.I. Sonny Bloch
Sonny Bloch Productions
40 East 63rd Street, #1
New York, New York 10021
(800) 745-TALK
FAX (212) 593-0963
Talk show/financial consumer
advocate radio program

ADDITIONAL AIDS

Creative Real Estate tools such as audio and video tapes, books, home study courses, live on-site seminar recordings, special reports, calculators, long-play tape recorders, *Who's Who in Creative Real Estate Annual Directory.*

The Mail Mart
Drawer L
Rancho Santa Fe, California 92067
(619) 756-1441
FAX (619) 756-1111

ACCOUNTANTS

Paul E. Berning, CPA
9639 Leebrook Drive
Cincinnati, Ohio 45231
(513) 521-8000
FAX (513) 521-2466

Timothy M. Considine, CPA
Considine & Considine
1501 Fifth Avenue, #400
San Diego, California 92101-3202
(619) 231-1977
FAX (619) 231-8244

ATTORNEYS

Arthur R. Carmano, Jr., JD
4681 Fox Road
Cincinnatus, New York 13040
(607) 863-4849
FAX (607) 863-4847

Danny C. Santucci, JD
1011 Brioso Drive #111
Costa Mesa, California 92627
(714) 650-2140
FAX (714) 650-2140

Shawn M. Casey, Esq.
Dream Development Corporation
1725 Washington Road, #407
Pittsburgh, Pennsylvania 15241
(412) 833-7890
FAX (412) 833-9284

Marvin B. Starr, Esq.
Miller, Star & Regalia
1650 Ordway Building
Kaiser Center
Oakland, California 94612
(510) 465-3800

FINANCIAL AND LEGAL ADVISORS

Judd S. Kessler, JD, CFP
Kessler Associates
6725 Mesa Ridge Road, Suite 204
San Diego, California 92121
(619) 452-1915
FAX (619) 452-2073

NATIONAL QUALIFIED INTERMEDIARIES

Central Coast Accommodators, Inc.
H.T. Frankhouser
P.O. Box 500
Solvang, California 93464
(805) 686-4944
FAX (805) 688-5183

R.J. Gullo, Inc.
Russell J. Gullo, President
490 Center Road, Suite E
Buffalo, New York 14224
(716) 677-2880
FAX (716) 675-0290

The National 1031 Exchange Corporation
Terry A. Heater,
   Vice President–Manager
4683 Chabot Drive, Suite 101
Pleasanton, California 94588
(800) TRY-1031
FAX (510) 416-1514

RETIREMENT PLAN ADMINISTRATORS

Entrust Administration
Hugh Bromma, CEO
P.O. Box 21529
Piedmont, California 94620-1529
(800) 392-9653
FAX (510) 654-5451

CONSULTING

The Brain Trust
Box E
Rancho Santa Fe, California 92067
(619) 756-1441
FAX (619) 756-1111

Claude W. Diamond
The Diamond Consulting Group
539 Telegraph Canyon Road, #145
Chula Vista, California 91910
(800) 324-4652
FAX (619) 421-5628

A.D. Kessler, Ph.D.
The Kessler Organization
Drawer E
Rancho Santa Fe, California 92067
(619) 756-1441
FAX (619) 756-1111

Terry L. Vaughan
T. Vaughan & Associates
183 Countryhaven Road
Encinitas, California 92024
(619) 633-1237
FAX (619) 633-1237

KEYNOTE SPEAKER

A.D. Kessler, Ph.D.
The Kessler Organization
Drawer E
Rancho Santa Fe, California 92067
(619) 756-1441
FAX (619) 756-1111

Index

A.D. Kessler . . .

. . . emerges clearly as a modern-day philosopher. Distilling the wisdom of the ages, he provides modern, practical solutions—applied in innovative ways—not only to real estate, but to the everyday task of living, providing rewarding fulfillment and pleasure for those who follow his advice.

Throughout *A Fortune at Your Feet,* the term "Creative Real Estate" is capitalized whenever it refers to the specific people benefits and can-do methods developed by A.D. Kessler. The name Creative Real Estate is a registered trademark and is also the title of the real estate magazine Dr. Kessler publishes. Other authors may write about creative financing and creative purchasing techniques, but only A.D. Kessler, the professional's professional, is the authentic spokesman for the style of Creative Real Estate that he founded more than 48 years ago. Any references to creative real estate transactions that are not directly related to Dr. Kessler's business methods will not be capitalized.

A highly decorated combat pilot, he was born on the east coast and educated across the country, earning a Masters Degree in Business Administration and Doctorates in Public Administration, Management and Behavioral Psychology.

An author, educator, problem solver, broker and investor, he got started in real estate while in a wheelchair as a result of war injuries, turning his last $100 into $1 million within 18 months.

He is translated and published in foreign languages, recognized and called on as an authoritative information resource by the major media. He has spoken in all 50 states, on six continents and on most of the high seas. His "Real Estate Answerman" and "Money Making Ideas" have aired on over 300 stations coast to coast and worldwide by satellite. His 30-minute feature television series, "A.D. Kessler's REAL ESTATE ROUNDTABLE," is aired nationwide on network, cable, and public television.

He is listed in *Who's Who in the World, Who's Who in America, Who's Who in the West, Who's Who in Finance and Industry, Who's Who in Real Estate, Who's Who in California, Who's Who in Creative Real Estate, Who's Who in Aviation and Aerospace, Who's Who in Association Management, Men of Achievement,* and *Leaders in International Achievement.*

His many business and organizational affiliations include:

- Publisher and Editor-in-Chief of the national *Creative Real Estate Magazine*. Published monthly since February 1972, each issue is read by more than 40,000 real estate and related professionals and serious investors. Incorporating *The Real Estate News Observer* and the National Real Estate Investors Newsletter, it is the bible of the Creative Real Estate industry.

- Founder, Producer and Chairman of the Annual Creative Real Estate EXPOsitions which became the keystone real estate educational and marketing events in the world.

- Chairman of the Board of Professional Educational Foundation, publishers and producers of seminar/workshops in real estate transactions and Continuing Education for real estate and related professionals. More than 300,000 real estate investors and experts have attended these workshops.

- Founding President of Educational Video Institute, pioneering the development of audio-visual educational materials and courses for real estate professionals.

- Founder, Chairman of the Board, International Director of IN-TEREX, the International Exchangors Association, which numbered more than 5,000 active members throughout the world in its first year.

- Chairman of the Board of Timeshare Resorts International, a resort development and marketing organization involved in more than $300 million worth of projects.

- Chairman of the Board of The Kessler Organization, performance based consultants specializing in implementation and activation of solutions.

- Chairman of the Board of The Brain Trust, an international real estate problem solving consortium whose clients include many Fortune 500 companies.

A.D. Kessler will tell you the affiliation he is proudest of and most grateful for is sharing with his spouse, Jaclyn, their six married children (five boys and one girl), their respective spouses, and eight grandchildren (six boys and two girls, with one more girl expected this year).